THE CIGARETTE UNDERWORLD

There are enough story ideas here to choke a camel—and maybe the entire tobacco industry as well. Underlying all of them, and a story in itself, are questions involving the coverage of smoking and health by the mainstream press, and the degree to which the $1.5 billion spent annually on cigarette advertising is blowing smoke in the media's greedy eyes. If the subject seems stale, think again: it is reignited with a fresh urgency that is not easily waved away.

—Gloria Cooper,
Columbia Journalism Review

Recommended reading: an important antismoking treatise. . . . [*The Cigarette Underworld*] is devoted to an exploration of all aspects of what is called in one article "the largest single avoidable cause of ill health and premature death in the industrialized world today."

This remarkable multiauthored monograph is not a tired reprise of the now well-known physiologic and pathologic consequences of smoking or of relevant morbidity and mortality statistics, although plenty of hard data of this type are presented for the reader seeking them. Rather, the contents explore smoking and its disastrous consequences from many standpoints, social, historic, economic, political, ethical, and legal, as well as medical. The roles of the tobacco industry, Madison Avenue, the media, the feminist movement, and government agencies at various levels throughout the world are examined in depth. That the stakes are high is made readily evident.

In spite of the "big business" of smoking, some progress has been made in the antismoking movement, with legislation in some areas now providing for relief for nonsmokers. Smokers have in many ways and mostly to their chagrin been put on the defensive. Incidentally, the medical profession, for a welcome change, comes off pretty well in terms of the role that it has played in this worthy campaign.

The victories as well as defeats of the antismoking forces are well chronicled in this important document. . . . It is fascinating, if chilling, reading.

—R.B.H., *Postgraduate Medicine*

THE BIG APPALL

Wayne Stayskal, editorial cartoonist of the Chicago Tribune, *created this cityscape especially for the* New York State Journal of Medicine.

THE CIGARETTE UNDERWORLD

Edited by Alan Blum, M.D.

(continued on following page)

Lyle Stuart Inc.   Secaucus, New Jersey

(Contents continued)

Published by Lyle Stuart Inc.
Published simultaneously in Canada by
Musson Book Company,
A division of General Publishing Co. Limited
Don Mills, Ontario

Queries regarding rights and permissions should be
addressed to: Lyle Stuart, 120 Enterprise Avenue,
Secaucus, N.J. 07094

Manufactured in the United States of America

5   4   3   2   1

Library of Congress Cataloging in Publication Data

Main entry under title:

The cigarette underworld.

    1. Cigarette habit—United States—Prevention—
Addresses, essays, lectures.   2. Tobacco—Physiological
effect—Addresses, essays, lectures.   I. Blum, Alan,
1949-
HV5740.C54 1985   362.2′9   84-26719
ISBN 0-8184-0375-6

Previously published as a special edition of the *New York
State Journal of Medicine* devoted to "The World Cigarette
Pandemic," December 1983.

Cigarette smoking and its promotion: Editorials are not enough

"One man's death is another man's living."
—IRA GERSHWIN

This issue of the *Journal* marks the 20th anniversary of the first report on smoking and health by the Surgeon General of the United States Public Health Service. Preparations for the issue began in 1982 with a letter to the present Surgeon General, C. Everett Koop, MD, requesting an interview on the subject of juvenile-onset cigarette smoking. Dr Koop's encouraging reply inspired other letters to individuals around the world who have been deeply committed to ending the cigarette pandemic.

Luther Terry, MD, one of those continuously involved during the last 20 years in seeking solutions to the smoking problem, supported the idea of an entire issue on the subject of the world cigarette pandemic. In his behind-the-scenes account in this issue of the origins of the 1964 report, Dr Terry describes the meticulous attention to objectivity exercised by his advisory committee and notes the efforts by the tobacco industry to cast doubt upon the findings. He credits his predecessor, Leroy E. Burney, MD, for a courageous policy statement in 1957 that left little doubt about the relationship between cigarette smoking and cancer of the lung. Each succeeding Surgeon General has been committed to curbing the use of tobacco. This issue of the *Journal* marks the first time that all Surgeons General who have spoken or written on the hazards of smoking have contributed to a single work on the subject.

In July in Winnipeg, Canada, at the Fifth World Conference on Smoking and Health (held at four-year intervals since 1967), the *Journal* invited several principal speakers to participate in this issue. Just as Sir George Godber, former chief medical officer of England, challenged his audience in Winnipeg to ask, "How many more such conferences is the world condemned to need?" so he urges the reader of this issue to become more actively involved in efforts to counteract smoking and its promotion. There are hopeful signs, he noted, in such disparate activities as Finland's North Karelia cardiovascular disease prevention project and Australia's BUGA-UP (Billboard Utilizing Graffitists Against Unhealthy Promotions).

Of all the sessions at the five-day conference, the most ominous—and least well-attended—were those that examined current efforts of the tobacco industry to open new markets and increase the level of smoking in developing nations. Not only does this portend a health catastrophe akin to that which has occurred in industralized countries but also a more immediate ecologic threat due to the mass destruction of trees used for flue-curing of tobacco. Several papers in this issue examine the tobacco dilemma of the Third World. Mike Muller's analysis of economic, social, and agricultural aspects of the situation leaves little doubt that the sole beneficiaries in the long run are the multinational tobacco companies. Profiles of four countries—Nigeria, Malaysia, India, and Brazil—offer a depressing scenario in which local health authorities seem powerless. An economic analyst, Frederick Clairmonte, DSc, believes that the first step toward finding a solution lies in looking not at the health consequences of smoking but rather at the interconnecting boards of directors of industry and banking, which he feels create obstacles to the provision of economic disincentives for the sale and cultivation of tobacco. Moreover, although the major cigarette manufacturers have dropped the word "tobacco" from their names in most instances and have diversified (ostensibly as the result of health concerns about tobacco), cigarette sales remain the number one profit maker for these companies. Dr Clairmonte points out that the tobacco industry is becoming synonymous with the selling of alcohol, and he raises the possibility that pharmaceutical research may be influenced by considerations of the cigarette industry. Indeed, it was noted in Winnipeg, the president of one of the largest pharmaceutical companies* serves on the board of a major tobacco company, and advertising accounts for many pharmaceutical products are held by advertising agencies that also promote various brands of cigarettes.

The most chilling realization of all is that the world headquarters of the cigarette industry lies not in the Deep South, but in New York City. New York is home to three of the six American cigarette manufacturers and the site of offices of two others. Nearly all of the advertising agen-

*CiBA-Geigy

cies that promote the products and objectives of the cigarette companies are located in New York. Most tobacco industry publications, including *The United States Tobacco Journal* (which became *The United States Tobacco and Candy Journal* earlier this year), are published in New York. The Council for Tobacco Research, which awards industry-financed grants for medical investigations, is based in New York.

In addition to hosting the headquarters of the three major broadcasting networks, New York is also home to one of the world's most influential newspapers. For more than a decade, several physicians, most notably George Gitlitz, MD, have challenged *The New York Times* to recognize the irony of repeated editorial accusations of financial self-interest on the part of the medical profession by acknowledging the newspaper's own role in promoting the major preventable cause of illness and avoidable medical costs. An eight-year correspondence between Dr Gitlitz and *The Times* is published in this issue, and the newspaper's rationalizations can only be read with disbelief.

At a time when newspaper editorialists across America are calling for greater accountability of physicians, it is dismaying that any editor or publisher can continue to defend the mass media's acceptance of cigarette advertising. Lest the position of a privately owned publication in a free society by misunderstood, there is no obligation to accept cigarette advertising merely because the product being sold is "legal." *The Times'* editorial opposition to teenage cigarette smoking and other forms of drug abuse is an insufficient rationalization for the newspaper's acquiescence in the promotion of cigarettes. Even the tobacco companies claim they do not approve of children smoking. The success of advertising campaigns for cigarette brands can be measured not only in terms of the continued high sales among young people in the face of all consequences but also in the continued complacency of editors and publishers who refuse to admit the connection between promoting cigarettes and the high economic and physical toll taken by smoking.

In recent years the mass media have played an increasing role both in reporting on health issues and also in determining the course of medical research. As the result of a news story on a puzzling disease, a threat to community health, or a laboratory finding, public pressure can be brought to bear on government to allocate additional funding for a line of research. If backed by the right publicity and the right people, a disease may even wind up with its own special institute at the National Institutes of Health. And whatever the disease, there is a presumption, fed by the mass media, that the key to better health lies in the research laboratory. According to the media, all carcinogens are equal—except that some carcinogens such as formaldehyde, asbestos, and dioxin (but not the carcinogens in cigarette smoke) are more equal than others. Coverage of Surgeon General Koop's statement that 170,000 Americans would die in 1983 due to smoking-related heart disease was confined to a wire service article on page D18 of *The Times*, while hearings on formaldehyde received greater attention in the main news section. The media claim that they are only reflecting the direction of modern medicine, and—publishers' and advertisers' concerns about coverage of smoking notwithstanding—they may have a point. One has only to read a fund-raising letter sent in September 1983 by a major

cancer treatment center* to understand how far prevention nihilism has gone:

> Last year in your home state of New York, 9,000 people died of lung cancer.
> Perhaps someone you know—a loved one or a friend—has lung cancer. It's quite possible, because this disease is the most common form of cancer, and one of the most difficult to control. . . .
> But some cancers—like lung cancer—do not respond well to existing forms of treatment. And because of this we must find new and different approaches for treating these difficult cancers. This is our goal, and we need your support to reach it.
> Because research efforts are so important, I want to ask you to consider making a generous gift. . . . You see, there are so many potential areas of research. So many new approaches we must try. But for that we need sufficient funds. . . .

The mass media are also reflecting the state of medical publishing in taking their cues for stories to cover. Because of the increasingly specialized nature of medical journals, smoking is considered only piecemeal, if at all, depending on the specialty. The pharmacotherapeutic objectives of controlled-circulation and single-sponsor publications have left little space for articles on preventive issues. One suspects that smoking may not be considered intellectually important enough: How often is smoking the topic of grand rounds? There may even be concern that those who propose such a conference might be carrying on a crusade—as if a campaign against an epidemic is something undignified or inappropriate. How, too, does one explain the reply of an editor of a national medical journal to a professor of public health in which a manuscript is rated "excellent, and a sure bet for a public health journal" but cannot be published in the general medical journal "because we've recently run an article on smoking"? Or the comment of another editor of a major medical journal which seldom publishes articles on the topic: "Saw your piece on cigarette advertising. Oh, I wrote that kind of thing 15 years ago." Apart from the *The Lancet, The British Medical Journal, The American Journal of Public Health*, and a few journals in respiratory diseases and preventive medicine, smoking is seldom addressed.

This issue, then, challenges preconceptions, not the least of which is that cigarette smoking is a moralistic topic. To believe this is to believe that suffering is a matter of informed consent, because an obscure and wordy warning has been placed in fine print on cigarette advertisements for the past 15 years. The key word to describe this issue is "context." Any textbook of pathology or public health can provide the grim details of the damage due to smoking. This issue attempts to place the subject in a variety of contexts, some of which most physicians may not have considered in depth—especially the man-in-the-street context of advertising. Medical training is geared almost exclusively to individual treatment and diagnosis. Very little of this issue is directed toward the cessation of smoking and the plethora of stop-smoking gimmicks, none of which has been shown to be as effective as the words and compassion of the physician himself or herself.

The intent of this issue is go beyond the posters, pamphlets, and palaver to the realm of primary prevention of the three million adolescents who take up smoking every year in this country. The term "peer pressure" is invoked in hand-wringing fashion to explain the seemingly insoluble

*Sloan-Kettering Cancer Center, New York.

dilemma of teenage self-destructiveness, while the *billions* of dollars spent on cigarette and alcohol advertising each year in the United States is seldom considered as the neglected cornerstone of drug abuse. Denial of our national drug abuse problem has become a cliché; but what is there to say when the major nationally televised program on adolescent drug abuse, "The Chemical People," contained not a single mention of smoking or of advertising for alcohol and cigarettes? (This in spite of a report issued earlier this year by the director of the National Institute on Drug Abuse, William Pollin, MD, indicting cigarette smoking as America's leading form of drug dependence.)

Because labels such as "antismoking," "smoker," "nonsmoker," "quitter," and "addict" may well have hampered a dispassionate analysis of the smoking problem on both individual and societal levels, contributors to this issue were encouraged to challenge the conventional vocabulary of smoking. Insofar as the average physician is concerned, smoking cessation has been regarded largely—if regarded at all—as a frustrating, futile, or hit-or-miss matter with little scientific basis. Not one of the nearly 9,000 continuing medical education courses offered in the United States in 1983 was devoted to scrutiny of methods for the treatment of the problem recognized by the World Health Organization and the Centers for Disease Control as the single most preventable cause of poor health in the world. One of the objectives of this issue is to encourage physicians to realize that not all of the onus for solving the smoking pandemic lies with themselves or with researchers or with governments—or, for that matter, with patients. But it is imperative that physicians overcome the misapprehension that patients "have heard it all before," for most information about smoking perceived on a day-to-day basis by the public and the medical profession alike has been put to them in the form of $1.5 billion worth of advertising images each year. As W. R. Rickert, PHD, implies in this issue, by advertising cigarettes as "low tar" (low poison? fewer carcinogen-containing compounds per puff?), the tobacco industry has become our leading health educator. At the very least—whether through the introduction of "toasting" in the 1920s, filters in the 1950s, or less "tar" in the 1970s, the industry has succeeded in allaying the health concerns about smoking on the part of millions of Americans and in undermining educational efforts—unimaginative, off-the-mark, and poorly promoted though most such campaigns may be—about the undeniable and irredeemably harmful consequences of cigarette smoking. The motto of the tobacco industry could well be "ubiquity, propinquity, iniquity," for it is by posting its cigarette brand images everywhere, by juxtaposing the images to enjoyable and healthful activities such as sport, and by reinforcing a sinful, rebellious idea of smoking that it keeps sales high.

Since the mass media will not report on the subject of cigarette smoking and its promotion to the extent that they cover even the rarest of diseases, physicians must choose whether to adapt to the mass media's concept of health and disease or to act on the basis of their own knowledge. Is it not our duty to work as hard to end the world cigarette pandemic as those who are paid to glorify the image of smoking?

ALAN BLUM, MD
Editor

Health versus greed

GEORGE E. GODBER, DM

The World Conferences on Smoking and Health began in New York at the instance of the American Cancer Society in 1967 and have continued at four-year intervals since. The conferences have been unusual in their provenance because none has been promoted by a government or a national medical organization. We have come together from many different backgrounds and with various support because we know what harm smoking does and want to see that harm reduced. In 1967 some of those attending may have thought there was still a case to prove, although I recall that even the television technicians had put out their cigarettes before Robert Kennedy was half way through his remarkable speech at the opening session. I do not imagine there is anyone attending the Fifth World Conference—even the odd agent from the industry—who still doubts that smoking is the largest single avoidable cause of ill health and premature death in the industrialized world today. Our problem is not whether but how we should persuade smokers to stop and others to refrain from starting. We all know that it is the active efforts of the promoters of smoking that has made it so difficult for the promoters of health.

Yet 1967 is only half way back to the time when we had the first unequivocal proof of the causal relationship of smoking to lung cancer. I remember that Alton Ochsner, MD who had suggested that there might be such a link 30 years earlier, was at that first conference. Richard Doll and Austin Bradford Hill in Britain and Ernst Wynder and Evarts Graham in the United States first gave us proof in 1950. By 1967 Doll and Hill had not only shown that smoking causes far more illness and death from other diseases than from cancer, but also that stopping smoking may reverse the effect. Hammond and Horn had reported on a far larger study in the United States. Hill, Hammond, and Horn were all at that first conference, which was chaired by Luther Terry. (Graham, who had smoked heavily until his own research convinced him otherwise, died of lung cancer.)

The epidemic of lung cancer in Great Britain alone has cost some three quarters of a million lives since we have known its origin and how to stop it. Thirty years ago, that epidemic was only half way to its present peak. Future generations will be aghast that so little had been done to stop it in the first decade or indeed by the time of the first conference. The most that health ministries were doing in the 1950s was some occasional propaganda which had little and transitory effect on most people, although the medical profession itself responded. The industry was all too alert to the threat to its market and rapidly increased its sales promotion. We were content to tell the public on a take-it-or-leave-it basis. Indeed, that is just the line some politicians take now because they maintain that people must be free to choose—and so they must, *provided it is an informed choice*. That choice is hopelessly prejudiced if it has to be made against the constant pressure of intensive sales promotion, always presenting smoking as a sociable, attractive activity of normal men and women in pleasant circumstances. By now we have come to realize that smoking is essentially a form of addiction, which is cleverly reinforced by sales promotion.

Two events of the 1960s changed public attitudes. In 1962 the Royal College of Physicians of London published their report on smoking and health, the result of a three-year study. That report had a tremendous impact and it sold even more copies in North America than in Britain. After the 1964 report of the United States Surgeon General there could no longer be any doubt of the enormity of smoking as a man-made threat to health. Since then the literature filling out information on every detail of the smoking menace has multiplied until it fills a modest book from the Technical Information Center of the US Office on Smoking and Health every two months. There have been yearly reports from the Surgeon General since 1964, two more reports from the Royal College, and reports in most industrialized countries from government or other committees, all presenting the same broad conclusions. Smoking is the largest single avoidable threat to health in the industrialized world today and the cigarette the most lethal instrument devised by man for peacetime use.

We are left with the problem not so much of deciding on the right action to take, but how to ensure it is taken. Looking back over 33 years, one can recognize three phases in the campaign, each lasting roughly a decade. First there was the period of proving the case, ending with the first major reports of 1962 and 1964. Second was the period of seeking ways of convincing the public and governments. Third came the period of more intensive study of the factors which make escape from cigarette dependence so difficult. It is probable that in the first phase the tobacco interests simply treated the health campaign as a scare which would

Dr Godber is former Chief Medical Officer of England and Chairman of the First and Second WHO Expert Committees on Smoking.

Based on a presentation delivered at the Fifth World Conference on Smoking and Health, Winnipeg, Canada, July 11, 1983.

Address correspondence to Sir George Godber, 21 Almonders Avenue, Cambridge CB1 4NZ, England.

die down. In the second phase they took a placating action which they implied would minimize the risk (a risk they have never acknowledged in the first place) of trying to make smoking materials less carcinogenic. That theory blown, in the third phase they have mounted a two-pronged promotional effort aimed at maintaining lucrative sales—namely, visible corporate philanthropy to cultural and sports organizations on the one hand and a barrage of sophisticated advertising imagery on the other—and the notion that the regrettable harm to health can be made to appear socially acceptable in return for the pleasure tobacco provides.

There can be no doubt about the need for an international approach. Work in one country has proved invaluable to others. This, after all, is how the tobacco industry operates. In 1975, the first Expert Committee of the World Health Organization (WHO) before the Third World Conference in New York proposed national comprehensive campaigns, which the conference endorsed and commended to all health ministers. Four years later a second Expert Committee reviewed and extended the measures proposed in a report, *Controlling the Smoking Epidemic*, and expressed great concern about the uninhibited way in which smoking was being promoted in less-developed countries. The third Expert Committee has been concerned with action leading to economic and agricultural changes.

In 1967, I first wondered just how useful a world conference could be. Now as I enter my membership of this, the fifth, I have no doubt that the series has helped to give the campaign against smoking an impetus it would not otherwise have had. But how many more conferences is the world condemned to need? We have made some real gains in reducing mortality in younger men, but women are now exposed much more to the damaging effects of smoking than they were 30 years ago and the result in rising cancer deaths is already apparent. Moreover, the danger to the fetus from smoking by pregnant women is now known and all too little has been done to reduce it. In the 16 years since the first conference, the people of our countries must have lost many millions of years of potential working lives because we have not succeeded to the extent we should have done. In recent years there has been a mounting threat to the less developed, less healthy, and less affluent countries of the world, promoted by the multinational conglomerates whose advances we are slowly containing at home. It is this last development that fully exposes the main support of the continued prevalence of smoking disease and explains the assignment given to WHO's third Expert Committee.

The commercial interests show no scruple about promoting a product with the devastating consequences we know all too well and of which they cannot be ignorant. The developed countries have begun to assert some control over promotion of tobacco—limited and ambivalent as governmental action has been—and the industry has used every endeavor to circumvent control, even in countries like Norway where forceful laws have been enacted. Politicians in some countries, like my own, have been so misguided as to accept inept and futile voluntary agreements about direct promotion which will never be effective so long as the indirect and supposedly innocent methods such as promotion of the arts and, most ironic of all, sports are left open. Those agreements would not be concluded if the commercial interests really believed that the result would be the end of their commerce.

Do governments have a secret reservation of their own that they can seem to fight for our cause so long as they do not actually win?

How many more times must we restate the formula? It has been set out by the last two conferences and the WHO Expert Committees and now again by the Ontario Task Force, each time with a wealth of added detail. But the essentials remain the same. Broadly, they are: Stop commercial promotion of tobacco products; limit smoking in public places; increase the cost of smoking by progressive taxation on tobacco products; and above all, improve education for health, especially of children. Let us stop deceiving ourselves by half measures and make a serious attempt to realize the target Sweden once set itself of a nonsmoking generation, and make it soon. Let no government hide behind the excuses that workers in the tobacco industry—producers, processors or sales force—will lose their incomes, or that taxes will have to be levied in different ways. There are other crops and other industries that might be far more beneficial to those people. We do not ask for laws against smokers, but against the promoters and reinforcers of tobacco addiction. If we in the industrialized world are beginning to win—and do not doubt that we will win—then it is the manifest duty of governments and international agencies to complete that victory within years, not decades, for all countries. Let that be our clear message to them.

HOLOCAUST

Every year cigarettes kill more Americans than were killed in World War I, the Korean War, and Vietnam combined; nearly as many as died in battle in World War II. Each year cigarettes kill five times more Americans than do traffic accidents. Lung cancer alone kills as many as die on the road. The cigarette industry is peddling a deadly weapon. It is dealing in people's lives for financial gain.

—from an address by the late United States Senator
Robert F. Kennedy of New York at the First World
Conference on Smoking and Health, New York, NY
September 11, 1967

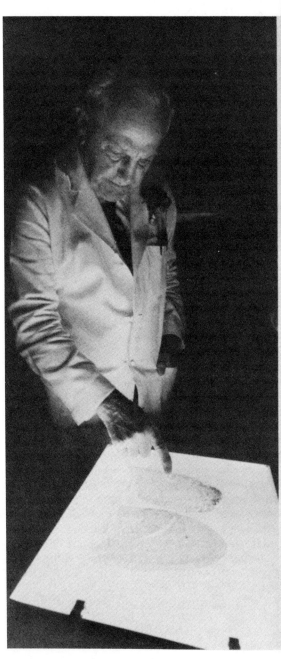

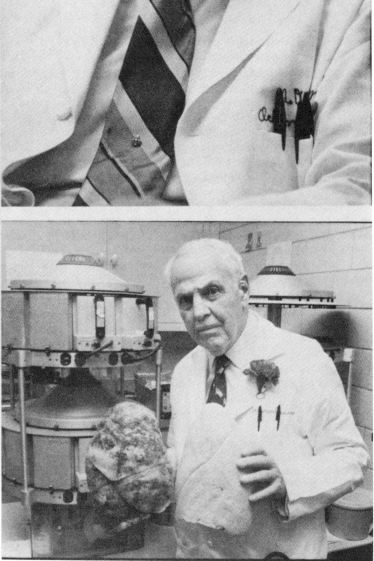

ALTON OCHSNER, MD

Alton Ochsner, MD, 1896–1981
He cleared the air

"In the early '50s, Alton Ochsner was coming to give a lecture to our medical school class at the University of Michigan. We thought we'd play the wise guys. So as soon as he was introduced, we all lit up cigarettes. But Ochsner never batted an eyelash. On the contrary, within only a few minutes of listening to him and seeing his vivid slides and x-rays of patients who died from lung cancer, not a soul was still smoking. And I doubt very many of us ever smoked again after that. I know I didn't."

The story was told by a physician who had just heard Dr. Ochsner, at age 84, deliver one of the major scientific addresses at the annual meeting of the American Academy of Family Physicians in 1980; the listener had found his presentation on the same topic as dynamic and compelling as it was 30 years before. Even if Ochsner, who died on September 24, 1981, had not been among the first physicians, in 1936, to make the connection between smoking and lung cancer, he would still be remembered as one of the foremost thoracic surgeons and medical teachers in history. Named chairman of surgery at Tulane University at the age of 30, he went on to found a leading medical center, the Ochsner Foundation Hospital (named after him as a sign of admiration by his physician-co-founders).

Ochsner's persistent belief that cigarette smoking was the principal cause of the growing epidemic of lung cancer—a theory he publicized throughout the 1940s in the face of ridicule and vituperative attacks even from within the medical profession—symbolized his energetic drive to improve public health. In 1919, lung cancer was such a rare disease that Ochsner's entire junior medical school class at Washington University's Barnes Hospital was asked to witness the autopsy of a man who had died from it. The professor, George Dock, MD, believed no one in the class would ever again see another such case. Seventeen years later, after having been a surgeon for more than a decade, Ochsner did see his next case of lung cancer—nine cases, in fact, in a period of just six months. Because all the patients were men who had taken up the newly mass-advertised practice of smoking while serving as soldiers in World War I, he had the temerity to suggest that cigarette smoking was responsible.

By 1952 he and his colleagues Paul DeCamp, MD, Michael DeBakey, MD, and C. J. Ray, MD, could write in *JAMA* (148:691–697), "There is a distinct parallelism between the sale of cigarettes and the incidence of bronchogenic carcinoma." They accurately predicted that the death rate from lung cancer would escalate as long as smoking continued to exist and that lung cancer would be the leading cause of death from cancer. So controversial was Ochsner that prior to an appearance on "Meet the Press" in the mid-1950s, he was told he would not be permitted to mention on the air the possible causal relationship between cigarette smoking and lung cancer.

In the 1960s and 1970s, Ochsner pointed out that as tragic as is the fatality rate from lung cancer due to smoking, it pales in comparison to cigarette-related deaths from heart attack and emphysema. After the widespread publicity accorded the breast cancer experiences of the First Lady, Mrs. Betty Ford, and the wife of the Vice-president, Mrs. Happy Rockefeller, Ochsner castigated the mass media for ignoring lung cancer—a more preventable problem and soon to become a greater cause of death among women. He also criticized insurance companies, having tried for years to get them to give preferential rates to nonsmokers. "The companies' own statistics show that heavy smokers live about $8\frac{1}{2}$ years less," he said, "but premiums appear to be set according to death rates for smokers. Company profits are thus boosted at the expense of nonsmokers who do not only pay extra but live longer." He surmised that insurance companies have tobacco stock in their portfolios.

Ochsner was among the first to debunk the government's $40 million research effort to develop a "safe cigarette." Whenever he was asked if filter cigarettes had any value, he would reply, "Yes, for the tobacco industry. They help sell more cigarettes."

Obituaries of Ochsner depicted him as a foe of smoking and a nemesis of the tobacco industry. It would be more accurate to describe him as a forceful advocate for good health. Although a surgeon, he preferred to speak out about measures that could prevent a need for the knife. "Even though relief of symptoms and prolongation of life can be obtained by surgery and other therapeutic measures," he wrote in *JAMA* in 1966 (196:852), "only through prevention, mainly abstinence from smoking, can one hope to attain better results in the treatment of lung cancer."

There is little on the horizon to challenge that statement.

ALAN BLUM, MD
Editor

Policy over politics

The first statement on smoking and health by the Surgeon General
of the United States Public Health Service

L. E. BURNEY, MD

In 1957, as Surgeon General of the Public Health Service, I issued a statement at a televised press conference that prolonged cigarette smoking was a causative factor in the etiology of lung cancer. This was the first time the Public Health Service had taken a position on this controversial subject and in fact was the first official national recognition provided to the public through the media of the relationship between cigarette consumption and the increasing incidence of lung cancer.

One does not make a decision of this importance in a vacuum. Michael Shimkin, MD, a friend and colleague in the Public Health Service at the National Cancer Institute, brought the overwhelming evidence implicating cigarette smoking to my attention; Ernst Wynder, MD, of New York City, an early investigator in this field, was also very convincing, as was Morton Levin, MD, an epidemiologist with the State of New York Department of Health working in the Roswell Park Memorial Institute.

The initial statement of 1957 was based on research conducted principally in Great Britain and the United States over many years, indicting cigarette smoking as responsible in large part for the increasing lung cancer death rate. Investigators in Great Britain, principally Doll and Hill, presented some of the earliest evidence. Their longitudinal study[1] included an analysis of over 40,000 British male physicians over 35 years of age. The age-adjusted death rate in their four-and-one-half-year study ranged from 7 per 100,000 for nonsmokers to 166 per 100,000 for heavy smokers.

One critic of this study suggested that the observed associations were spurious and the result of the interplay of various subtle and complicated biases. However, the British government accepted the causative relationship as valid and instituted public educational programs directed at reducing the prevalence of cigarette smoking.

In the United States, Hammond and Horn, supported by the American Cancer Society, were among the early investigators together with Dorn of the Public Health Service, Cornfield, Breslow, and many others.

In 1956, the American Cancer Society, American Heart Association, National Cancer Institute, and National Heart Institute organized a Study Group on Smoking and Health, which, after many conferences, issued a statement that "the sum total of scientific evidence established beyond reasonable doubt that cigarette smoking is a causative factor in the increasing incidence of human epidermoid carcinoma of the lung." [2]

In 1957, the British Medical Research Council stated that ". . . a major part of the increase [in lung cancer] is associated with tobacco smoking, particularly in the form of cigarettes" and further stated that "the relationship is one of direct cause and effect." [3]

In 1959, as a result of additional evidence, I stated in an article in the *Journal of the American Medical Association* that "the weight of evidence at present implicates smoking as the *principal* factor in the increased incidence of lung cancer." [4]

Further investigations in subsequent years substantiated both the 1957 and 1959 statements and also presented evidence implicating cigarette smoking in heart disease, emphysema, and other conditions. There were then compelling reasons for the Public Health Service to make a firm statement in 1957 on the hazards of cigarette smoking. Cancer of the lung was increasing more rapidly and causing more deaths than any other form of cancer in the adult male population. The death rate in white males had increased from 3.8 per 100,000 in 1930 to 31.0 in 1956, resulting that year in 29,000 deaths.[5]

The Public Health Service, from its origin in 1798 as the primary health agency of the national government, had a responsibility, through its Surgeon General, to inform the public and members of the health professions on all matters relating to public health problems and issues.

To comply with this responsibility and mandate, a copy of the Surgeon General's statement and supporting evidence was sent to (1) all state medical societies with the request that they forward the material to all local societies, and (2) (with the assistance of the Office of Education) all state superintendents of education to inform and assist them in the preparation of materials and teaching content of health and physical education programs in local schools.

It is one thing to make a decision, but quite another to have the freedom to implement that decision. This freedom was available to me under the Secretary of the Department of Health, Education and Welfare, Marion B. Folsom, former official of Eastman Kodak Company. When I informed him of the data and my plans to hold a press conference and issue a statement, his response was typical for

Dr Burney served as Surgeon General of the United States Public Health Service from 1957 to 1961.

Address correspondence to Dr Burney, 901 Rock Creek Road, Bryn Mawr, PA 19010.

him: this was a professional program decision for me to make, and he would support my decision.

The White House was informed and all that press secretary James Haggerty requested was a copy of the proposed press release.

One major reason the statement on cigarette smoking in 1957 caused such alarm among those in the cigarette business was the shared confidence of the public, Congress, and the mass media in the integrity and credibility of the Public Health Service.

As a courtesy to the tobacco industry, which was attempting to refute all evidence on the hazard of cigarette smoking, I sent a copy of the press release to their representative a few days prior to the conference. My courtesy was repaid by their simultaneously releasing a lengthy, harsh rebuttal to the statement. I continue to be surprised by any action of a vested interest which puts profits above human welfare.

The reaction of organized medicine was muted—and for several years after 1957. The American Medical Association (AMA) had a rather detached, arms-length attitude.

This disappointment was compounded by a highly critical editorial in 1959 by the Editor of *JAMA*,[6] John Talbott, MD, following publication of my article entitled, "Smoking and lung cancer—a statement of the Public Health Service." [4] One never questions the freedom of an editor to express his views, but in the absence of any official AMA position on the hazards of cigarette smoking and lung cancer, an editorial by the editor in the official publication of the organization could very well lead the medical profession, the public, and the media to assume that the editor was in fact expressing the unspoken position of the AMA.

This attitude appears to have changed during the last few years, and it is encouraging to observe the positive position and direct actions of physicians in informing the public and influencing the smoking habits of their patients. This issue of the *New York State Journal of Medicine* on the cigarette pandemic is an outstanding example of medical leadership and involvement—the kind of action the public wants, needs, and expects from their physicians.

Progress has occurred during these 26 years but the battle is far from won. Special economic interests and the politicians they influence still refuse to drop their membership in the Flat Earth Society and acknowledge that cigarette smoking is killing hundreds of thousands of Americans each year.

In the continuing efforts to reduce and prevent the mortality and disability from lung cancer, emphysema, heart disease, and other diseases in which cigarette smoking has a causative role, physicians have the most important role in changing the smoking habits of the public. They will not, I am sure, adopt the life style of Henry Adams who described himself (in *The Education of Henry Adams*) as follows:

> As it happened, he never got to the point of playing the game at all; he lost himself in the study of it, watching the errors of the players.[7]

I hope that this issue of the *Journal* will inspire the physicians of New York State to take the lead in this most important issue of the public's health.

REFERENCES

1. Doll R, Hill AB: Lung cancer and other causes of death in relation to smoking: Second report on mortality of British doctors. *Brit Med J* 1956; 2:1071–1081.
2. Joint Report of Study Group on Smoking and Health. *Science* 1957; 125:1129–1133.
3. Tobacco smoking and cancer of lung, statement of British Medical Research Council. *Brit Med J* 1957; 1:1523–1524.
4. Burney LE: Smoking and lung cancer: A statement of the Public Health Service. *JAMA* 1959; 171:1829–1837.
5. National Office of Vital Statistics: *Vital Statistics of the United States: Mortality Data*, Government Printing Office, vol 2, 1945–1956.
6. Smoking and lung cancer, editorial. *JAMA* 1959; 171:2104.
7. Adams H: *The Education of Henry Adams*, Samuels E (ed). Riverside ed series, Cambridge, Houghton Mifflin Co, 1973 p 4.

ETIOLOGY OF LUNG CANCER: PRESENT STATUS (1954)

The fact that 13 separate studies have shown the same result is strong presumptive evidence that an association exists between cigarette smoking and lung cancer, i.e., that lung cancer occurs more frequently among cigarette smokers than among nonsmokers. Indeed, one may predict that the "prospective" studies now under way will fully confirm the fact of a substantially increased risk of lung cancer among cigarette smokers . . . .

Lung cancer is a rapidly increasing cause of death in this country. In New York State it now exceeds tuberculosis in number of deaths among males.

Between 1931–1933 and 1948–1950, age-adjusted lung cancer mortality increased among males in New York State by 385 per cent, among females by 68%. Since cancer is a reportable disease in New York State, it is possible to calculate the probability of developing cancer of various sites throughout the life span. For lung cancer, within the short period between 1942–1944 and 1949–1951, this probability has more than doubled for males. At present rates of incidence, 2% of males may be expected to develop lung cancer. If the present rate of increase continues, this figure may double again within the next fifteen years.

Lung cancer is a public health problem rapidly mounting in importance. Public health authorities as well as private medical practitioners must take cognizance of the available facts regarding its occurrence and etiology.

—MORTON L. LEVIN
New York State Journal of Medicine 1954; 54:769–777.

Dr. Levin, Professor of Epidemiology, Johns Hopkins University, was Assistant Commissioner for Medical Services of the New York State Department of Health when he wrote this article.

The Surgeon General's
first report on smoking and health
A challenge to the medical profession

LUTHER L. TERRY, MD

Many Americans believe that the Surgeon General's Advisory Committee report, *Smoking and Health*, of 1964 was America's first recognition of the enormous toll taken by tobacco. But in fact, it was the culmination of growing scientific concern over a period of more than 25 years. In 1928 Lombard and Doering[1] reported a relationship between smoking and health when they noted that heavy cigarette smoking was more common among patients with cancer than among controls. In 1938 Pearl[2] found that heavy smokers had a shorter life expectancy than nonsmokers. During the 1930s there were many other reports by medical scientists of smoking associated with lung cancer, chronic pulmonary disease, emphysema, and coronary artery disease.

One of the most outspoken opponents of smoking was Alton Ochsner, MD, of Tulane University. (His convictions in this regard were so strong that he would not permit any of the members of his staff to smoke. There are many stories of interns who burned their hands or ruined uniforms in an attempt to conceal their smoking.) In 1939 he and Michael DeBakey, MD, reported their observations on the association between cigarette smoking and lung cancer.

Many of the studies on smoking and health were interrupted during World War II. However, by the early 1950s several major prospective and retrospective epidemiologic studies had been published. In 1954 cigarette companies set up the Tobacco Industry Research Committee in an effort to question the increasing evidence unfavorable to their product.

A year later Surgeon General Leroy E. Burney, MD, aided the establishment by the National Cancer Institute, the National Heart Institute, the American Cancer Society, and the American Heart Association of a scientific study group to assess the problem. The group concluded that a causal relationship existed between excessive smoking and lung cancer. On July 12, 1957 Dr Burney placed the Public Health Service on record as accepting the cause-and-effect relationship between smoking and lung cancer. Cornfield et al[3] analyzed the scientific data and confirmed the causal relationship. In November 1959 Dr Burney published an article in *JAMA*[4] confirming the position of the Public Health Service on the issue. Still, the subject received little scientific and public attention.

On June 1, 1961 the presidents of the American Cancer Society, the American Heart Association, the National Tuberculosis Association, and the American Public Health Association submitted a joint letter to President Kennedy, pointing out the increasing evidence of the health hazards of smoking and urging the President to establish a commission to study the tobacco problem.

On January 4, 1962 I met with representatives of these organizations and then submitted to the Secretary of Health, Education and Welfare, Abraham A. Ribicoff, a formal proposal for the establishment of an Advisory Committee on Smoking and Health to report to the Surgeon General. At that time I reported on the mounting evidence of the adverse health effects of tobacco smoking, a request from the Federal Trade Commission for guidance on labeling and advertising of tobacco products, a resolution introduced in the Congress by Senator Maureen Neuberger urging a presidential commission on the subject, and a recent report by the Royal College of Physicians of London concluding that "cigarette smoking is a cause of lung cancer and bronchitis, and probably contributes to the development of coronary heart disease."

After discussions between the staffs of the White House and HEW, President Kennedy announced that he was assigning the responsibility of a study on smoking and health to the Surgeon General. At the same time, I was given the personal assurance of the President that he expected an expert scientific review of the subject and that he would not allow any political interference with the study. I am happy to report that this commitment was rigidly observed until the report was published.

On July 27, 1962 my staff and I met with representatives of the various medical associations and volunteer organizations, the Tobacco Institute, the Food and Drug Administration, the Federal Trade Commission, the Departments of Agriculture and Commerce, the Federal Communications Commission, and the President's Office of Science and Technology. These representatives were given a list of 150 eminent biomedical scientists (none of whom had taken a major public position on the subject of smoking and health) from which we expected to appoint a committee of about ten members. The attendees were given the opportunity to delete from the list anyone to whom they objected, and they were not required to give reasons for their objection.

Ten individuals were picked from various areas of the medical sciences, and I personally invited each of them to serve. Every one of the first ten selected agreed to serve. This assured me that these scientists were convinced of the importance of the subject and of the complete support and confidence of the Public Health Service.

The committee first met on November 9, 1962, at which time it was agreed that all of the methodology and conclusions of the report would be kept secret until publication. Although I was the nominal chairman of the committee, it

---

Dr Terry served as Surgeon General of the United States Public Health Service from 1961 to 1965.

Address correspondence to Dr Terry, Emeritus Professor of Research and Medicine, University of Pennsylvania, 2035 Delancey Place, Philadelphia, PA 19103.

was agreed that I would not participate in any of the deliberations or conclusions of the group. All of the members of the committee and the supporting staff were pledged to secrecy, a pledge which was rigidly observed.

In the next 14 months the members of the committee worked at the National Library of Medicine and at their home institutions. The committee sought research data and other relevant material from all interested organizations and persons, including the tobacco industry. I had instructed members of my staff not to acquaint me with the work or conclusions of the committee. Thus, I could not be pressured into hinting to the press, in spite of daily inquiries, the conclusions of the committee. When the 387-page report was completed, it was printed with strict security by the US Government Printing Office. I did not see the report until it was in final print, and I did not participate in the preparation of any of the report.

The report was released on Saturday, January 11, 1964 at a press conference held in the conference room of the State Department, which was chosen because of its communications facilities. Congress was not in session, and we were assured of the full attention of the press.

All those attending the press conference were required to remain for the entire presentation. Each person was given a copy of the final report. After allowing an hour for the press to study the report, the members of the committee, a few members of my staff, and I held an open press conference. The report hit the country like a bombshell. It was front page news and a lead story on every radio and television station in the United States and many abroad. The report not only carried a strong condemnation of tobacco usage, especially cigarette smoking, but conveyed its message in such clear and concise language that it could not be misunderstood.

At the time of the press conference I gave my verbal support of the report and a few days later issued a formal written endorsement. Since that time the Public Health Service has stood fully behind the report. In addition to the 7,000 scientific articles reviewed by the committee, there have been more than 30,000 articles published in the 20 years since the report. Almost without exception they confirm the committee's findings and extend the knowledge of the health hazards of smoking.

In the face of this overwhelming scientific evidence, the tobacco industry has continued to maintain that the evidence is not complete and that more research is needed. Of course, these companies do not want more evidence on the subject, preferring to fund certain researchers who accept grant money in exchange for attempting to divert attention from the bleak facts about smoking and helping to perpetuate such myths as the safe cigarette.

Immediately after the Advisory Committee's report, tobacco company executives became agitated about the possible collapse of the industry. They established the position of Commissioner (similar to the appointment of Judge Kennesaw Mountain Landis by professional baseball after the "Black Sox Scandal"), who was to review all tobacco advertising prior to publication. The first such commissioner was a former governor of New Jersey, who soon resigned. Another prominent public figure, a former US ambassador, also found the job meaningless and quit. So much for the self-proclaimed integrity and public health concern of the tobacco industry!

The same is true of the "code of ethics in advertising" after the report was published. Among other things the tobacco companies announced that they would no longer use prominent sports figures or sporting events in their advertising. This, too, has been violated at every turn, as a look at professional soccer, tennis, auto racing, or football will confirm.

In 1970, when cigarette advertising on the broadcast media was banned, the industry spent about $300 million to promote smoking. Today, the six American cigarette companies spend $1.5 billion annually for advertising on billboards, in newspapers and magazines, and on countless promotions, many of which are televised. There is heavy targeting of cigarette advertising toward teenagers, women, blue collar workers, and cultural minorities—vulnerable groups that now have the highest level of smoking and the lowest rate of smoking cessation. The hirelings of the advertising industry are out to get them at any price.

Today, less than 15% of our physicians and dentists smoke, the smallest level of smoking in any segment of our population. On the other hand, I am disappointed in the number of nurses and other health workers who smoke and the lack of a more positive antismoking posture of many of our physicians.

The abuses by cigarette companies are too numerous to mention. It is clear that they do not want the public to recognize the health hazards and the enormous financial cost to society caused by smoking. Therefore, health professionals must take back the leadership role. Physicians must not only serve as exemplars, they must also be the leaders who take the message to their patients, friends, and associates, and to the general public. The one person who can have the most influence in determining whether one starts or continues to smoke is the physician.

I hope that every member of the medical profession will recognize this responsibility and will be committed to spreading the message that tobacco smoking is the single most preventable cause of disability and death in the United States today.

One further thought. There was a time when it appeared that women were less susceptible than men to the health hazards of smoking. More recent evidence had indicated that women are as vulnerable and that in certain circumstances, such as while taking pills for birth control or during pregnancy, women face a more serious risk than do men. The comment of former Secretary of Health, Education and Welfare, Joseph Califano, Jr, rings in my ears: "Women who smoke like men, die like men!" I would only add that women who smoke during pregnancy not only carry the same personal risk to their health, but that they are imposing an additional risk to their unborn child. In other words, *cigarettes are child abuse.*

REFERENCES

1. Lombard HL, Doering CR: Cancer studies in Massachusetts: Habits, characteristics, and environment of individuals with and without cancer. *N Engl J Med* 1928; 198:481-487.
2. Pearl R: Tobacco Smoking and Longevity. *Science* 1938; 87:216-217.
3. Cornfield J, Haenszel W, Hammond, EC, et al: Smoking and lung cancer. *J Nat Cancer Inst* 1959; 22:173-203.
4. Burney LE: Smoking and lung cancer: A statement of the Public Health Service. *JAMA* 1959; 171:1829-1837.

A warning against complacency

WILLIAM H. STEWART, MD

For 20 years, since the Surgeon General's benchmark report proclaimed smoking as one of the major public health problems in this country, a titanic struggle has been waged between health professionals supporting this contention and an industry trying to persuade people to smoke for pleasure and emotional support.

No winner can yet be declared. However, in spite of the lopsided media exposure given to the promotion of tobacco products in our society, there is enough evidence of rejection of cigarette smoking to provide a glimmer of hope that the struggle may be successful.

In his forward to the 1982 annual report of the Surgeon General on smoking, Edward Brandt, Jr, MD, Assistant Secretary of Health, wrote, "I am encouraged by the recent decline in cigarette smoking rates in this country. Today, only one third of adults smoke, a decline from 42% in 1965."[1]

The sentiment expressed by Dr Brandt is strengthened by an analysis, also found in the 1982 report, of the changes in the presence of cigarette smoking among successive birth cohorts for men and for women between 1900 and 1980. Men born in the decade 1911–1920 turned out to be the champion smokers of the twentieth century, reaching 70% smokers during the decade 1941–1950 when they were 20 to 40 years of age. In men born after 1920, the peak prevalence has been declining for each successive cohort. For those born in the decade 1951–1960, the last cohort to reach smoking ages by 1980, the peak prevalence rate seems to have been reached at about 40%.

Among women, those born in the decade 1931–1940 win the women's title of champion smokers of the twentieth century, reaching a peak prevalence rate of 45% in the decade 1961–1970. This is considerably lower than the peak prevalence rate for women for each successive cohort born later than 1940. For those born during the decade 1951–1960, the peak prevalence rate was about 37%, a less dramatic fall than has occurred in men.

Because of the long latency period between the initiation of smoking and the appearance of lung cancer, the decline in the prevalence rates of smoking in men and women would not be reflected, as yet, in a decline in the mortality rates due to lung cancer. There has been a drop in the age-specific mortality rates for lung cancer at the earlier ages for both men and women. This may be the beginning of a downward trend, but it is too early to tell if this is so.

The 1982 Surgeon General's report should encourage health promotion activists that they are having an effect on the prevalence rate of smoking. Ironically, the fact that nearly all of the best-selling brands are promoted as having lower levels of "tar" suggests that even among those who have not yet stopped smoking, the message that smoking is harmful is filtering through. But it would be a great mistake if this is taken as a sign the struggle is over. On the contrary, it should stimulate and encourage the campaign against smoking to new and greater efforts.

The truth about cigarette smoking needs to be promoted by a variety of means in order to offset the constant drum beat of the cigarette companies' marketing messages. Yet continually chiding that cigarette smoking is harmful to health is not enough. Special efforts are called for to reach specific groups with a health message that is effective. For instance, as the number of persons who smoke declines, those who continue to smoke are the most resistant to change and will require the most help to stop smoking. Similarly, it is not enough to direct a campaign to adolescents without recognizing there are several subcultures in the teenage population with quite different perceptions of reality. Each must be approached through an individualized world of awareness.

Dr Stewart served as Surgeon General of the United States Public Health Service from 1965 to 1969.

Address correspondence to Dr Stewart, Head, Department of Public Health and Preventive Medicine, School of Medicine in New Orleans, Louisiana State University Medical Center, New Orleans, LA 70112.

REFERENCE

1. *The Health Consequences of Smoking—Cancer. A Report of the Surgeon-General, 1982.* Rockville, MD, US Department of Health and Human Services, Public Health Service, Office of Smoking and Health, p ix.

"NO MINORITY REPORT WAS WRITTEN ..."

The final conclusions of the Advisory Committee were based upon systematic evaluations of clinical, pathological, experimental, and epidemiologic evidence. Judgments of causality followed predetermined criteria on the associations between smoking and a disease entity or process. The elucidation, exposition, and application of these criteria were a notable epidemiologic accomplishment of the Advisory Committee, whose members learned from each other and taught each other the rules and scientific percepts of their individual disciplines. No minority report was written. Scientific evaluations were objective, and the Report represented conclusions unanimously acceptable to every member of the committee. . . . .

The Advisory Committee proved to be an influential force in the policy process of government. As a committee it was not a continuing one, for its official life lasted but fifteen months. Its influence, however, through the various wheels it set in motion, continues to be felt in the years of successive events, favorable for the most part to the health of the public. The Report to the Surgeon General, born despite adversity, may have served to weaken the power of the tobacco subsystem to a modest extent, but it enhanced the resolve, unity, and power of the health forces immeasurably more.

—LEONARD M. SCHUMAN
The origins of the Report of the Advisory Committee on Smoking and Health to the Surgeon General.
J Pub Health Pol 1981; 2:19–27

Women and children last?

Attitudes toward cigarette smoking and nonsmokers' rights, 1971

JESSE L. STEINFELD, MD

By January 1971 Dan Horn, PhD, and his staff at the National Clearinghouse for Smoking and Health had reviewed with the government's internal and external scientific authorities all the evidence available on smoking and health in order to produce a single comprehensive volume critiquing the literature and updating the 1964 report. However, this new Surgeon General's report had not been cleared by the Office of the Secretary of Health, Education, and Welfare (HEW) or by the Executive Office of the President. This meant that at the January 11, 1971 meeting of the Interagency Council on Smoking and Health, which coincided with National Education Week on Smoking and Health, I would not be permitted to summarize the report. Rather, three days before the meeting I was told to write a personal speech and not discuss the report. This I did with my own review of the scientific data, followed by some personal observations. I was promptly and severely criticized by my superiors in HEW. Following are excerpts of that speech.

There is one hazard associated with smoking which concerns me particularly, and should concern all members of the Interagency Council: the effects of cigarette smoking in pregnancy. The 1964 Surgeon General's Report noted that smoking during pregnancy could result in babies of lower than average birthweight. At that time there was no evidence that this necessarily affected the biological fitness of the infant. In our 1967 *Health Consequences of Smoking*, we advised that in light of this prematurity factor it was "prudent" for pregnant women not to smoke. In 1969, it was suggested that there was a relationship between smoking during pregnancy and spontaneous abortion, stillbirth, and neonatal death. Now there is a substantial body of evidence which clearly supports the earlier view that maternal smoking during pregnancy harms the unborn child by exerting a retarding influence on fetal growth. In addition to the already established data on low birth weight in the pregnancies of smoking mothers, there is new data on fetal wastage and neonatal death. One study showed that these women have 20% more unsuccessful pregnancies than they would have if they had not smoked. The British Perinatal Mortality Survey, the largest prospective study to deal with this question, demonstrated that smoking mothers have significantly more stillbirths and neonatal deaths than non-smoking mothers.

Fetal wastage is a terrible tragedy, as is the loss of an infant, and let me suggest that certain purveyors of cigarettes stop making awkward remarks about how some young mothers in childbirth might welcome smaller babies. The mother who smokes is subjecting the unborn child to the adverse effects of tobacco and as a result we are losing babies and possibly handicapping babies.

The influence of smoking upon pregnancy brings up the whole problem of women and smoking. One third of all women in the childbearing years are smokers and their numbers are building up as more and more teen-age girls get started on the smoking habit. In the past seven years, there has been an appreciable drop in smoking among men but regrettably there has been no comparable drop among women. . . .

From the very beginning the cigarette industry has done everything it could to bring women into the smoking population. In the early days of advertising, a nonsmoking lady would be shown appealing to her gentleman companion, "Blow the smoke my way," or saying, "Reach for a Lucky instead of a sweet." The latter slogan caused considerable furor in the candy industry, but lured many weight-conscious women to take up smoking. In the past half century the advertising has become more blatant; women have been enticed by endorsements from ladies of fashion and even opera stars; they have been led to the bait by young, modish, sophisticated models who live and play in elegant settings, accompanied by male companions who are handsome and virile. To all of this has been added cigarettes just for women, and what could be a more effective way to advertise them than to suggest that the fair sex has come a long, long way since the days when they could smoke only behind closed doors? The makers of one brand which has just come on the market have promised a veritable flood of print advertising in women's magazines, entertainment programs, newspapers and Sunday supplements, and on billboards.

One of the most important reasons for the low cessation rate among women is the fact that they have yet to experience the toll of death and disease from smoking which men have had. Partly this is because women, until now, have smoked somewhat differently than men. As a rule they smoke fewer cigarettes per day, inhale less frequently and less deeply, use lower tar and nicotine cigarettes, and consume smaller portions of each. Primarily, however, the difference may be explained by the shorter period in which women have smoked. We know, for instance, that women did not start to smoke in any great numbers before World War I; thus few in their 70s and 80s have had the same exposure to this health hazard as men of the same ages. With each succeeding decade more women did take up smoking, and they started at earlier ages; yet there have always been fewer women smokers, proportionately, than men. This holds true today despite the changes in smoking habits I have already noted.

Since there are fewer women smokers to be affected, the relative death rates from smoking-associated diseases are going to be smaller than those of men. Furthermore, their overall death rate from almost all other diseases is generally lower than that of men. A man will see his friends, co-workers, and relatives dying at relatively young ages from heart disease, lung cancer, and other smoking-related diseases. A woman may be less conscious of such deaths among her women friends and relatives and consequently feel herself somehow safe from the hazards of smoking. But this may change. I want to emphasize that while men's death and disability days are higher than women's, the woman smoker has a higher death rate than the nonsmoking woman.

Currently, girls are rushing to emulate the cigarette smoking practices of boys. What will happen to these young smokers? Some will stop once the glamour wears off and their crowds disperse after high school days are over. A very large number will undoubtedly continue to smoke, for a habit started that early in life is one that is hard to break. . . .

The plethora of ads promised by the tobacco industry is of concern on two counts. First, it may encourage young people to

Dr Steinfeld served as Surgeon General of the United States Public Health Service from 1969 to 1973.

Address correspondence to Dr Steinfeld, Medical College of Georgia, Augusta GA 30912.)

17

take up smoking; but, more important, it may tend to shake the resolve of those who sincerely want to quit. An overwhelming dose of ads in women's magazines could have such an effect, for women basically find it harder to give up smoking than men and even those who quit are more likely to return to smoking than men. Data for 1970, for instance, shows that above 25% of all men smokers managed to quit, while only 15% of women smokers were able to give up the habit.

We do not know why women have not made a better showing. Perhaps it is an affirmation of the desire to break away from old social restrictions. Certainly advertising has played a part. It may be that the housewife's basic environment is more conducive to continue smoking, particularly if she is alone part of the day. In the business world, smoking undoubtedly helps create a sense of equality with men. Some women keep up the smoking habit because of the fear of weight gain that may accompany cessation.

Today, January 11, 1971, even though cigarette commercials are now off the air, a new broadside attack through the print media is bound to have considerable impact. The onslaught has already started. My staff counted a total of 36 cigarette advertisements currently carried in eight of the leading magazines aimed exclusively at women. One of them has eight such ads in the current issue. These journals are not just the kind that stress hair styling, grooming, and the secrets of being popular. Those surveyed included homemaking magazines which carry articles on child care and household hints—journals that have wide popular appeal to women in all walks of life. . . .

The health professions must become more active in the smoking and health field. Obstetricians and gynecologists should have a particular concern about smoking's effect on their patients. One group of professionals has a particular stake in this effort— not only because they are women, but because they have an opportunity to exert a considerable influence on other women. I refer to our nurses who play an important role in so many areas of health care—in hospitals, clinics, physicians' offices, industrial health units, school health programs. The American Nurses' Association two years ago passed a resolution calling on its members to be informed about the health hazards of cigarette smoking and encouraging them to involve themselves in positive health education programs to prevent nonsmokers, particularly youngsters, from starting to smoke. I regret to say that there are

still more smokers proportionately among nurses than among women generally. Of course I do not mean to suggest that our efforts should be limited to women or that men and boys should be neglected in future educational campaigns. Our obligation is to all segments of the population; our challenge is to turn back the new rising tide of cigarette consumption.

Finally, evidence is accumulating that the nonsmoker may have untoward effects from the pollution his smoking neighbor forces upon him. Nonsmokers have as much right to clean air and wholesome air as smokers have to their so-called right to smoke, which I would redefine as a "right to pollute." It is high time to ban smoking from all confined public places such as restaurants, theaters, airplanes, trains, and buses. It is time that we interpret the Bill of Rights for the Nonsmoker as well as the smoker.

Although this call for a nonsmokers' rights movement was not looked upon approvingly within the Office of the Secretary of HEW, it brought forth a blizzard of mail with an overwhelmingly favorable response. I had previously asked the individuals responsible for the scientific content of the Surgeon General's report to summarize all available data on the effects of smoking on the passive or involuntary smoker. This material was published in a subsequent Surgeon General's report. In the wake of this report, the General Services Administration, which operates all government office buildings, required its tenants for the first time to make some provisions for nonsmokers. My feeling in 1971 was that continued warnings regarding the health hazards of smoking would be less effective in controlling the smoking epidemic than social actions such as peer pressure, other social pressures, and legislation to protect the nonsmoker. This "semi-official" call for social activism has been followed during the past 12 years by a number of city, state, and even federal regulations protecting the nonsmoker. Perhaps the consequence I could have least likely foreseen after the January 1971 speech was to be named "Public Enemy Number One" by the tobacco industry.

THE EVOLUTION OF THE FEMALE CIGARETTE AND THE SILENCE OF THE WOMEN'S MOVEMENT

Cigarette advertisements increasingly directed at women have escaped the notice of feminists campaigning to remove sexist stereotypes in advertising. Ironically, this is because cigarette advertisements rarely portray women in overtly dumb-blonde or passive roles. The National Advertising Review Board (NARB), part of whose job is to make recommendations on "matters of taste and social responsibility" in connection with US advertising, specified 14 negative and undesirable (or sexist) ways in which current advertising portrays women. Of these, I could find only three which cigarette ads breached. Furthermore, the ads actually fulfilled six of the nine proposals from the NARB on how women could be portrayed constructively. . . .

A peculiar silence — almost a resistance — surrounds the question of smoking among women's organizations. As far as the women's movement is concerned, smoking is someone else's problem. The now prolific literature on women's health and health care is remarkable for lack of attention to the issue. . . .

I contacted more than fifty women's organizations on both sides of the Atlantic, some feminist, some not, some national and some local, but most failed to reply. The National Organization of Women (NOW), for instance, which has taken a highly active role on many women's health issues in the USA, was not prepared to comment, and in its 40-page submission to the 1979 Kennedy hearings on women's health, NOW did not make a single reference to the problem. Indeed, had the American Cancer Society not referred to the rising lung-cancer rates in women in its own evidence to the hearings, the issue would not have been raised at all.

The National Women's Health Network, which represents over a thousand women's health organizations, has "no formal position on smoking."

It is the same story in Britain . . . The Birmingham Women's Health Group seemed to sum up the prevailing attitude among many British women's groups:

When we read your letter there was a great reluctance in the group to spend a whole meeting discussing smoking. Most members (despite being smokers themselves) felt there were more important issues to discuss.

—BOBBIE JACOBSON
The Ladykillers-Why Smoking is a Feminist Issue,
London, Pluto Press, 1981, pp 60, 78-79.

Ending the cigarette pandemic

JULIUS B. RICHMOND, MD

A year after the issuance of the original Surgeon General's report, Congress passed the Federal Cigarette Labeling Advertising Act, which required that all cigarette packages distributed in the United States carry a Surgeon General's warning that smoking may be a hazard to health. In 1969, Congress passed the Public Health Cigarette Smoking Act, which banned cigarette advertising from radio and television.

In 1979, on the fifteenth anniversary of the first report, the Surgeon General published the most comprehensive volume on smoking ever issued in the United States. The data on cigarette smoking's adverse effects on health were overwhelming, and the press recognized this. No longer able to count on journalists to cast doubt on the reliability of the data, the industry changed its strategy by attempting to portray smoking as a civil rights issue. The tobacco industry began pouring millions of dollars into campaigns to prevent the passage of municipal, state, and federal legislation that would ban cigarette advertising or restrict smoking in public places and at the work site.

The publication, also in 1979, of *Healthy People*, the Surgeon General's first report on health promotion and disease prevention, emphasized the necessary future direction of medicine: prevention.

In the years ahead, efforts to end the cigarette pandemic will need to focus on the following:

An end to the victimization of women. In 1980, the Surgeon General's report predicted that women *en masse* would suffer a fate similar to that of men if they continued smoking: By the mid-1980s, lung cancer would surpass breast cancer as the leading cause of death among women. This prediction is a nightmare come true. The death rate from cancer of the lung has increased from 4.6 per 100,000 in 1950 to a projected rate of 20.9 per 100,000 in 1982. In 1983, 17% of cancer deaths in women will be due to lung cancer; 18% will be due to breast cancer.

Dr Richmond served as Surgeon General of the United States Public Health Service from 1977 to 1981.

Address correspondence to Dr Richmond, Professor of Health Policy and Director, Division of Health Policy at Harvard Medical School, 398B Brookline Avenue, Boston, MA 02215.

A greater focus on adolescents. Seventy-five per cent of those who smoke become dependent on cigarettes by age 20. It goes without saying that the medical profession can no longer remain indifferent to the exploitation of adolescents by cigarette advertisers. All future efforts to curtail smoking must center on the age of onset of this form of drug dependence.

More effective strategies for smoking cessation. Over 90% of adults who smoke say they would like to stop smoking. It is incumbent on the medical profession to reinforce this choice among their patients and to encourage legislators, government officials, and industry to develop strong positive incentives for not smoking. It is time to stop pretending that smoking is not a preventable problem.

More attention to clean indoor air rights. It is astounding to contemplate how a single industry has been allowed to undermine not only the health of three generations of Americans but also a treasured age-old amenity like common courtesy. Persons who still smoke are no longer encouraged to ask whether anyone else objects or to be concerned if children are present. Advertising images encourage smoking as the social norm. Physicians must help mobilize greater respect for the rights of the vast nonsmoking majority, especially children.

Abandonment of recommendations to switch to low-tar, low-nicotine cigarettes. Of the many lessons we have learned about smoking, one of the harshest is that low-tar, low-nicotine cigarettes do not lessen the risk for myocardial infarction or impaired pulmonary function. Unfortunately, there is no safe cigarette.

Revelation of chemical additives in cigarettes. In the development of so-called low-tar, low-nicotine cigarettes as a means of allaying health concerns about smoking, the tobacco industry has added hundreds of chemicals and artificial tobacco substitutes to enhance palatability. The industry has prevented the public from learning the names of these chemicals. This information must be revealed.

The epidemiologists have now documented the devastating nature of the health problems attributable to cigarette smoking. But the minimal budgetary allocations to fight smoking testify to the lack of political will of government to meet the challenge. The medical profession must take the lead in making the cigarette issue our number one health priority.

CHEST PHYSICIANS PLEDGE TO ELIMINATE SMOKING

"As a new Fellow of ACCP and a leader in the most important struggle faced by chest physicians, the prevention and control of our major health problems of lung cancer, cardiovascular and chronic pulmonary disease, I shall make a special personal effort to control smoking and to eliminate this hazard from my office, clinic and hospital. I shall ask all of my patients about their smoking habits and I shall assist the cigarette smoker in stopping smoking. I make this pledge to my patients and to society."
—from the Fellowship Pledge of the American College of Chest Physicians

Confronting America's most costly health problem

In November 1981, C. Everett Koop, MD, became Surgeon General of the United States Public Health Service and deputy assistant secretary for health in the Department of Health and Human Services. Born in Brooklyn in 1916, he received his MD from Cornell in 1941. In a 35-year career spent in large part as Professor of Surgery and Surgeon-in-Chief at Children's Hospital of the University of Pennsylvania, Dr Koop became one of the nation's foremost pediatric surgeons. Dr Koop also served as editor of the Journal of Pediatric Surgery. *Most of the surgeons who trained under him now either head departments of surgery or hold the title of professor.*

Early this year, Dr Koop responded with enthusiasm to a request from Journal *editor Alan Blum, MD, for a dialogue on the subject of smoking. They met for two hours on February 26, 1983, in Dr. Koop's office in the Department of Health and Human Services.*

Alan Blum, MD: Current headlines and news stories reflect a concern for the environment. Politicians are venting their anger over dioxin, nuclear radiation, or formaldehyde foam. The public has been put into an uproar over the question of toxic dumping. Why don't we have that same kind of environmental concern about what Surgeons General over the past 25 years have described as the most harmful product in our society—cigarettes?

Everett Koop, MD: I have that concern. And the environmental issue of second-hand or passive side-stream smoking is a very important priority of mine. I think that we are going to prove without any doubt how dangerous this is to the nonsmoker, starting with the unborn and going right on through to the elderly.

AB: If there is any doubt at all, why do we err on the side of harm?

EK: We didn't err on the side of harm in the last Surgeon General's report (on cancer). We quoted studies from Japan, Greece, and the United States. The American study was small and not statistically valid, but the Greek study and the larger Japanese study of lung cancer in the spouses of those who smoke showed beyond any shadow of a doubt side-stream smoking is very dangerous to your health.

AB: But what about the more elemental things like the smoke-filled work place—the kind of disability that so many more people are exposed to?

EK: Take the incidence of colds and pneumonia in toddlers whose parents smoke. It is very clear. There is no doubt about it, and I think that it is a very serious environmental hazard. And one that I object to having to put up with as a nonsmoker.

AB: The data on tobacco smoke pollution in the indoor environment seem to imply at least as compelling a public health hazard as Legionnaire's bacilli cultured in air-conditioning systems. But what will it take to bring about a public outcry on the side-stream issue?

EK: I think certain things are coming up. You mention the issue of not being able to work and feeling uncomfortable due to asthma and having exacerbations. There are a couple of lawsuits going on now that I think will tend to elevate this in the eyes of the public. The other thing that I have always felt strongly about is that the present Surgeon General's warning on cigarettes has been there so long and has been stated in the same way so frequently that no one notices it any more. I think if we had rotating labels and if one of them said, "The smoke from the cigarette you are about to exhale is dangerous to the health of your children," it would have far greater effect than saying "dangerous to your health."

AB: You are presuming that people truly care for children in society. And you may not recall Senator Frank Moss who said it is absurd to talk about the warnings on billboards and the like when nobody can see them. So you are honing in on the *content* of the warning. Whether it be rotating or not, what gives you any hope that the warning is anything more than an "out" for the industry to prevent it from being sued?

EK: There is no doubt that it is the latter, but I am also a firm believer in anecdotal information that comes my way; and one of the things that I do hear repeatedly from people is that "If I had seen that warning on cigarettes when I was a teenager, I wouldn't have started." Maybe that is hindsight, I don't know. But I think we've got to go with everything that we have. One of those things is to change the size of the label, or to vary it so that it sticks out in a different way: When you just see that little box, it isn't hard to ignore the fact that it is there.

AB: What about enlarging the warning on billboards to the size of the Marlboro man and bringing the Marlboro man down to the corner to say, "Hi, smoke Marlboro and be macho"?

EK: For your kinds of spoofs, I know you'd love that.

AB: Seriously, what's wrong with that? The industry is fond of saying that everybody's heard about the "alleged dangers" of smoking and now has a free choice of what to do. What kind of sense of fairness says that camouflaging an industry-approved warning down in the corner of a huge billboard of a cowboy or other hero model enables a child to have a free choice about smoking?

EK: I am not coining a statement to tell you that life isn't fair.

AB: Well, if it is not fair, then what kind of commentary is it on our political system? In *Private Practice*, you have described your role as being one of an apolitical advisor. You could say to people, "Smoking is injurious to your health," but you couldn't tell people, "Don't smoke."

EK: I do tell people not to smoke all the time. I say it publicly. I say it on radio. I say it on television spots. Any place people will listen to me, I say, "Don't smoke." I say "Smoking kills you."

AB: And how are you received?

EK: Of course, I am not out there in the television audience, so I don't know. But when I can talk to young kids and ask them, for example, "How would you feel if instead of the newspaper saying that somebody died of cancer of the lung, it just said 'He died of smoking'? Would that have an effect on you?" And the answer is "yes." As a matter of fact, several suggestions have been made that we should change death certificates: instead of saying "died of cancer of the lung," we'd write "died of smoking complicated by . . . ."

AB: Dr Joe Davis, the Medical Examiner of Dade County, Florida, has written about this. There is a doctor, Charles Tate, MD, of Miami who does just that, and he has raised some eyebrows. People don't like change or rocking the boat. That's the whole point: again it seems as if we are almost hovering defensively, trying to think of strategies to counteract an industry that has every incentive in the world to entice children to buy cigarettes, including tax write-offs for its advertising. It can do whatever it pleases with full impunity.

Is this not demoralizing to you?

EK: It is terribly frustrating to me that the budget of the tobacco industry set aside to lobby here in Washington is five times that of the budget of the Office on Smoking and Health. It is frustrating to me that the money spent on advertising for cigarettes is more than on any other product in the United States (nearly $1.5 billion). And I guess it is demoralizing to me rather than frustrating when I realize that the target of that advertising is the young individual who everybody knows will become hooked to the most addictive drug that we use in this country—nicotine—if he starts when he is 14, 15, 16 years old.

AB: But they say they are only after " 'adult smokers'. We only want to keep our customers. We don't want kids to smoke."

EK: There is some discrepancy between those statements and the obvious thrust of the advertising.

AB: At hearings in Chicago and at AMA meetings, Ron Davis, MD, has shown that children are being given free packages of cigarettes on street corners and at state fairs. What better kind of proof do we need that these people are pushing at children? What will it take to energize public reaction?

EK: If you'd like my real belief about how this is going to turn around, it is not going to come from a governmental effort. It is going to come from the private sector.

AB: And which corporations have come to you and said, "Gee, I am so captivated by your statements I want to help you?"

EK: I haven't found anyone clamoring to come in here. I would think it would be a real natural for insurance companies, though.

AB: You would think that there are some child-oriented industries that would want to show how concerned they are for kids; that might want to sponsor a *real* "Smoke-Out"

C. EVERETT KOOP, MD

364 days a year and give the tobacco companies one day for a fund-raising "smoke-in." Are the health charities doing all they can do?

EK: I think they are beginning to do more.

AB: Immediately after the comprehensive Surgeon General's reports were published in 1964, 1971, and 1979, the per capita consumption of cigarettes declined. Doesn't that suggest that people do follow the Surgeon General's advice but then something happens, which obviously is the money spent on advertising, to undermine that belief?

EK: My concern is the same about many things in the Public Health Service, and that is that this country is geared to reparative and rehabilitative concerns about health. To give an example that has nothing to do with smoking, I am having a lot of trouble getting a preventive program for hip fractures organized in this country. We have 300,000 hip fractures that cost a tremendous amount of money; we can prevent perhaps half of them with an educational program—how to choose a chair, how to get up from a chair, how to get out of bed, how to get out of a car, how to wear the right shoes, and so forth. But the thing is that reparative surgery, such as Teflon hip joints, is much more glamorous.

AB: This is akin to what seems to have happened with medical students. Those who might have become involved in tackling and making real progress against the pandemic of smoking-related diseases seem to have bypassed the smoking issue to cry out against nuclear war. Frankly, I don't know anyone who is *for* nuclear war, and I am finding it difficult to understand the neglect for the very concrete issue of the smoking holocaust, as opposed to the more timeless and abstract issue of war.

EK: I think it is the glamor issue again. This is the year for joining an antinuclear movement.

AB: But could it also be that the smoking issue is too intellectually simplistic for the medical community to deal with? "Okay, fine, it causes disease, so what else is there to do?" I don't know of a single course in medical schools related to techniques for improving the primary prevention of disease. I had a one-hour lecture on smoking in four years, and most people I speak with didn't even have that. Could we not mandate or suggest that there be additional physician training in this? To my knowledge there is not a single full-time physician in the world involved in mass media ways to counteract cigarette smoking. How would you like to get physicians involved, apart from those crazies of us who don't mind the lack of glamor of this issue?

EK: I think it is those crazies who will eventually prevail, because they will attract more people to them—innovative people who are different and who will approach this in an off-beat way.

AB: There was a comment in *Public Health Report** to the effect that no student should get out of medical school without going down to a cigarette billboard and writing a skull and cross bones on it. Is that too radical? Is taking to the streets like that, as physicians are doing in Australia, going too far? Or have we come to a point where property is more valued than life.

EK: I think people who feel strongly enough to take to the streets are ridiculed by the press in this country. And I think that keeps a lot of physicians, who are more or less staid people, home. There are a number of physicians in this country—I would suspect more than half—who are incensed about abortion. But they see a radical fringe doing things that the press ridicules, and rather than have somebody say, "Well, he is part of that," they just stay quietly at home. I have been very outspoken about my opposition to abortion, to infanticide, and to euthanasia. Every place I go, I meet silent physicians who say, "I am with you all the way." But they are not verbally with me, they are not visibly with me, and I think this is true about smoking.

In the last 20 years, I have been talking against smoking. Now I feel I have a mandate. I am in a job that demands that I do this, and I do it to the best of my ability. But it is a very big job, and we are a small cadre. I am concerned that people are terribly critical of things that government tries to do—critical to the point where they cease to be neutral and become almost opposed to you.

AB: I know that you do get involved in advising the World Health Organization (WHO) and other international agencies. Where has the United States stood on the promotion of cigarettes in the Third World, where people may not have the sophistication or knowledge that we have about smoking?

EK: In representing the United States at the WHO, I have begged the Third World countries who do not yet have cigarette advertising to stop it before it begins. But you know what happens? The money that can come to a country by increasing the sale of cigarettes and increasing the tax on them seems beneficial to that country's economy at the moment, until the health problem catches up with them many years later.

AB: Is that argument still valid today? I notice that there

*Neuhaser D: Don't teach preventive medicine: A contrary view. *Publ Hlth Rep* 1982; 97:220–222.

has never been a Surgeon General's report on the health costs attributable to cigarette smoking. That's been alluded to, but why not get rid of the myth that the sale of cigarettes is a boon to the economy?

EK: We've said that. I say it when I talk. I say it when people ask me questions about smoking. We can give them figures about what it costs in actual health care as far as we can figure—$13 billion the last year that we calculated, which I think was 1979. But an additional $23 billion work loss and the morbidity that goes with that is not included. They are also not measuring something else far worse—the cost of human dignity and quality of life of the families left behind by people who die due to smoking.

AB: Yet developing countries from New Guinea to Namibia are under a veritable siege by the tobacco industry, which is still using movie stars and athletes to sell cigarettes. I wonder, too, if there is not a regression in our own country with the introduction of the slogan, "Camels. Where a man belongs." When will this type of exploitation—the vulnerability aspect that is exploited through advertising—be a main part of a Surgeon General's report? Or will that have to be studied and "proved" before it becomes something that can be acknowledged by the Public Health Service?

EK: I think that you are touching on one of the reasons why the private sector has to do it. The government has to be extraordinarily careful when it makes a statement. It has to be able to back it up from every conceivable point of view, whereas the private sector can take liberties. I could say things in my former life that would be considered outrageous for me to say here, but they were true statements; it's just that I couldn't nail them to the wall in the way that the government has to do, because of all the pressures that you get—the lawsuits and that sort of thing. But you have asked me questions that are really prophetic, and I can't give you those answers.

I think that what you are asking me is, "You are the Surgeon General and you say these things. And you are not afraid to say these things. And you believe these things. Therefore, why doesn't the government get behind you?"

I wish they would.

AB: One issue that consumers of cigarettes and nonusers alike agree on is the need to force manufacturers to remove the chemical additives to cigarettes that prevent them from self-extinguishing and are responsible for 2,000 burn deaths a year in the United States.

EK: I spoke to that issue at a symposium in Houston in early 1983 on the injured child. There was a half-day on burns, and I said if we are going to talk about prevention one of the things that has to be addressed is the removal of these chemical additives. This measure is succeeding in the private sector, and the AMA has at last supported the proposed regulation.

AB: Overall, is the AMA doing enough on this issue?

EK: I don't think anybody is doing enough. Let's just say that tomorrow a new something came along that was going to kill 340,000 people next year. Would there be any kind of an outcry? Suppose the killer bee was coming in from South America and they said there were going to be 340,000 people who would die. Would there be a tremendous public response to surround people with something to protect them, to give them something to fight the bee, to take them to a different country until the bee was gone? Of course there would. I think that one of the things about human nature is that if it comes slowly and very gently into your life and all of a sudden it is there and surrounded by advertising, by glamor, by all the things we have been talking about, then it is very hard to see it. You look back on history and you wonder why those idiots didn't see what was happening at a certain time. When you and I, when we're in history, we are those idiots, and we don't see it happening because it is very hard to look at history developing around you. You can't see from the perspective of distance. And I think this is one of the things that has happened with cigarette smoking.

AB: It is fascinating, though, to listen to the initial denial of people who don't believe that they are affected by advertising, least of all when it comes to smoking. But I am encouraged by the number of people who later tell me that once they started paying attention to cigarette advertising, perhaps after having seen a spoof of a cigarette ad, they didn't realize how pervasive and insidious this propaganda is.

EK: There are two things that encourage me about the smoking issue. One is that the per capita use of cigarettes is dropping, and the second is that young people have turned the corner and are coming down. When you quiz them on the high school survey, they do recognize that maybe it is not terribly important to be macho like the Marlboro man. Maybe it is not so smart to be as thin as the girl in the Virginia Slims ads. If you were to ask me what would I do if I could do anything about the problem of teenage smoking, I would like to go back before kids start to smoke—perhaps at about age 12—and start showing them how their lives can be influenced by things like advertising that don't tell the whole story.

AB: This approach, combined with local mass media advertising, is what the group of physicians, DOC, has done in junior high schools. Not that huge grants are required, but it is discouraging that the curative research field gets so well funded in contrast to the preventive strategy you just mentioned.

EK: I think it gets back to what we have discussed. It's part of the American system that reparative techniques and other glamorous things are funded and garner the attention. To stop kids from smoking is not glamorous, and it is very hard to make it glamorous.

AB: The Office on Smoking and Health hasn't been given much money, I know. But has it ever considered paid counter-advertising in the mass media?

EK: I can't answer that. We don't even have enough money to think about it right now. We just barely have enough money to get out the annual report.

RELATIVE IMPORTANCE OF CIGARETTE SMOKING IN OCCUPATIONAL LUNG DISEASE

Since the turn of the century the burden of respiratory disease on our community has changed. Some of the benefits have been due to improved social conditions and some to more effective medical care. There remains a serious level of disease and premature death due to chronic bronchitis and asthma that is unlikely to respond further to social change or to treatments available at present. The incidence of lung cancer has increased alarmingly. These three diseases—bronchitis, asthma, and lung cancer—are at least in part due to materials inhaled into the lungs and to this extent are preventable.

Much has been done at the result of the Clean Air Act to improve the general level of atmospheric pollution, and this may be the reason for the recent improvement in morbidity and mortality for bronchitis. But the other two important sources of pollution of inhaled air (the work place and tobacco smoking) could be reduced further. In this age of financial stringency, cost effectiveness is often the ultimate determinant as to which we should tackle first.

I have reviewed the evidence of the relative importance of smoking and dust in coal miners, slate quarry workers, iron and steel workers, and those working with asbestos. The evidence is scanty and in many instances unreliable. But it indicates that although dust may cause the symptoms of bronchitis in young men, these symptoms may persist but are unlikely to cause serious airways obstruction or premature aging of the lung (emphysema). In most cases smoking is the main cause of bronchitic symptoms in all age groups and may lead to airways obstruction and emphysema. . . .

Only in the archaic conditions of the slate industry did dust exposure exceed cigarette smoking as a cause of disabling disease. In all the other situations reviewed, cigarette smoking was the dominant cause of symptoms, of disability, and of premature death from respiratory disease. Bearing in mind that smoking also causes serious cardiovascular disease, there is no question that even in these dusty industries stopping smoking would have a greater effect on the burden of disease than the complete suppression of all the dusts and fumes.

—P C ELMES
(The Ernestine Henry Lecture delivered at
the Royal College of Physicians, London, November 6, 1979)
Br J Ind Med 1981; 38:1-13.

The three review articles in this section were invited in anticipation of the 1983 report of the Surgeon General, The Health Consequences of Smoking: Cardiovascular Disease.

Effects of cigarette smoking on systemic and coronary hemodynamics

LLOYD W. KLEIN, MD

The mechanisms by which cigarette smoking contributes to the development and clinical manifestation of cardiovascular disease continue to be investigated. The epidemiologic association of smoking with atherosclerosis is established,[1,2] although the pathophysiologic process responsible for this effect remains unknown.[3] Cigarette smoke contains over 1,200 substances and their combustion products,[4,5] several of which could potentially be involved. A recent epidemiologic study suggests that nicotine and carbon monoxide may be less important to the subsequent development of atherosclerosis than previously believed,[6] although the basic premise of that study has been questioned.[7] The increased risk of sudden death in chronic smokers, however, is probably related to the arrhythmogenic potential of nicotine.[8,9]

This paper will review the proved physiologic effects of smoking on the cardiovascular system. Through a better understanding of the ways in which cigarette smoking affects the balance between myocardal oxygen supply and demand, the relationship of smoking to the pathophysiologic process can be better appreciated.

SYSTEMIC HEMODYNAMIC EFFECTS OF CIGARETTE SMOKE AND NICOTINE

The inhalation of cigarette smoke and the parenteral administration of nicotine lead to a well-defined acute cardiovascular response. This response in normal human and animal subjects includes increases in blood pressure, heart rate, and cardiac output.[10,11] Although myocardial contractile force and velocity of contraction also increase,[12] changes in stroke volume vary.[11] These acute physiologic effects last for about 15 minutes, gradually returning to baseline values.

The mechanism by which these physiologic events occur has been extensively studied. Nicotine stimulates all sympathetic ganglia,[13] resulting in the release of norepinephrine from post-ganglionic adrenergic terminals.[14,15] Consequently, peripheral vasoconstriction is produced from direct ganglionic stimulation,[16,17] by facilitation of conduction

of impulses through ganglia,[18] and through chemoreceptor activation in the medulla and the aortic and carotid bodies;[18] therefore, systemic blood pressure rises consequent to the increased peripheral resistance. Heart rate increases, both due to catecholamine release[18,19] and to direct chronotropic effects. Myocardial contractility increases as the result of catecholamine release,[12] an effect that can be prevented by adrenergic beta receptor blockade.[20] Cardiac output increases,[21] primarily as the result of the increase in heart rate. Stroke volume changes can vary depending on the relative effect of increased afterload.

In the presence of left ventricular dysfunction, these systemic hemodynamic changes could be markedly altered. Depending on the degree of systolic dysfunction, one might anticipate that increased afterload could cause the stroke volume to fall dramatically, perhaps accompanied by a decreased cardiac output. In a preliminary study of patients with coronary artery disease, a smaller increase in blood pressure was observed in patients with abnormal systolic function as determined by left ventriculography as compared with those with a comparable extent of coronary disease but with normal left ventricular function. This difference was statistically significant despite nearly identical changes in arterial-coronary sinus oxygen difference and double product (heart rate × systolic blood pressure). In several such patients, the systolic blood pressure was noted to fall with smoking.

INFLUENCE OF CIGARETTE SMOKING ON CORONARY BLOOD FLOW

As the result of the increased double product and increased myocardial contractility observed with smoking, myocardial oxygen demand is increased. In addition, the oxygen-carrying capacity of the blood is diminished in smokers as a result of elevated carboxyhemoglobin levels.[22] Carbon monoxide, a major component of cigarette smoke, is irreversibly bound to hemoglobin. This limits the oxygen supply transported to the microcirculation and, hence, available for myocardial cellular aerobic metabolism.[23] The net result of these factors is to increase myocardial oxygen demand and to limit myocardial oxygen supply,[24] which would potentially precipitate myocardial ischemia.[25]

In response to the increased oxygen demand, there are two compensatory responses available to the coronary vasculature that may result in increased oxygen delivery to the myocardium. First, the myocardial cells could improve

Address correspondence to Dr Klein, Assistant Professor of Medicine, Mid-Atlantic Heart and Vascular Institute, Presbyterian–University of Pennsylvania Medical Center, 39th & Market Streets, Philadelphia, PA 19104.

their efficiency in exchanging CO_2 for oxygen; however, it is well known that myocardial oxygen extraction is nearly maximal at rest.[26] The second possibility is for coronary artery dilation to occur, allowing increased coronary blood flow.

It has been well demonstrated that there is an increase in coronary blood flow following the administration of cigarette smoke or nicotine accompanying increased myocardial oxygen demand in normal animal models.[27-29] Nicotine administration directly into the coronary arteries of dogs has similar effects.[30] When positive chronotropic and/or inotropic effects were produced during left circumflex artery injections, there invariably was an increase in coronary flow.

In those animal models with experimental coronary lesions and atherosclerosis,[31-33] no change, or a mild decrease in coronary blood flow, commonly occurs. Presumably, these observations reflect the inability of some diseased coronary arteries to conduct an increased amount of blood. Thus, when the coronary vasculature is unable to compensate for an increased workload, such as might occur in atherosclerotic coronary disease, cigarette smoke or nicotine elicits an increase in the metabolic requirements of the myocardium which cannot be supplied. In human subjects, cigarette smoking in the presence of coronary artery disease can lead to deleterious clinical effects, inducing angina pectoris at a lower than unusual workload[34] and of a more severe nature.[35]

Bargeron et al[36] were the first to investigate alterations in coronary blood flow during cigarette smoking in normal human subjects. Utilizing the nitrous oxide method with a coronary sinus catheter, coronary flow was measured at rest and again following smoking. Increased coronary flow was observed, and this is the generally cited "normal" physiologic response. However, Regan et al[37,38] studied both patients with coronary artery disease and normal patients. Despite increases in heart rate, cardiac output, and blood pressure, there was no change in coronary flow as determined by the nitrous oxide method in either group. How-

There is, in fact, a marked difference between the response to smoking in normal individuals and those with coronary artery disease. A recent study[39] has shown that the presence, severity, and distribution of coronary lesions have an important effect on the coronary vascular response to smoking. In patients with proximal coronary lesions, coronary blood flow decreased and coronary resistance increased with smoking a single cigarette. Those vasoconstrictor responses that occurred in patients with distal lesions were less prominent. In the normal patients, coronary blood flow increased and coronary resistance decreased; in no individual did coronary resistance increase with smoking.

On the basis of these findings, it is proposed that smoking increases coronary tone at the site of a coronary stenosis. Such dynamic vascular activity in and around a stenotic area has important clinical and physiologic implications quite apart from the effects of smoking. In addition, collateral circulation could also modify this response, if present.

Coronary artery spasm related to cigarette smoking has never been reported in a normal individual. Several patients with severe left main or proximal anterior descending artery lesions have been observed to develop a 10% increase in coronary resistance, but without concurrent electrocar-diographic or clinical signs of ischemia.

A recent report[40] on the effects of chronic smoking on the coronary circulation in 22 patients with angiographically normal coronary arteries and left ventricles found that the coronary vascular reserve, or the capacity of the coronary arteries to dilate and increase blood flow on increased demand, is significantly less in chronic smokers than in nonsmokers. Furthermore, we found that this decrease is more pronounced in heavy smokers. The implication of this observation is that chronic smoking affects coronary artery reactivity, perhaps through a neural mechanism, resulting in a limitation in the ability of the coronary vasculature to respond to increased myocardial oxygen demand.

SUMMARY

Cigarette smoking has important effects on both the coronary and peripheral vasculature. Both acute and chronic effects on coronary artery reactivity have been documented. These physiologic changes have potential implications for both the development of atherosclerosis as well as for the intensity of symptoms when coronary artery disease is present. A major segment of the population continues to consume tobacco despite its proved adverse cardiovascular consequences. Therefore, it is imperative for every member of the medical community to play a greater role in communicating this information to the public and assuring that it is heeded.

REFERENCES

1. *The Health Consequences of Smoking.* US Department of Health, Education and Welfare, Public Health Service, Center for Disease Control 1976. HEW Publication No. (CDC)78-8357.
2. McGill HC: Potential mechanisms for the augmentation of atherosclerosis and atherosclerotic disease by cigarette smoking. *Prev Med* 1979; 8:390.
3. Rogers WR, Bass RL, et al.: Atherosclerosis-related responses to cigarette smoking in the baboon. *Circulation* 1980; 61:1188-1193.
4. Kensler CJ: Components of pharmacologic interest in tobacco smoke. *Ann Intern Med* 1960; 90:43-47.
5. Johnstone RA, Plimmer JR: The chemical constituents of tobacco and tobacco smoke. *Chem Revs* 1959; 59:885-936.
6. Kaufman DW, Helmrich SP, Rosenberg L, Miettinen OS, Shapiro S: Nicotine and carbon monoxide content of cigarette smoke and the risk of myocardial infarction in young men. *N Engl J Med* 1983; 308:409-413.
7. Benowitz NL, Hall S, Herning R, et al: Smokers of low-yield cigarettes do not consume less nicotine. *N Engl J Med* 1983; 309:139-142.
8. Bellet S, Fleischmann D, Roman L, Degugman N: The effect of cigarette smoke inhalation on the ventricular fibrillation threshold. *Circulation* 1970; 42(suppl3):135.
9. Greenspan K, Edmands RE, Knoebel SB, Fisch C: Some effects of nicotine on cardiac automaticity, conduction, and inotropy. *Arch Int Med* 1969;123:707-712.
10. Thomas CB, Murphy E: Circulatory responses to smoking in healthy young men. *Ann NY Acad Sci* 1960; 90:266-276.
11. Thomas CB, Bateman J, Lindberg E, Bornhold H: Observations on the individual effects of smoking on the blood pressure, heart rate, stroke volume and cardiac output of healthy young adults. *Ann Intern Med* 1956; 44:874-892.
12. Leaders FE, Long JP: Action of nicotine on coronary vascular resistance in dogs. *Am J Physiol* 1962; 203:621-625.
13. Comroe JH: The pharmacologic actions of nicotine. *Ann NY Acad Sci* 1960; 90:48-51.
14. Hall G, Turner D: Effects of nicotine on the release of 3H-Noradrenaline from the hypothalamus. *Biochem Pharmacol* 1972; 21:1829-1838.
15. Cryer P, Haymond M, Santiago J, Shah S: Norepinephrine and epinephrine release and adrenergic mediation of smoking-associated hemodynamic and metabolic events. *N Engl J Med* 1976; 295:573-577.
16. Burn JH: The action of nicotine on the peripheral circulation. *Ann NY Acad Sci* 1960; 90:81-84.
17. Freund J, Ward C: The acute effect of cigarette smoking on the digital circulation in health and disease. *Ann NY Acad Sci* 1960; 90:85-101.
18. Gebber GL: Neurogenic basis for the rise in blood pressure evoked by nicotine in the cat. *J Pharmacol Exp Ther* 1969; 166:255-263.
19. Rehder K, Roth G: Effect of smoking on the fasting blood sugar and pressor amines. *Circulation* 1959; 20:224-228.
20. Westfall T, Cipolloni P, Edmundowicz A: Influence of propranolol on

hemodynamic changes and plasma catecholamine levels following cigarette smoking and nicotine. *Proc Soc Exp Biol Med* 1966; 123:174–179.

21. Irving DW, Yamamoto T: Cigarette smoking and cardiac output. *Br Heart J* 1963; 25:126–132.

22. Ayers S, Mueller H, Gregory J, Gianelli S, Penny J: Systemic and myocardial hemodynamic responses to relatively small concentrations of carboxyhemoglobin. *Arch Environ Health* 1969; 18:699–709.

23. Aronow WS, Rokaw SN: Carboxyhemoglobin caused by smoking non-nicotine cigarettes: effects in angina pectoris. *Circulation* 1971; 44:782–788.

24. Oram S, Sawton E: Tobacco angina. *Quart J Med* 1963; 32:115–143.

25. Kien GA, Sherrod T: Action of nicotine and smoking on coronary circulation and myocardial oxygen utilization. *Ann NY Acad Sci* 1960; 90:161–173.

26. Messer JV, Wagman RJ, Levine HJ, Neill WA, Krasnow N, Gorlin R.: Patterns of human myocardial oxygen extraction during rest and exercise. *J Clin Invest* 1962; 41:725–742.

27. Kien G, Lasker N, Sherrod T: Action of cigarette smoke on cardiovascular hemodynamics and oxygen utilization in the dog. *J Pharmacol Exp Ther* 1958; 124:35–42.

28. Ross G, Blesa MI: The effect of nicotine on the coronary circulation of dogs. *Am Heart J* 1970; 79:96–102.

29. Leb G, Derntl F, Robin E, Bing RJ: The effect of nicotine on effective and total coronary blood flow in the anesthetized closed-chest dog. *J Pharmacol Exp Ther* 1970; 173:138–144.

30. West J, Guzman S, Bellet S: Cardiac effects of intracoronary arterial injections of nicotine. *Circ Res* 1958; 6:389–395.

31. Bellet S, Kershbaum A, Meade R, Schwartz L: The effects of tobacco smoke and nicotine on the normal heart and in the presence of myocardial damage produced by coronary ligation. *Am J Med Sci* 1941; 201:40–51.

32. Rinzler S, Travell J, Karp D, Charleson D: Detection of coronary atherosclerosis in the living rabbit by the ergonovine cigarette test. *Am J Physiol* 1956; 184:605–612.

33. Travell J, Rinzler S, Karp D: Cardiac effects of nicotine in the rabbit with experimental coronary atherosclerosis. *Ann NY Acad Sci* 1960; 90:290–301.

34. Aronow WS, Kaplan M, Jacob D: Tobacco: a precipitating factor in angina pectoris. *Ann Intern Med* 1968; 69:529–536.

35. Fox KM, Jonathan A, Williams H, Selwin A: Interaction between cigarettes and propranolol in the treatment of angina pectoris. *Br Med J* 1980; 281: 191–193.

36. Bargeron LM, Ehmke D, Gonlubol F, Castellanos A, Siegal A, Gorlin R.: Effect of cigarette smoking on coronary blood flow and myocardial metabolism. *Circulation* 1957; 15:251–257.

37. Regan T, Frank M, Mc Ginty J, Zobl E, Hellems H, Bing RJ: Myocardial response to cigarette smoking in normal subjects and patients with coronary disease. *Circulation* 1961; 23:365–369.

38. Regan T, Hellems H, Bing RJ: Effect of cigarette smoking on coronary circulation and cardiac work in patients with arteriosclerotic coronary disease. *Ann NY Acad Sci* 1960; 90:186–189.

39. Klein LW, Ambrose J, Pichard AD, Holt J, Gorlin R, Teichholz LE: Acute coronary hemodynamic response to cigarette smoking in patients with coronary artery disease. *J Am Coll Cardiol* 1984; 3:879–886.

40. Klein LW, Pichard AD, Holt J, Smith H, Gorlin R, Teichholz LE: Effects of chronic tobacco smoking on the coronary circulation. *J Am Coll Cardiol* 1983; 1:421–426.

courtesy DOC archive

"I've looked at life from both sides now." —Judy Collins. Top L: A cigarette-sponsored religio-cultural exhibition, "The Vatican Collection," sponsored by Philip Morris, makers of Marlboro and other cigarette brands. Top R: Balanced coverage of a cause and cure of cardiovascular disease. Bottom: Public service advertisement and paid advertisement.

Constituents of cigarette smoke and cardiovascular disease

DAVID W. KAUFMAN, ScD

There is now little doubt that cigarettes play a major role in the cause of heart disease, and increasing attention has been focused on which constituents of cigarette smoke might be harmful. Most of the interest has centered on nicotine and carbon monoxide, which are known to affect the cardiovascular system in potentially adverse ways.[1] Nicotine raises systolic blood pressure and cardiac output; it increases the levels of free fatty acids, which may promote atherosclerosis; and it may lead to increased platelet adhesiveness. Carbon monoxide reduces the amount of oxygen available to the heart; it decreases the threshold for ventricular fibrillation in animals and may promote atherosclerosis by increasing vessel-wall hypoxia and permeability.

It is not clear whether or not these effects are sufficient at the levels present in cigarette smoke to account for the elevated risk among smokers. Despite one earlier study[2] which indicated that low-tar/nicotine cigarettes might be somewhat safer with respect to coronary heart disease, recent evidence has tended to suggest that smoking such cigarettes may not reduce the risk relative to smoking other brands. In two prospective studies, death rates from ischemic heart disease,[3] and rates of myocardial infarction (fatal and nonfatal),[4] were similar among smokers of filter and nonfilter cigarettes. In a case-control study of nonfatal myocardial infarction which linked the brand smoked to levels of nicotine and carbon monoxide published by the Federal Trade Commission,[5] the estimated magnitude of the risk was not related to the level of either substance. In all three studies, the risk was considerably higher in those who smoked than in those who didn't.

The public health importance of these findings is evident, but the biologic implications are less clear. It is possible that the nicotine and carbon monoxide in cigarette smoke are not the factors that contribute to the cause of coronary disease, and that one or more of the many other constituents is responsible. Alternatively, an effect of the two substances could be masked by differences in smoking behavior. Individuals who smoke cigarettes that are "low" in nicotine and carbon monoxide according to machine testing may actually be absorbing as much as those who smoke the "high" brands.

The latter possibility is supported by a growing body of data. It has been noted that smokers of low tar/nicotine cigarettes inhale more deeply, or otherwise smoke more intensively.[6,7] In a small study,[8] smoking behavior was a better predictor of blood nicotine levels than were the nicotine yields of different cigarettes as determined by machine smoking. Most recently, in a study of nearly 300 smokers,[9] it was observed that blood levels of cotinine, a metabolite of nicotine, were unrelated to the machine-determined levels of nicotine published by the Federal Trade Commission. The investigators concluded that "smokers of low-nicotine cigarettes do not consume less nicotine" than smokers of higher-rated brands.

It may be reasonable to presume that if nicotine intake is unrelated to the type of cigarette, then the same may be true for carbon monoxide; however, the evidence for this presumption is weaker. In one study, carboxyhemoglobin levels were highest among smokers of cigarettes with traditional unperforated filters, intermediate among smokers of newer-type cigarettes with perforated filters, and lowest among smokers of unfiltered cigarettes.[10] The picture that emerges is equivocal: cigarettes with unperforated filters were machine rated at higher levels of carbon monoxide than unfiltered cigarettes, but those with perforated filters were rated at lower levels. At the least, the data suggest that smoking the newest low-level cigarettes did not correlate with the lowest blood levels of carboxyhemoglobin.

What of the possibility that factors other than nicotine and carbon monoxide cause the smoking-related increase in the risk of coronary heart disease? Very little is known about the effects of the many other constituents of cigarette smoke. It has been suggested that cadmium might be related to hypertension,[1] although smoking itself is not known to cause hypertension. Other hypotheses include tobacco antigens causing increased endothelial cell damage, and atherosclerosis resulting from monoclonal smooth muscle cellular proliferation.[1] The latter hypothesis implies that tar might be atherogenic. There appears to be no relationship between the tar level of cigarettes and coronary disease,[5] but there is the same problem of interpretation as with nicotine and carbon monoxide.

In summary, although it is clear that cigarettes increase the risk of cardiovascular disease, the existing evidence concerning the role of particular constituents of cigarette smoke is inconclusive. There are biologic grounds to suspect that nicotine and carbon monoxide increase the risk. Although the direct evidence does not show any relationship between the machine-determined levels of these substances in cigarettes and risk, it now appears that smokers of low-level cigarettes compensate and absorb as much as smokers of other brands. Thus, the jury is still out on nicotine and carbon monoxide. It is also possible that some other substance may be the culprit, but the information is very sketchy indeed.

One statement can be made with some confidence: the newer low-level brands of cigarettes, as smoked, seem to carry the same risk of coronary heart disease as other brands. Those who smoke these cigarettes in the belief that

Address correspondence to Dr Kaufman, Senior Investigator, Drug Epidemiology Unit, Boston University School of Medicine, School of Public Health, 1371 Beacon Street, Brookline, MA 02146.

they are reducing their risk of heart attacks should be warned that they are deluding themselves.

REFERENCES

1. *The Health Consequences of Smoking—the Changing Cigarette: A Report of the Surgeon General.* Washington, Department of Health and Human Services, 1981.

2. Hammond EC, Garfinkel L, Seidman H, Lew EA: "Tar" and nicotine content of cigarette smoke in relation to death rates. *Environ Res* 1976; 12:263–274.

3. Hawthorne VM, Fry JS: Smoking and health: the association between smoking behavior, total mortality, and cardiorespiratory disease in west central Scotland. *J Epidemiol Commun Health* 1978; 32:260–266.

4. Castelli WP, Garrison RJ, Dawber TR, et al: The filter cigarette and coronary heart disease: the Framingham Study. *Lancet* 1981; 2:109–113.

5. Kaufman DW, Helmrich SP, Rosenberg L, Miettinen OS, Shapiro S: Nicotine and carbon monoxide content of cigartte smoke and the risk of myocardial infarction in young men. *N Engl J Med* 1983; 308:409–413.

6. Wald NJ, Idle M, Boreham J, Bailey A: Inhaling habits among smokers of different types of cigarettes. *Thorax* 1980; 35:925–928.

7. Russell MAH, Jarvis M, Iyer R, Feyerabend C: Relation of nicotine yield of cigarettes to blood nicotine concentration in smokers. *Br Med J* 1980; 2:972–976.

8. Herning RI, Jones RT, Benowitz NL, Mines AH: How a cigarette is smoked determines blood nicotine levels. *Clin Pharmacol Ther* 1983; 33:84–90.

9. Benowitz NL, Hall SM, Herning RI, Jcaob P, Jones RT, et al: Smokers of low-yield cigarettes do not consume less nicotine. *N Engl J Med* 1983; 309:139–142.

10. Wald N, Idle M, Smith PG, Bailey A: Carboxyhaemoglobin levels in smokers of filter and plain cigarettes. *Lancet* 1977; 1:110–112.

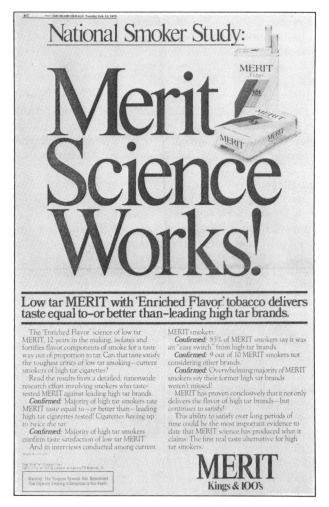

Advertising headlines touting certain "low tar" cigarette brands use words such as "science," "study," and "research." The reader of such advertisements might not realize that such terms refer to *marketing* research.

"Less hazardous" cigarettes: fact or fiction?

W. S. RICKERT, PhD

INTRODUCTION

Since many individuals either cannot or will not give up smoking, a great deal of effort has gone into the development and marketing of cigarettes that are potentially "less hazardous," that is, cigarettes with reduced chemical yields and less biologic activity.[1] This "less hazardous" cigarette concept rests on three basic assumptions: (1) Large scale commercial production of cigarettes with reduced activity is feasible, (2) Given the option, those who cannot or will not stop smoking will switch to this sort of product, and (3) Persons who do switch will experience a reduced risk of smoking-related diseases compared with those who continue to smoke the higher-yield products.

Considerable effort has been expended in attempting to verify these assumptions, including monitoring of cigarette characteristics by several countries, investigation of smoking behavior, and large-scale epidemiologic studies. What follows is a limited review of the results from some of these investigations.

CHANGES IN CIGARETTE YIELDS, 1969 TO 1982

Although numerous compounds have been identified in tobacco smoke, there are only about 10 constituents that are both biologically active and present in amounts exceeding 1 μg per cigarette.[2] Of these, carbon monoxide (CO) is generally found in the highest concentration (1 to 26 mg), followed by tar (1 to 21 mg), nicotine (0.1 to 1.3 mg), aldehydes (0.08 to 1.2 mg) and hydrogen cyanide (0.04 to 0.25 mg).[3] When inhaled, the CO in tobacco smoke results in the formation of carboxyhemoglobin (COHb), so that approximately 80% of persons still smoking have COHb levels of from 2% to 8%.[4] COHb levels are better correlated than smoking history with the development of angina pectoris, myocardial infarction, and intermittent claudication; the relative risk of developing coronary heart disease is about 20 times greater in individuals with COHb levels of 5% or greater than in those with levels below 3%.[5] "Tar" is a complex mixture of compounds including a number of identifiable carcinogens and cocarcinogens, while nicotine is generally accepted as the principal constituent responsible for the cigarette smoker's pharmacologic response.[2] Aldehydes, such as acetaldehyde, are toxic to cilia as is hydrogen cyanide (HCN), which also interferes with respiration.[6] A single cigarette delivers 40 to 250 μg of HCN.[3] In rats a dose range of 170 to 230 μg per kilogram of body weight causes unconsciousness and 590 to 640 μg per kilogram of body weight is lethal.[7]

Yields of these compounds were evaluated for the 1969 and 1978 versions of 25 brands of Canadian cigarettes representing more than 70% of sales in each year.[8] During this 10-year period significant decreases in average tar (2.5 mg), nicotine (0.34 mg), HCN (69 μg), total aldehydes (114 μg), and acrolein deliveries (5.2 μg) have been reported but no significant change in average CO yields. With respect to tar, this decline has continued with a further decrease in average yields of from 14.4 mg in 1978 to 11.7 mg in 1982. During this same period there was a marked decrease in average CO yields of 17.7 mg in 1978 to 13.0 mg in 1982. This abrupt change can be attributed to a recognition of the potential health effects of low-level CO exposure and the fact that an average consumer can obtain as much as twice the recommended industrial limit for CO exposure from his cigarette brand based on the following simple calculation.

Smoking a single cigarette with a CO yield of about 18 mg will result in average alveolar CO concentration of about 475 ppm (parts per million) for six minutes.[9] For an average pack-a-day smoker (20 cigarettes), this lung level of exposure can be expressed as 950 ppm-hours as compared with the industrial limit of 400 ppm-hours (50 ppm × 8-hour working day). Since the levels of CO in the breath of many heavy smokers often exceeds 50 ppm, a limit of 50 ppm for industrial exposure to CO is unrealistic for those who smoke. Similar arguments can be made with respect to other smoke constituents that have industrial limits.[6]

The 27% decrease in average CO yields over the past five years has come about due to major changes in the construction of most cigarette brands. In 1978, there was no significant correlation between tar and CO yields for brands whose tar yield exceeded 13 mg. As a result, for a given tar yield, CO deliveries could vary by as much as a factor of two. In addition, the higher tar brands on the average delivered less CO per unit tar than did the lower yield brands. By 1982, this circumstance had changed somewhat due to an increased use of high porosity papers and filter tip ventilation, but there is still considerable variability in CO yields for a given tar yield, particularly for the higher tar brands.

CONSUMER ACCEPTANCE

The critical factor with respect to any "less hazardous" product is consumer acceptance and, with respect to the low-tar brands, consumer response has been extraordinary. Data from the United States indicate that sales in the low-tar segment (that is, tar ≤ 15 mg) have tripled from 17% in 1976 to 59% in 1982.[10] A similar pattern has occurred in Canada.[8]

There are several possible explanations for this explosive

From the Smoking and Health Program of Labstat Incorporated, a project receiving financial support from Health and Welfare Canada, Bureau of Tobacco Control and the National Health Research Development Program.

Presented in part at the Fifth World Conference on Smoking and Health, Winnipeg, Canada, July 13, 1983.

Address correspondence to Dr Rickert, Labstat Incorporated, 262 Manitou Drive, Kitchener, Ontario N2C 1L3 Canada.

growth, but the major contributor would seem to be an increased public awareness that cigarette smoking, and in particular exposure to cigarette tar, is detrimental to health. Cigarette companies have capitalized on this perception by advertising tar levels as the basis for brand selection.

In Canada, the tobacco industry does not promote the tar yields of brands as an advertising device but rather focuses on the usage of words such as "light" (extra light, ultra light) and "mild" (extra mild, special mild, superior mild, ultra mild) to convey the impression of low or reduced yields. Unfortunately, this is misleading to the consumer since there is no general agreement as to the meaning of these descriptors in relationship to brand characteristics. As shown in the Table, it is possible to purchase a brand with no "special" designation having a tar yield of 1 mg and another described as "light" with a tar yield of 15 mg. Even within a category such as that labeled as "D" in this table, yields can vary by as much as tenfold and more. The inference is that descriptors such as "light" and "mild" are so well established in the public's mind as meaning "less" that their usage can increase sales irrespective of tar yields (Fig 1).

HEALTH CONSEQUENCES FROM "LESS HAZARDOUS" CIGARETTE USAGE

Given the now widespread usage of lower-yield brands, there have been several large-scale investigations into the resulting consequences for the health of smokers, and with respect to lung cancer they are significant. One major 12-year study of more than 1 million smokers reported that smokers of low-tar/nicotine cigarettes (tar $\leq$ 17.6 mg) had a 26% lower lung cancer mortality than those who reported smoking high tar (25.8 to 35.7 mg) cigarettes.[11] From this same study, with respect to overall mortality, there also appeared to be a relationship to stated brand yield since smokers of medium-tar (17.6 mg to 25.8 mg) had a 9% lower mortality rate than did smokers of high-tar cigarettes. The differences between high- and low-tar, and high- and medium-tar groups were reported as "highly significant."[12]

With respect to heart disease, the results are far less encouraging, since several studies have concluded that men who smoke cigarettes with reduced yields do not have a lower risk of myocardial infarction when compared with those who use the higher-yield products.[13,14] In summary, then, although there may be a lower risk of death due to lung cancer resulting from the usage of lower-yield ciga-

NOW EVEN MILDER

FIGURE 1. Point-of-purchase advertisement for a brand of Canadian cigarettes.

rettes, the overall risks to health are far less dramatic than would have been predicted based on changes in tar deliveries alone. In the hands of many smokers, the so-called "less-hazardous" product carries much the same risk as that associated with the usage of the higher-yield brands.

A partial explanation for the discrepancy between anticipated and observed reduction in lethal risk is a tendency toward increased consumption, which often occurs on switching to a low-yield brand.[15,16] This increase has been ascribed to a nicotine dependency which may also cause more subtle changes in smoking behavior. This conclusion results from studies of cigarette yields as measured by smoking machines in relation to smoke absorption estimated from levels of smoke constituents in body fluids. For ex-

A Comparison of Brand Descriptors and Tar Yields of Brands of Canadian Cigarettes*

Category	Brand Designation	No.	Tar Yields (mg)		
			Average	Median	Range
A	Light	18	11.1	11.5	5–15
B	Ultra Light, Extra Light	4	6.0	7.5	1–8
C	Mild	2	12.5	12.5	12–13
D	Extra Mild, Special Mild, Ultra Mild, Superior Mild	23	6.3	4.0	0.4–13
E ·	Others	73	13.9	14.0	1–18
	TOTAL	120			

* List produced by the Canadian Tobacco Manufacturers Council, March 31, 1983.

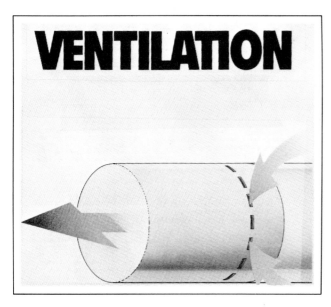

FIGURE 2. Fluted filter construction: vents to promote air dilution.

ample, if a cigarette is smoked in a manner similar to the conditions used in cigarette testing then the stated yield of HCN should provide a reasonable measure of the amount of HCN to which a smoker is exposed. However, in one study involving 240 subjects, no correlation was found between brand yield and smoke absorption after standardizing for level of consumption.[17] Others have reported similar results.[18]

The question of nicotine compensation also has been approached using volunteers who were made to switch to progressively lower-yield brands. Measures of smoking exposure such as blood COHb, serum cotinine, and plasma

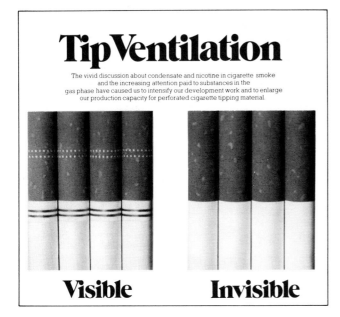

FIGURE 3. Laser perforating as a means of reducing the visibility of cigarette ventilation. (Source: Advertisement in Tobacco Reporter, October 1981. *Deutsche Benkert* GMBH and COKG.)

thiocyanate all demonstrated that more smoke was absorbed than would have been predicted from the values on the packages. In fact, the lack of major differences between the treatment and control groups in this study suggested that most subjects obtained just as much nicotine from the so-called less-hazardous products as they did from their original brand.[19,20] For most subjects in these studies, switching to low-yield brands did not result in a significant decrease in the amount of smoke absorbed, due primarily to a tendency to increase puff volume and/or depth of inhalation when such products are smoked.[21] Unfortunately, these maneuvers are an unconscious response to a nicotine dependency and, as such, are difficult for the smoker to control. However, there are more obvious ways to increase cigarette yields. For example, one major factor that most low-yield brands have in common is the presence of air dilution devices, an example of which is shown in Figure 2. This filter type is used on a number of US cigarette brands and presents some difficulty with respect to appropriate conditions for testing since blocking of these vents would allow a smoker to obtain more from a cigarette than the stated contents would imply.[22] Fifty percent of those who smoke low-tar cigarettes admit to blocking the holes; thus, there could be little, if any, change in the risk of smoking-related diseases.[23] But although consumers can be warned of the danger of hole blocking, the vents on many brands are all but invisible to the human eye, as illustrated in Figure 3.

The extensive use of air dilution devices to effect reduced yields has other consequences as well. Although mainstream yields to the smoking machine are reduced by these devices, sidestream yields to the environment are not. For example, it has been reported that under standard testing conditions a 3-mg tar cigarette produced a total of 39 mg of tar, as did a 17-mg cigarette. Similarly, with respect to carbon monoxide, a 3-mg cigarette produced a total of 56 mg of CO, a value close to that recorded for a 17-mg CO cigarette. Thus, when mainstream and sidestream yields are added together, the total appears to be largely independent of cigarette tar classification.[24] This implies similar hazards to those exposed to the smoke of others regardless of whether or not the brand being smoked is described by the manufacturers as "light" or "mild."

Unfortunately, most persons who still smoke cigarettes do not realize that the numbers so heavily exploited by industry are based on the average smoking habits of a male smoker of nonfilter cigarettes as determined 25 years ago.[25] Today, fewer than 10% of all smokers in the United States appear to follow this pattern.[26] Thus, on this basis alone, it is not surprising that yields to the smoker will bear little resemblance to the yields to the smoking machines that have been used as the basis for comparisons in epidemiologic studies.[11-13] In addition, human smoking behavior is so variable that it is questionable as to whether or not any single set of conditions for machine smoking will provide "reasonable" values for smoke constituents.[27] For example, recently it has been reported that a cigarette brand that delivered 39 μg of HCN under standard conditions produced from 5 to 241 μg HCN when tested under conditions defined by observations of current smoking behavior. This range for a *single cigarette brand* is greater than the range recorded for all 115 brands of cigarettes that were tested.[28]

With respect to the tobacco industry, the "less-hazardous" cigarette program has focused to a large extent on pressuring manufacturers to reduce yields as measured by smoking machines. But, given the ease with which a smoker can modify these yields, the vanishingly small-tar deliveries of many brands can only be guaranteed to smoking machines that smoke each and every cigarette under "standard" conditions.

REFERENCES

1. Hoffman D, Tso TC, Gori GB: The less harmful cigarette. *Prev Med* 1980; 9:287–296.
2. *Smoking and Health*. A report of the Surgeon General. DHEW Publication No. (PHS), 79-50066, US Department of Health, Education, and Welfare, 1979.
3. Rickert WS, Robinson JC, Young JC: Estimating the hazards of less hazardous cigarettes. I. Tar, nicotine, carbon monoxide, acroelin, hydrogen cyanide and total aldehyde deliveries of Canadian cigarettes. *J Toxicol Environ Health* 1980; 6:351–365.
4. Heliovaara M, Karvonen MJ, Vilhunen R, Punsar S: Smoking, carbon monoxide and atherosclerotic diseases. *Br Med J* 1978; 1:268–270.
5. Wald N, Smith HS: Association between atherosclerotic diseases and carboxyhemoglobin levels in tobacco smokers. *Br Med J* 1973; 1:761–765.
6. Petersen C: The effect of inhibitors on the oxygen kinetics of cytochrome C oxidase. *Biochem Biophys Acta* 1977; 460 (2):299–307.
7. Bell RH, Stemmer KL, Barkley W, Hollingsworth LD: Cyanide toxicity from the thermal degradation of rigid polyurethane foam. *Am Indust Hyg Assoc J* 1979; 40:757–761.
8. Rickert WS, Robinson JC: Yields of selected toxic agents in the smoke of Canadian cigarettes, 1969 and 1978. A decade of change? *Prev Med* 1981; 10: 353–363.
9. Goldsmith JR, Terzaghi J, Hackney JD: Evaluation of fluctuating carbon monoxide exposures. Theoretical approach and a preliminary test of methods for studying effects of human populations of fluctuating exposures from multiple sources. *Arch Environ Health* 1963; 7:647–663.
10. Cigarette Report: Low Tar in Command. *Tobacco International*, April 1, 1983, pp 68–69.
11. Hammond EC, Garfinkel L, Seidman H, Lee EA: Tar and nicotine content of cigarette smoke in relation to death rates. *Environ Res* 1976; 12:263–274.
12. Lee PM, Garfinkel L: Mortality and type of cigarette smoked. *J Epidemiol Community Health* 1981; 35:16–22.
13. Kaufman DW, Helmrich SP, Rosenberg L, Miettinen OS, Shapiro S: Nicotine, carbon monoxide content of cigarette smoke and the risk of myocardial infarction in young men. *N Engl J Med* 1983; 308:409–413.
14. *The Health Consequences of Smoking. The Changing Cigarette*. A Report of the Surgeon General US Department of Health and Human Services. DHHS(PBS), 81-50156, 1981.
15. Stepaney R: Consumption of cigarettes of reduced tar and nicotine delivery. *Br J Addict* 1980; 75:81–88.
16. Garfinkel L: Changes in the cigarette consumption of smokers in relation to changes in tar/nicotine content of cigarettes smoked. *Am J Public Health* 1979; 69:1274–1276.
17. Rickert WS, Robinson JC: Estimating the hazards of less-hazardous cigarettes. II. Study of cigarette yields of nicotine, carbon monoxide and hydrogen cyanide in relation to levels of cotinine, carboxyhemoglobin and thiocyanate in smokers. *J Toxicol Environ Health* 1981; 7:391–403.
18. Benowitz NL, Hall SM, Henning RI, et al: Smokers of low-yield cigarettes do not consume less nicotine. *N Engl J Med* 1983; 309:139–142.
19. Robinson JC, Young JC, Rickert WS: A comparative study of the amount of smoke absorbed from low yield ("less hazardous") cigarettes. Part 1: Non-invasive measures. *Brit J Addict* 1982; 77:383–397.
20. Robinson JC, Young JC, Rickert WS, Fey G, Kozlowski LT: A comparative study of the amount of smoke absorbed from low yield ("less hazardous") cigarettes. Part 2: Invasive measures. *Br J Addict* 1983; 78:79–87.
21. Henning RI, Jones RT, Bachman J, Mines AH: Puff volume increases when low nicotine cigarettes are smoked. *Br Med J* 1981; 283:1–7.
22. Kozlowski LT, Rickert WS, Pope MA, Robinson JC, Frecker RC: Estimating the yield to smokers of tar, nicotine and carbon monoxide from the "lowest yield" ventilated filter cigarettes. *Br J Addict* 1982; 77:159–165.
23. Lombardo T, Davis CJ, Prue DM: When low tar cigarettes yield high tar: cigarette filter ventilation hole blocking and its detection. *Addict Behav* 1983; 8: 67–69.
24. Rickert WS, Robinson JC, Collishaw N: Yields of tar, nicotine and carbon monoxide in the sidestream smoke from 15 brands of Canadian cigarettes. *Am J Public Health* 1984; 74:228–231.
25. Brunnemann KD, Hoffman D, Wynder EL, Gori GB: Chemical studies on tobacco smoke. XXXVII. Determination of tar, nicotine and carbon monoxide in cigarette smoke. A comparison of international smoking conditions, in: Wynder EL, Hoffman D, Gori GB (eds): *Modifying the Risk for the Smoker*. Proceedings of the Third World Conference on Smoking and Health, New York, June 2–5, 1975. Vol. 1. US Department of Health, Education and Welfare, Public Health Service. National Institutes of Health, National Cancer Institute, DHEW Publication No. (NIH) 76-1221, 1976, pp 441–449.
26. *The Health Consequences of Smoking. Cancer*. A report of the Surgeon General US Department of Health and Human Services. DHHS(PBS) 82-50179, 1982.
27. Rickert WS, Robinson JC, Young JC, Collishaw NE, Bray DF: A comparison of the yields of tar, nicotine and carbon monoxide of 36 brands of Canadian cigarettes tested under three conditions. *Prev Med* 1983; 12:682–694.
28. Rickert WS, Robinson JC, Collishaw NE, Bray, DF: Estimating the hazards of "less-hazardous" cigarettes. III. A study of the effect of various smoking conditions on yields of hydrogen cyanide, and cigarette tar. *J Toxicol Environ Health* 1983; 12:39–54.

L: In 1936 even Santa smoked Luckies; the word "light" could describe an unfiltered cigarette with over 30 mg tar. Middle: In 1983 promotion for the revived brand received a boost from *TIME*. R: Young man in newspaper sports section advertisement tries his luck with this "mild" smoke.

The economics of smoking: dollars and sense

KENNETH E. WARNER, PhD

The Surgeon General has identified cigarette smoking as the nation's most significant source of preventable morbidity and premature mortality.[1] The annual death toll—some 350,000 people—exceeds the number of American lives lost in all of the wars this country has fought in the 20th century.

The economic toll of smoking is both less familiar to the general public and less readily comprehensible. Smoking-related diseases annually consume approximately $15 billion in medical care resources, or more than 5% of the nation's total direct health care costs, and cause a productivity loss (due to excess morbidity and disability and premature death) of $34 billion. (These and succeeding dollar figures are updated by the author from the referenced sources to approximate 1983 dollars.) The sum of these numbers—$49 billion—may be considered a first approximation to the social economic cost of smoking.[2] If New York's share of this burden is proportionate to its population share, this means that smoking costs the State and its residents approximately $4.4 billion each year. In ignoring important economic intangibles, such as the cost of pain and suffering, all of these figures must be considered a substantial underestimate of the true social cost of smoking.

A figure in the billions of dollars is difficult for most people to comprehend. To put it into perspective, the measurable annual social cost of smoking per capita is on the order of $200. Medical care necessitated by smoking-related illness translates into an annual economic burden on the typical nonsmoking, working-age adult in excess of $100 in taxes and health insurance premiums to pay for the health care needs of the victims of smoking.

If smoking is so socially costly, how can one explain the fact that over the years the federal government has spent hundreds of millions of dollars subsidizing the growing of tobacco, while the Office on Smoking and Health and its predecessor, the National Clearinghouse on Smoking and Health, have received a total of only $33 million to convey the health hazards of smoking to the public? Why, two decades after the original Surgeon General's report,[3] do large pockets of ignorance about the health effects of smoking remain?[4] Why is the nonsmoking majority unaware of the expenditures they must make to support the habits of the smoking minority?

The answers lie in the unique interface of tobacco eco-

nomics and politics, a powerful phenomenon driven by the former and converted into social impacts by the latter. Smoking is big business. In 1982, consumers spent close to $25 billion on cigarettes. When the indirect expenditures associated with cigarette sales are added in, the total annual contribution of cigarettes to the national economy exceeds $60 billion, or roughly 2.5% of the gross national product, accounting for some 2 million jobs, 2.5% of total private sector national employment.[5] The national economic significance of tobacco is further illustrated by the fact that, in 1976, Americans spent one and a half times as much on tobacco as they did on drugs and sundries, and 40% of what they spent on new automobiles.[6]

These economic statistics offer some insight into the significance of cigarettes, but they do not begin to explain the political power of tobacco. The latter results primarily from the *concentration* of economic interests and their historically successful translation into political influence. The process is circular, with this political influence having fed the economic interests of the industry for half a century. To gain some perspective on the nature and consequences of this political-economic force, consider the following[6,7]:

- The growing of tobacco is highly concentrated geographically, with two states (North Carolina and Kentucky) accounting for half the national acreage and the top six states, all clustered in the South, accounting for three-quarters. The annual raw crop value of tobacco in these states ranges from $150 million to close to $1 billion in North Carolina. In no other states does the value of raw crop exceed $50 million.

- Several hundred thousand farm laborers work on the close to 100,000 tobacco farms, though the majority of nonowner laborers typically work on tobacco farms for under 25 days per year. By contrast, cigarettes are manufactured by only six major firms, two of which account for over 60% of retail sales.

- In addition to subsidies through the price support system (reduced but not eliminated by recent legislation), holders of allotments benefit substantially from a system that legally restricts tobacco growing. These two features make tobacco farming one of the most anticompetitive structures in US agriculture and industry. Yet such vocal proponents of free enterprise as Senator Jesse Helms consistently and vigorously support this self-serving, anticompetitive system.

- One of the results of this system is that the gross income per acre of tobacco can range from $3,000 to $4,000. By way of comparison, the comparable figures for corn and soybeans are, respectively, $150 and $300.[8]

Address reprint requests to Dr Warner, Professor and Chairman, Department of Health Planning and Administration, School of Public Health, University of Michigan, Ann Arbor, MI 48109.

The force of these concentrated and intense economic interests combined with the seniority system in Congress, which historically has disproportionately produced southern leadership, has led to decades in which passage of major federal antismoking legislation was unthinkable. Non-southern legislators learned quickly that they could garner votes on issues of importance to them in exchange for support of pro-tobacco votes; this vote-trading is alive and flourishing, quite openly, in 1983.[8]

Similarly, the economic muscle of the tobacco industry—which invested some $1.5 billion in cigarette advertising last year—has translated into anemic coverage of smoking-and-health issues by the nation's media. Media that depend heavily on tobacco advertising, including newspapers and magazines, are victims of both implicit and explicit intimidation intended to suppress such coverage.[9] The product diversification of the cigarette manufacturers means that the threat of loss of advertising, as a response to antitobacco coverage, extends to beer, soft drinks, crackers, catsup, and dog food.

Despite these discouraging situations, there are new circumstances that give reason for cautious optimism. Competition from tobacco grown overseas is making the price support system less economically tenable. More important, the politics of smoking have been changing. In 1983, pressure from an invigorated antismoking lobby forced tobacco legislators to support a "no net cost" bill which was passed into law. While the purported intent of the bill—to eliminate the taxpayers' subsidization of tobacco—has not been entirely realized, the symbolism of the law is clear and important. In 1984, a successful battle was waged in Congress to strengthen the health warning system on cigarette packs. More legislation can be expected.

The traditional antismoking forces, including the major national voluntary health associations, have finally banded together to constitute the first serious antismoking lobby in Washington. Perhaps equally important, if much more subtle, has been the shift in the nation's attitude toward smoking. Concerns about "passive" smoking and the simple right to breathe clean air, combined with a growing appreciation of the health and economic costs of smoking, have created a social climate in which the smoker no longer asks, "Would you like a cigarette?" Today the question is, "Do you mind if I smoke?" As this question is increasingly answered in the affirmative, Congress will gradually catch up with a public that is kicking its collective cigarette habit.[10,11]

REFERENCES

1. *Smoking and Health—A Report of the Surgeon General.* US Dept Health, Education, and Welfare publication NO. (PHS) 79-50066, Government Printing Office, 1966.
2. Luce BR, Schweitzer SO: Smoking and alcohol abuse: A comparison of their economic consequences. *N Engl J Med* 1978; 298:569–571.
3. *Smoking and Health: Report on the Advisory Committee to the Surgeon General of the Public Health Service.* US Dept Health, Education, and Welfare—Public Health Service, Government Printing Office, 1964.
4. Myers ML, Iscoe C, Jennings C, et al: *Staff Report on the Cigarette Advertising Investigation.* Federal Trade Commission, May 1981.
5. *A Study of the US Tobacco Industry's Economic Contribution to the Nation, Its Fifty States, and the District of Columbia.* Philadelphia, Wharton Applied Research Center and Wharton Econometric Forecasting Associates, Inc, August 1980.
6. Tobacco's economic importance, *Congressional Record* 1978; 124 (May 25) pp S8328-S8334.
7. Two invisible sides of the smoking and health issue. *Perspective* 1981; 16: 1–12.
8. Waldmon MS: Jobs, health key to price support battle. *Ann Arbor News*, June 21, 1983.
9. Whelan M, Sheridan J, Meister, A, et al: Analysis of coverage of tobacco hazards in women's magazines. *J Public Health Policy* 1981; 2:28–35.
10. Warner KE: Cigarette smoking in the 1970s: the impact of the antismoking campaign on consumption. *Science* 1981; 211:729–731.
11. Warner KE, Murt A: Impact of the antismoking campaign on smoking prevalence: a cohort analysis. *J Public Health Policy* 1982; 3:374–390.

THE INDIVIDUALISTIC LEGACY

The dominant perspective that has defined the issues and directed the tasks of health workers in attempting to reduce smoking prevalence has been individualistic, viewing smoking through informational, educational and motivational programs directed at individuals or small groups. Because the ravages of smoking finally present as medical problems, and because epidemiology as a branch of medical science was first able to describe the relationship between smoking and disease, the great part of smoking control activity has been overseen by the medical profession. The reports of the Royal College of Physicians and the US Surgeon General stand as landmarks to the widespread social recognition of smoking as a major health epidemic but also to the prevailing and limiting definition of the problem as fundamentally medical.

Accordingly, smoking control has been dominated worldwide by medical interests. Medical agencies have tended to fund only work that fits in with established notions of what the role of medicine ought to be—biochemical, clinical, individualistic. Interventions are often sterile, over-theorized and trivial, having been stultified by research conditions that enable peer acceptance in the scientific, conferencing community. Scarce monetary grants capable of financing substantial interventions are emasculated by up to a third going to support the research interests of academic hoop-jumpers. Such notions of "the way to go about it" are recycled in medical and the less radical public health curricula and have effectively limited the role of medicine in addressing smoking control in its political, economic and cultural dimensions.

—SIMON CHAPMAN
The Lung Goodbye—A manual of tactics for counteracting the tobacco industry in the 1980s,
Sydney, Australian Consumers Association, 1983.

The politics of tobacco: curse and cure

COMMISSIONER MICHAEL PERTSCHUK*

If a prescription for a cure to the smoking pandemic could be made up, it would likely comprise 10% medical and behavioral ingredients and 90% political effort. Indeed, a model national cure has been available for the taking for years, in the splendid green-clad pill published by the UICC (International Union Against Cancer) *Guidelines for Smoking Control* (Technical Report Series, Vol. 52, Edited by N. Gray and M. Daube, Geneva, Switzerland, 1980). That it is a practical prescription has been established through the experience of the Scandinavian countries, which after years of struggle have emerged as national laboratories for rational, successful smoking-control programs. But the rest of the world lags far behind: physiologically, economically, ideologically, and politically addicted to the cigarette. And what an ecumenical addiction it is: liberal and conservative regime; democracy and dictatorship; socialist and capitalist—all equally debilitated in disarming the cigarette.

In moments of discouragement we tend to dismiss this failure of national will as the inevitable product of the awesome and diabolic political power of tobacco.

Social psychologists have charted the chronic tendency of warring nations to distort both the motives and power of their adversaries. As Ralph K. White has observed, "Always there seems to be a tendency to exaggerate the virtues on one's own side and the diabolical character of the opposite side, and especially of the leaders on the opposite side."

We need to resist a diabolic view of our adversaries; that way leads to despair and resignation. And the truth is that tobacco interests are not omnipotent. To be sure, they have powerfully retarded progress in national smoking control programs. But they, too, have lost battles. Reluctantly, they have been forced to give up cherished marketing tools and to withdraw from markets among important population segments. Indeed, they face an inexorable pattern of long-term, steady retreat.

DISPASSIONATE ACTIVISM

What is critical is that there be a cool assessment of the sources and strengths of the tobacco industry's political power, and the power of those who oppose tobacco, and that strategies be based on sound political analysis. Neither wishful thinking nor the exaggerated bloating of the power of tobacco serves the public interest.

Of course, the political power of the cigarette does rest on a broad foundation, and greed is not its only motivating force. When the budget director of Brazil excoriates tobacco

companies for their lack of aggressiveness in promoting the sale of cigarettes, he is rightly condemned by a committee of leading physicians. But he is not in the pay of the cigarette companies. His is the anguished voice of a regime desperate for cigarette tax revenues, which make up ten percent of the national Brazilian budget.

The Republic of China can hardly be viewed as the handmaiden of the multinational cigarette companies. Yet in that "rational, scientific" socialist country the cigarette tax is a prime means of capital formation, a central economic fact that largely accounts for the tepid government efforts to discourage smoking.

In the United States, CBS-TV produced a report on the politics of smoking, entitled "The Golden Leaf," in September 1982, one of the first such documentaries on television. Some health advocates were disappointed because the program did not revel in shots of slick lobbyists slinking through the corridors of power in Washington. Instead the camera dwelled on small tobacco farmers in North Carolina, where it was pointed out that the farmer reaps $3,000 an acre for his tobacco, over 10 times the value of an acre of corn. The truth is that if the Washington lobbies and public relations firms were to disappear, other forces would remain: dozens of congressmen whose farmer-constituents are dependent on tobacco, school systems sustained by tobacco taxes, large and small magazines and newspapers surviving on cigarette advertising revenues, advertising agencies, small news stands, wholesalers, retailers, truckers, and tobacco worker unions, all dependent on the maintenance of the cigarette habit.

Perhaps an equally formidable block to effective national action is the anger of people who smoke. As Lee Fritschler observes in *Smoking and Politics* (New York, Appleton-Century Crofts, 1975), "Smokers dislike being told, particularly by politicians, that their pleasures could be injurious to their health. Consequently, health-oriented politicians are likely to devote their time to more popular activities."

Cultures and myth maintain a hold independent of economic interests. In China, Chairman Mao's cigarette box is displayed at a shrine along with other cherished artifacts. The offering of the cigarette as a symbol of hospitableness dies hard, as does the folk wisdom, especially for leaders under stress, that "smoking quickens the senses."

Tobacco is also, whether we like it or not, a solace for people in misery. In Krakow, Poland, a young guide was chastised for smoking by a visiting American congressional representative, whereupon she replied quietly, "Poland is a very poor country and we have few consolations." These myths, legends, and addictions buttress passive popular resistance to national smoking-control programs.

To rationalize is human. And those dependent on tobacco have seized on powerful symbols in their need to rationalize their economic role: they are the defenders of freedom—

Mr. Pertschuk served as a Commissioner of the Federal Trade Commission from 1977 to 1984.

* The views expressed in these comments are those of Commissioner Pertschuk and most likely do not reflect the views of the Federal Trade Commission.

Based on a presentation delivered at the Fifth World Conference on Smoking and Health, Winnipeg, Canada, July 11, 1983.

Address correspondence to Commissioner Pertschuk, Federal Trade Commission, Washington, DC 20580.

freedom of choice. They are in the thick of the fashionable neoconservative revolt against regulatory programs characterized as oppressive, bullying government, run by unelected bureaucrats endlessly intervening in the lives of individuals. They are defenders against moral zealotry. They evoke history and tradition. "Tobacco," boasts Senator Wendell Ford of Kentucky, "is part of the character of Kentucky: beautiful women, fast horses, bourbon and cigarettes."

Do they believe it? Cognitive dissonance suggests that this would be so. There are fire and passion in the voice of cigarette spokesmen defending their business, and it is sadly true that the conscientious objector or defector from the cigarette camp is rare.

THE OPPONENTS' PSYCHE

It is important to understand how the cigarette industry's defenders view themselves and their opponents. They see themselves as victims of regulators' hunger for power and puritanical zeal. It may be hard to visualize Philip Morris Incorporated or R.J. Reynolds Industries as victims. But it is nonetheless the way in which they view the world. They are genuinely frightened, not only by the public health establishment but by other industries. They view—probably with some validity—the enthusiastic embrace by textile plants or asbestos companies of antismoking programs as a ruse for diverting attention away from other health hazards at the workplace. They see themselves as weak and the opposition as powerful. And although that may sound absurd, that is their perception and is part of the political reality that must be recognized. There is also a germ of truth in it.

For just as the political supporters of the tobacco industry are not all fairy tale villains, although their cause may be villainous, neither are they invincible. And public health activists possess potent political resources of their own. Foremost among these is the power of scientific truth, and the truth is that the cost to society of cigarette smoking dwarfs all other public health hazards. When the Surgeon General of the United States Public Health Service proclaims, as Dr. Koop did in his 1982 report, that "cigarette smoking is clearly identified as the chief preventable cause of death in our society, and the most important public health issue of our time," his message rings with authority and potent political force. Public health leaders are credible in large part not only because of their scientific credentials, but also because they have no apparent economic self-interest in the cause they espouse. Over many cultures and political systems, their symbols are stronger, more persistent, and deeper than the industry's: the defense of children from commercial exploitation; the defense of family from the premature loss of father or mother; the relief of overburdened health care systems; the preservation of labor productivity from the debilitation due to smoking-related diseases. The case against smoking rests not only on traditional symbols relating to childhood, family, and productivity, but on emerging symbols of political potency as well, such as the rise of the health ethic reflected in exercise, diet, and the care of one's own body: Anyone who knows anything about health does not smoke. There also has been a dramatic shift in the prevailing view of public smoking from the assumed right of the smoker to light up virtually anywhere, to the emerging right of the nonsmoker to a pollution-free public environment.

Finally, the very power and influence of the tobacco interests themselves contain the seeds of tobacco's political vulnerability. More often than not their crude expressions of greed and overreaching political power furnish the fuel for public outrage. When a Federal Trade Commission report released by a congressional committee quoted tobacco marketing specialists coolly advocating exploitation of the sexual and social insecurity of adolescents, that story was national news. When a congressional committee dominated by tobacco-state representatives favorably reported a bill in 1970 which "prohibited the states and federal agencies from taking any action on cigarette advertising," Fritschler reports, "the reaction in the Senate and elsewhere in government was severe. The tobacco interests were regarded as having overplayed their hand." The cumulative expressions of public and editorial outrage contributed to the withdrawal of cigarette advertising from television and radio in 1970. This was not an unalloyed victory for public health interests, but it was far better than the bill first bludgeoned through the committee by tobacco's representatives.

Thus, the public health forces are not lacking in political resources. Yet political power, even benign political power, is not self-executing.

The UICC's *Guidelines for Smoking Control* is no utopian fantasy. It contains a practical, informed blueprint for national political strategies to achieve attainable goals. But its effectiveness depends greatly on the willingness of public health advocates to shed fastidiousness toward political involvement and to recognize that the press conference, the campaign, and the ballot box hold a potential for the saving of lives lost to smoking as great as any combination of medicines. Papers and speeches decrying the power of the tobacco lobbies and the unresponsiveness of public officials may be satisfying to the soul of the speaker. But if the work of the public health advocate ends with the speech or the paper, it is as if the physician were to end his treatment with his diagnosis.

ACHIEVABLE OBJECTIVES

A dispassionate view of the motives, perceptions, strengths, and vulnerabilities of the various tobacco interests is a necessary first step toward the development of sound national political strategies to advance smoking-control programs.

Even public health advocates need to remind themselves that their real end objective is the reduction of smoking-related disease, *not* retribution against all those with an economic stake in tobacco. In the United States, for example, the mere fact that tobacco farmers and their representatives passionately defend the tobacco price-support program should not trigger automatic public health opposition to the program. It should be recognized that the federal government in the United States does not actually "subsidize" cultivation of tobacco. Rather it *restricts* the production of tobacco as part of a program for maintaining the price of tobacco and hence the income of tobacco farmers.

Nearly all smoking-control advocates in the United States warmly embraced an increase in cigarette taxes last year in the belief that a rise in the price of cigarettes will discourage smoking. But it may be equally in the interest of public health to keep the price of tobacco, the raw ingredient of cigarettes, high. The result of abolishing the tobacco price-support program might well be a return to the conditions that spawned the program in the great depression: overproduction of tobacco and a precipitous price drop, impoverishing and transforming tobacco farmers into virtual economic serfs of the cigarette companies.

If public health advocates were to drop their opposition to tobacco price supports, they could enhance the opportunities for the passage of legislation strengthening cigarette warnings and other restraints on promotion. How does this translate into practical politics? Legislators have an incurable aversion to hard choices; they invariably seek to split the baby down the middle: "I can't be with you on this vote, but I'll support you on that one." When a Kentucky congressman says to his friend and colleague from neighboring Missouri: "I need your help on tobacco, it's my people's economic lifeblood," few congressmen will look him in the eye and say, "Sorry, I'm going with the public health." But many would be comfortable saying: "O.K., I'll go with you on price supports, but I can't vote against stronger warnings."

A MATCHSTICK PENTAGON

Political scientists speak of the ability of certain entrenched economic interests to maintain control of public policy through "iron triangles." Thus the tobacco industry—a concentrated, organized, and politically sophisticated economic interest—retards change through close political alliance with government agencies, principally the Department of Agriculture, which has nurtured the tobacco industry for decades, and key congressional leaders and committees such as the agriculture committees of Congress.

To combat these iron triangles, the public interest often requires the initiative of a countervailing political geometry. Although its configuration may vary from country to country and issue to issue, its most common form might resemble a pentagon. The first side, or base, requires public health, education, and consumer authorities who are prepared to provide a solid foundation of scientific and behavioral expertise to support smoking-control efforts, to respond to the propaganda and dissembling of tobacco spokesmen, and to take the initiative in launching public policy initiatives.

A second side is formed by elected representatives who are willing to step forward and lead.

A third side must be supplied by organized communities of concerned professionals and ordinary citizens. At the national level are the health charities and public health organizations. At the local level there are medical societies, parent-teacher associations and nonsmokers' rights groups.

A fourth side of the pentagon requires the existence of a critical network of public interest lobbyists—typically, lawyers, doctors, teachers, and students who share a zest for combat in the arena of public policy formation and for development of the political skills, if not yet the numbers of resources, to match those of the most sophisticated tobacco lobbyists.

The fifth and perhaps most critical side of the pentagon is represented by journalists not only dedicated to the rooting out of truth, but determined to overcome the not uncommon resistance of publishers and editors to stories inconvenient to advertisers.

The alertness and independence of the mass media will ultimately determine whether the cigarette story is told in terms of the spurious but seductive symbols offered in defense of a beleaguered industry, or by the symbols of public health and concern whose violation properly evokes public outrage.

This pentagon—perhaps visualized as a matchstick configuration to contrast its fragility with that of the more solidly welded iron triangle—is slowly becoming bound together by an international network of concerned citizens.

In the United States at this moment one can glimpse the effective workings of the matchstick pentagon, as Congress moves toward the strengthening of health warnings in cigarette advertising. The initiative in unmasking the ineffectiveness of the current warning and in presenting a blueprint to Congress for stronger warnings came from the Federal Trade Commission, but the history of the smoking-restraint effort in the United States over the last two decades has also been marked by uncommon courage from successive Surgeons General, the Federal Communications Commission, and cabinet secretaries such as Joseph Califano, Jr. The legislative initiative has been taken by outstanding public health advocates in the Congress over the last 25 years from both parties, including Representatives John Blatnik, John Moss, Robert Drinan, Henry Waxman, and Don Edwards and Senators Maurine Neuberger, Warren Magnuson, Frank Moss, Edward Kennedy, Bob Packwood, Thomas Eagleton, and Orrin Hatch. The voluntary health associations have hired skilled lobbyists to help develop and implement a sound strategy for strengthening legislation aimed at cutting the death toll due to smoking.

The tobacco industry is rich and powerful. But it is also vulnerable to astute political action. Like it or not, lobbying in support of smoking-control programs is a requisite public health need. The ultimate political weapon of the public health forces is broad, sustained public outrage provoked and stimulated by a responsible press, tempered by strategic realism. No public health issue offers greater grounds for such public outrage. And public outrage, channeled intelligently, can move mountains.

ALL'S FAIR

So where do we go from here? I believe we go to war. We recognize quite clearly that this is a war with a determined enemy . . . The tobacco industry has demonstrated in every continent that it has forfeited any right to be regarded as anything other than the opposition . . . The merchants of death are the manufacturers, and we must confront them on every battlefield, whether it be health, political, social, environmental, economic, or any other.

—MIKE DAUBE
Closing remarks, Fourth World Conference
on Smoking and Health, Stockholm, Sweden, 1979

Why Uncle Sam is still smoking

JAMES H. LUTSCHG, MD

Tobacco and government have been closely tied since the beginning of this nation. George Washington, who grew tobacco in Virginia, is honored with his likeness on a package of tobacco still available today. For years Congress Perfecto, Senate Bouquet, President Extra, and Uncle Sam were popular cigar brands (Fig). The formation in 1958 of the Tobacco Institute, the main public relations and lobbying arm of the tobacco industry, merely formalized the long-standing alliance of cigarette manufacturers, agricultural officials, and congressmen from tobacco-growing areas. The staff of the Tobacco Institute is headed by a former congressman. More than 100 congressmen from states that grow little or no tobacco received funds from the Tobacco People's Public Affairs Committee (TPPAC) in 1979, and more than 200 of the current members of Congress received PAC funds from the TPPAC and the tobacco industry oligopoly during the elections of 1981 and 1982. Honoraria for speaking at tobacco industry functions represent another source of funds to congressmen, including the Speaker of the House of Representatives, Thomas P. "Tip" O'Neill, Jr (D, Massachusetts).[1]

Political connections of the tobacco industry with the Executive Branch, especially in the Carter administration, have not been uncommon. For instance, the director of corporate relations at Philip Morris took a full-time leave to serve Mr Carter's campaign in 1976 as liaison with the business world.[2] President Carter appointed a board member of Philip Morris as chairman of the President's Council on Physical Fitness and Sports.

In 1980, Ronald Reagan stated, while campaigning in North Carolina, "My own Cabinet members will be far too busy with substantive matters to waste their time proselytizing against the dangers of cigarette smoking." In 1981 the Department of Health and Human Services (HHS) canceled a new kind of advertising campaign aimed at teenagers and featuring actress and model Brooke Shields. One of the officials responsible for snuffing the campaign (allegedly because the Madison Avenue approach and Ms Shield's line, "Smokers are losers," would be offensive) had previously served as a legislative aide to Senator Jesse Helms (R, North Carolina). In 1982, the budget of the Office on Smoking and Health of HHS was cut from $2.6 million to $1.9 million—less than 1/600th of the estimated $1.3 billion spent advertising cigarettes in 1982.

The National Cancer Institute's (NCI) record on smoking is disappointing at best. At a time when lung cancer rates were soaring, the NCI's major smoking research project was a $40 million effort to develop "less hazardous cigarettes"—the assumption being that people will continue to smoke regardless of warnings. This effort

Dr Lutschg is a chest specialist.
Address correspondence to Dr Lutschg, Baton Rouge Clinic, 8415 Goodwood Blvd, Baton Rouge, LA 70806-7899.

was finally abandoned, and its project director now works under a grant from Brown & Williamson (BAT) for the tobacco industry-financed Franklin Institute. (The cigarette company had earlier offered to endow a $400,000 chair for this individual at a medical school in Washington, DC.)

In NCI's status report of December, 1978,[3] it was noted that in 1977 there had been 354,200 premature deaths related to cigarette smoking, and it was estimated that there had been over four million premature deaths related to cigarette smoking since the issuance of the Surgeon General's initial report in 1964. Yet a privately published anniversary book, *Decade of Discovery: Advances in Cancer Research 1971–1981*[4] (aimed at promoting the NCI among the affluent and influential), did not acknowledge the failure of research to lessen cigarette-related cancers. Included in this publication was a half-page graph labeled "Five-Year Relative Survival Rates for Whites for Seven Leading Cancer Sites." The seven sites depicted all showed five-year survival rates ranging from 45% to 81%. Lung cancer, the leading cancer site, was omitted from the graph. Also not mentioned was the five-year relative survival rate for lung cancer (less than 10%), unchanged in the last 40 years.

Similarly, the NIH Publication No. 82-1635 *What Black Americans Should Know About Cancer* offers to dispel a number of myths. To the rhetorical question, "What are the chances of surviving cancer?" the booklet responds:

Today, the chances of surviving cancer are better than ever before. For example, the five-year survival rate for patients with cancer of the uterus has risen to 81%, breast 68%, prostate 63%, bladder 61%, colon 49%, and rectum 45% . . .[5]

The leading cancer site is omitted, as are the survival rates for several other cancer sites associated with cigarette smoking (larynx, esophagus, and pancreas).

Governmental regulation of carcinogens has avoided cigarettes. In 1981, Congress' Office of Technology Assessment issued *Technologies for Determining Cancer Risks from the Environment*, listing 102 substances regulated as carcinogens in the United States. Tobacco is not listed. This same publication estimates that approximately one third of all malignancies are due to smoking.[6]

The value of the mandated Surgeon General's warning must be questioned in light of evidence that only one in fifty persons buying cigarettes acknowledges reading it.[7] A single component of cigarette tar, benzo(alpha)pyrene, has 50,000 times the experimental carcinogenic potency of saccharin.[8] Yet the word "cancer" appears in the warning on "diet" drinks and not on cigarette packs. Packets of snuff, cigars, or loose tobacco for hand-rolled cigarettes (all increasingly advertised to a young male audience) contain no warning at all. Even candy bars must carry a label listing ingredients and additives, but there is no such requirement for cigarettes. In 1985, 100,000 Americans will die as the result of lung cancer due to cigarette smoking, and twice that many

Patriotic American cigar brands: testimony to the smoke-filled room?

will die due to other cigarette-related diseases; but there remains no noticeable governmental effort to discourage the consumption of cigarettes.

In contrast, the government has declared AIDS as health priority number one and has pulled out all the stops—from hotlines to crash research programs to crack epidemiologic team investigations. The Assistant Secretary of HHS has noted that there have been approximately 2,000 cases of AIDS and that the two-year mortality rate for AIDS is approximately 80%. This is the same mortality seen in lung cancer.

Fifty years ago a United States Senator and a President's daughter endorsed Lucky Strikes. Although such images would seem ridiculous today, the tobacco industry's love affair with government is still as torrid as ever.

REFERENCES

1. Jackson B, Pound EF: Legislative lucre—Fees for congressmen from interest groups doubled in past year. *Wall St. Journal*, July 28, 1983.
2. Sapolsky H. The political obstacles to the control of cigarette smoking in the United States. *J Health Politics, Policy, Law* 1980; 5:277–290.
3. *Status report of December 1978.* Smoking and Health Program 1978. Division of Cancer Cause and Prevention, NCI, National Heart, Lung, and Blood Institute.
4. *Decade of Discovery: Advances in Cancer Research 1971–1981.* US Department HHS, Oct 1981, NIH 81-2323:36, 73–74.
5. *What Black Americans Should Know About Cancer.* US Department HHS, NIH, Public Health Service, NIH Publication 82-1635, 1982.
6. *Assessment of Technologies for Determining Cancer Risks from the Environment* Office of Technology Assessment, 1982, pp 205–207.
7. Myers ML (ed): *Staff report of the cigarette advertising investigation.* Federal Trade Commission, 1981, Ch 4.
8. Repace J: Indoor air pollution, tobacco smoke, and public health, et al. *Science* 1980;208:471.
9. Brandt E: The Public Health Service's number one priority. *Public Health Reports* 1983;98:306–307.

The research smokescreen
Moving from academic debate to action on smoking

MICHEL COLEMAN, BM, BCH

Smoking is a major health hazard for individuals, and a massive drain on the health resources of nations; but smokers accept the risk, and governments accept the cost.

Behind this apparent paradox lie the tobacco companies, exploiting every available means of persuading people to smoke. Tax revenue from tobacco sales then becomes the incentive for government to tolerate their activities. Until these activities are brought under control, smoking will remain the greatest single cause of premature death and preventable illness in developed countries. Still worse, it will become a new and major cause of equally avoidable illness and death in developing countries, in which the industry is now promoting tobacco products with appeals to sexual and commercial success, and without health warnings. Cigarette consumption is rising rapidly as a result. Before the health risks of tobacco can be overcome, physicians and public health specialists will need more effective weapons; academic research, health education, and advice to government have clearly been inadequate for the job. It may be instructive to consider why this is so.

The success story of medical research over the last 30 years has been the production of unassailable evidence that cigarette smoking is the cause of the 20th-century epidemic of lung cancer, and a major etiologic factor in ischemic heart disease and peripheral vascular disease, in chronic obstructive lung disease, in cancers of oropharynx, esophagus, and bladder, and in low-birth-weight deliveries. But this success has not been translated into the great improvements in public health which might have been expected.

In the United Kingdom, for example, the proportion of adult males who smoke has fallen from 62% to 42% since 1960, and for adult females from 44% to 32% since 1966.[1,2] These encouraging trends are at least partly due to vigorous health education campaigns, using evidence supplied by medical research. But smoking is now responsible not only for one in seven deaths—over 90,000 premature deaths from heart and lung disease each year in the UK—but also for an enormous toll of morbidity and lost economic activity. Although fewer children now take up smoking than previously, one in three girls and almost as many boys become regular smokers by 19 years of age—not far short of the adult proportion.[3]

Physicians can and do influence the smoking behavior of their patients. But what about sources of advice to dissuade the young never-smoker from starting? In the United Kingdom, research charities founded to combat cancer and heart disease spent £14 million on research in 1978, but less than 2% of this on health education.[4] So far, there is little evidence of a change in approach.[5,6] The health education bodies funded by government could only spend £2.1 million to run their spirited antismoking campaigns in 1981.[7] By contrast, the UK tobacco industry spends £100 million a year on advertising,[8] much of it aimed at youth. Such an imbalance cannot be said to permit a truly free choice on whether to smoke, yet it is clear that long-term prospects for improvement in public health depend on never-smokers never becoming smokers.

Medical advice to government could not be more blunt than that given by the Royal College of Physicians in 1971: "Action to protect the public against the damage done to so many of them by cigarette smoking would have more effect upon the public health in this country than anything else that can now be done in the whole field of preventive medicine."[9] Five years later, in a statement on prevention and health, the Department of Health said: "No one can seriously doubt any longer that the habit of cigarette smoking has been responsible for an enormous amount of preventable disease and untimely death in this country".[10] Good medical advice, unreservedly accepted by government. Seven years later, the government still has no overall strategy to deal with the damage done by smoking to the health of its electorate, and its legislative and political efforts have been uncoordinated and ineffective. Tobacco advertising was banned from television in 1965 and from radio in 1973. Health warnings appeared on packs in 1972.[1] But no fewer than 16 parliamentary bills to provide more effective control of advertising have been defeated by political opponents with financial interests in the tobacco industry, although government support would have ensured the passage of any one of them into law. Since 1975, further controls on advertising have been achieved through a series of "voluntary agreements" between the tobacco industry and government. But the law of 1933 prohibiting tobacco sales to children under 16 is almost never enforced and is openly ignored. Cigarettes are now 15% cheaper in real terms than in 1960. The tobacco companies simply flout the television ban by sponsoring televised sport, obtaining prolonged exposure of their name and logo far more cheaply than if they paid for advertising directly. They have diversified into sponsoring adventure holidays and books on sport—all aimed at young people. As one executive admitted, such promotions are "an extension of the marketing arm for cigarettes."[15] *The Lancet* summed it up well: "Voluntary agreements do not stop epidemics."[5] As the British experience clearly shows, neither do they stop advertising.

The culmination of this series of "voluntary agreements" came in October 1982, when the tobacco industry endowed a Health Promotion Research Trust with £11 million to

Address correspondence to Dr Coleman, Clinical Lecturer, Department of Medical Statistics and Epidemiology, London School of Hygiene and Tropical Medicine, Keppel Street, London WCIE 7HT, England.

fund three years of research into the promotion of health. But studies "designed directly or indirectly to examine the use and effects of tobacco products" are specifically excluded.[12] The agreement was condemned by Sir George Godber, lately chief medical adviser to government, as "a sick joke at the public's expense."[13] The research limitation, however, was defended by Health Minister Kenneth Clarke on the grounds that it would not prevent the trust sponsoring research which threw further light on the damage to health caused by smoking.[12] This is broadly equivalent to the government welcoming Mafia investment into research on the promotion of law and order, providing organized crime rackets are excluded from study. Seen in this light, the UK government's claim to have a public health policy based on prevention is like the emperor's new clothes—barely credible.

In short, successful medical research, vigorous (if ill-funded) health education, and strong advice to government have all failed to prevent the health hazards of smoking. Governments have simply failed to respond, largely because their national economies are deeply penetrated by tobacco. The Food and Agriculture Organisation, in its report on the economic significance of tobacco, baldly states: "Until world demand, which was still rising in 1977–80, can be curbed sufficiently to make tobacco growing less profitable, it will be difficult to induce growers to curb production."[14] Demand, however, is stimulated and maintained by advertising: fewer than 20 nations, 12 of them European, have actually banned tobacco advertising.[15] In the United States, 13% of excise tax receipts (1% of all taxes) are derived from tobacco—$6.8 billion in 1981.[14] In the countries of the European Economic Community, 2% to 8% of all tax revenue derives from tobacco.[14] In such circumstances, it is not surprising that attempts to mobilize a government to control tobacco will always meet powerful opposition. In the 120 countries producing tobacco around the world, the scale of the problem may vary, but its nature is the same.

The British and American governments, in common with many others, now display a corporate addiction to tax revenue from tobacco. All the signs of addiction are there. They regret the damage it causes to health, and they say they honestly want to give it up; but they have an irresistible craving for more, and they collude with their suppliers to protect the supply from law.

Civilized government has a clear duty to protect the health of its people. The legislative means by which this may be achieved for the health hazards of smoking have been discussed in a thorough review by Roemer.[15] A copy should be sent to every legislator in the land, with instructions to read it, and to act on it. The Scottish Health Education Committee has produced a concise and exemplary guide[8] to the fiscal, legislative, and other measures which can be taken by a government "to convince the public that smoking really is a major threat to health and one which the government takes seriously."

There is an urgent need to create such a powerful expression of public desire to be rid of this dangerous poison, that governments rediscover the political will to confront the tobacco industry, since "these industries can diversify into other products; dead men and women cannot."[8]

Physicians have a duty to throw their weight into the argument,[16] even if it means ditching the usual caveat that academic integrity demands political neutrality. To be silent during a public health tragedy is not honest medicine, and this is no longer simply an academic debate. William Osler and John Simon fought tuberculosis and cholera in the corridors of power, not just at the bedside and in the laboratory. Today, if we fail to make use of our influence, as physicians, to arouse public opinion on this most grave of public health issues, then we forfeit any claim to be concerned about the prevention of ill health as well as the cure of disease.

REFERENCES

1. Calnan M: A review of government policies aimed at primary prevention, in Alderson M (ed): *The Prevention of Cancer*. London, Arnold, 1982, pp 101–183.
2. Cox H, Marks L: Sales trends and survey findings: A study of smoking in 15 OECD countries. *Health Trends* 1983; 15:48–51.
3. The children who smoke. *Lancet* 1983; 1:943–944.
4. Medical charities and prevention. *Brit Med J* 1979; 2:1610.
5. Voluntary agreements do not stop epidemics. *Lancet* 1982; 2:855.
6. Kemp NH, Hince TA, Mohun R, et al: Smoking and the cancer charities. *Lancet* 1982; 2:1050.
7. Token offering to health research from the tobacco industry. *Lancet* 1982; 2:1055.
8. Scottish Health Education Coordinating Commitee: *Health Education in the Prevention of Smoking-Related Diseases*. Edinburgh, 1983.
9. Royal College of Physicians: *Smoking and Health Now*. London, Pitman, 1971.
10. Department of Health and Social Security: Prevention and Health: Everybody's Business. A Reassessment of Public and Personal Health. London, Her Majesty's Stationery Office, 1976.
11. Smoking promoted by sly new methods. *Brit Med Assoc News Rev* 1983; 9:1–3.
12. Healy P: Tobacco industry to cut spending on advertising. *The Times*, Oct 28, 1982.
13. *The Health Services*, Jan 14, 1983, p 2.
14. Food and Agriculture Organisation: *The Economic Significance of Tobacco*. Rome, Commodities and Trade Div ESC: Misc 83/1, 1983.
15. Roemer R: *Legislative Action to Control the World Smoking Epidemic*. Geneva, World Health Organization, 1982.
16. Lessof MH: Tobacco advertising. *Lancet* 1983; 1:596.

OCCUPATIONAL HEALTH SHOULD NOT ACCEPT TOBACCO INDUSTRY SPONSORSHIP

Tobacco industry sponsorship of sport, opera, and the visual arts is objectionable enough, but when it comes to the industry providing money for the Institute of Occupational Health, things have gone too far. Yet the *Financial Times* of June (1981) carried a half-page advertisement appealing for £2½ million for the institute, and listed among the companies that have contributed already was Imperial Tobacco. Included in the advertisement ironically is a chest radiograph showing advanced silicosis: the radiograph could equally well have shown a carcinoma caused by cigarette smoking . . .

The Institute of Occupational Health is still at an early stage in its development. Its aims deserve generous support from individuals and corporate bodies, but the enthusiasm of the fund raisers should be tempered by discretion. The *BMJ* believes that no medical body should accept money from the tobacco industry, and that the Institute of Occupational Health should recognise its mistake and sever the connection.

—Editorial
Br Med J 1981; 283:4.

Culpable negligence: a case for the courts?

MAURICE H. LESSOF, MD

The fall in cigarette smoking is gathering pace—enough to make the tobacco companies diversify their financial investment but as yet insufficient to affect the deaths caused by smoking. Between 1960 and 1980, the annual consumption of tobacco by adults in the United Kingdom declined by 16%, followed by a further 9% fall in cigarettes sold in 1981 and a 7.5% fall in 1982.[1]

The scale of the death and destruction caused by the tobacco industry remains astronomical. Fifty thousand premature deaths from cancer, heart disease, chronic bronchitis, or obstructive airways disease in Britain alone, 50 million lost working days a year, nearly 2,000 people seriously burned or killed in fires started by cigarettes.[2] Increasing quantities of cigarettes are now exported to the Third World—an idea that is as deplorable as the sale of opium in the 19th century.

The steps taken by governments have been feeble, and politicians who speak against the tobacco industry have tended to disappear without trace. Mr Laurie Pavitt placed a bill before the British parliament in 1982 which would have outlawed the promotion of tobacco. It ran out of time, because the previous item of business had suddenly been delayed by 164 last-minute amendments.

When Norway banned tobacco advertising, the previously steady rise in cigarette smoking was reversed and there was a 5% reduction in the number of smokers over a two-year period.[2] Even more encouraging, in young men in the age group 16 to 24, there was a fall from 49% of smokers in 1974 to about 33% eight years later. In another survey[3] it has been suggested that only a small number (7%) in this age group consider that they will become permanent smokers. However, a more detached follow-up study[4] puts the chance at 85% that early smoking will become a habit. The struggle for the minds of the young is at the heart of the matter. Although smoking is a potent cause of respiratory symptoms, even in childhood,[5] addiction to nicotine is hard to cure.

The belief that smoking is fun, that it makes people confident, or that it makes them look tough may be losing sway. A survey of nearly 16,000 children in 65 schools and colleges reflects the results of health education policies and the influence of key role-models.[3] Among those children who thought their parents, teachers, or friends would object very few smoked, as opposed to nearly half who thought their parents would not mind. In Britain there is also a wider change in attitudes. As smoking has slowly moved towards becoming socially unacceptable, the Trades Union Congress decided, in 1981, to support antismoking campaigns and the rights of nonsmokers. There has also been an increased demand for nonsmoking areas in public places.

Not surprisingly, the tobacco lobby has fought back. After a ban on television advertising came the gift-coupon schemes and the claim that advertising bans would cause unemployment and close down newspapers (contrary to the experience in Norway[2]). After this came health promotion schemes—paid for by the cigarette companies on condition that they must avoid the investigation of tobacco.[6] There has also been the sponsorship of sport and the arts, aiming both at acquiring prestige and at developing the idea of financial dependence on tobacco interests.[7] Television coverage of tobacco-sponsored events has also served to keep cigarette advertising in the public eye and may explain the triumphant claim that in Finland, Poland, and Italy a "ban" on advertising had absolutely no effect. Why ban advertising, said the tobacco lobby, when it is so lucrative a source of revenue for the mass media and does not have any influence anyway?[8]

One particular promotion method now rivals all the rest—an investment in the holiday business. Silk Cut Masterclass Holidays (Gallaher), Marlboro Adventure Holidays (Philip Morris), and Peter Stuyvesant Travel (Rothmans International) seek, once again, to link the names of tobacco products with glamorous activities.[9] To the extent that the tobacco companies are diversifying their investments, this should perhaps be welcomed, but as a way of advertising brand names "through the back door" this practice is open to question.

To many, the concept of a business which promotes cancer and death is obscene, and the growing unpopularity of the tobacco barons is being translated into political pressure. Physicians, informed as they are about the dangers of cigarettes, smoke less than any other group. With evidence such as this, many more physicians are joining the antitobacco lobby and are now attempting to exert a political influence. Action is still needed from government on two fronts—a ban on all promotion or advertising and a realistic increase in tobacco taxes. Viewed as a health tax on tobacco, the income could be used to provide extra government money for the hospital service, the Health Education Councils, and the sponsors of sport. This would go some small way towards providing compensation for the harm that tobacco undoubtedly does.

There are other ways in which physicians can help. Giving health information to the newspapers has been a disappointing endeavor because the facts so often have been suppressed. But if physicians can use their influence to achieve a ban on advertising and promotion, it should follow that investigative reporters will be allowed or even encouraged to speak up—in particular, about the continued recruitment of new, young smokers who will become the cancer victims of the future. If this fails, the time has come to marshal the evidence that will allow tobacco companies

Address correspondence to Dr Lessof, Professor of Medicine, Department of Medicine, Guy's Hospital Medical School, London, SE19RT England.

to be sued in the courts for the years of willful neglect when, knowingly, they continued to cause deaths before they even agreed to introduce a warning on the label.

The evidence is now strong enough to convince any impartial judge or jury of the complicity of cigarette manufacturers in causing death and disability; but it will need the help of the medical profession to see the argument through. It will also need the organizational and financial help of an antismoking group that is willing to support an individual claimant in a lengthy legal battle with a giant industry.

REFERENCES

1. Cigarette sales on the decline. *Lancet* 1983; 1:886.
2. Gillie O: Citizen's Bill. *Sunday Times;* May 12, 1982.
3. The children who smoke. *Lancet* 1983; 1:943.
4. Rimpelä M, Rimpelä A: *Incidence of Smoking Among Finnish Youth—A Follow-up Study.* Tampere, Kasanterveystieteen laitosket, 1980.
5. Rimpelä A: Occurrence of respiratory diseases and symptoms among Finnish youths. *Acta Paediat Scand* 1982; (suppl). 297:1–77.
6. Token offering to health research from the tobacco industry. *Lancet* 1983; 2:1055.
7. Marks L: Policies and postures in smoking control. *Brit Med J* 1983; 284: 391.
8. Norris: Hypocrisy of tobacco levy. *Sunday Times,* Dec 19, 1982.
9. Smoking promoted by sly new methods. *BMA News Review* March 1983; 9:1–3.

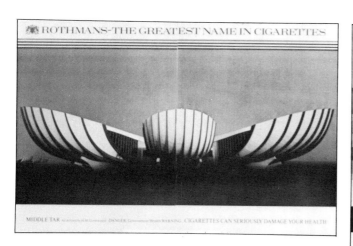

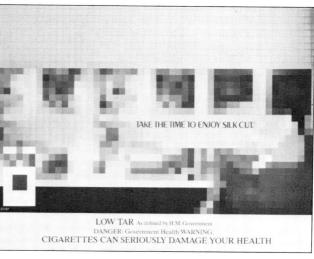

In Great Britain tobacco companies are undaunted in the face of partial advertising bans, mandated enlargement of the warnings, and prohibitions against the depiction of people smoking. The companies' psychologists appear to have learned that associating brand names with mysterious images, striking colors, and fast-action sporting events can keep cigarette sales high. Many brands also continue to feature the Royal crest and the words "by appointment to Her Majesty the Queen." Noted *The Lancet* in 1978 (ii:880): "Some cynics refer to the warrant as the Royal Health Warning, the last four monarchs having died of diseases related to smoking."

Cigarette advertising and *The New York Times:* An ethical issue that's unfit to print?

GEORGE GITLITZ, MD

Since 1975, George Gitlitz, MD, a vascular surgeon and past president of the Broome County (NY) Medical Society, has written letters to the editor and publisher of The New York Times *challenging them to discuss on the editorial page their reasons for continuing to accept advertising for cigarettes. Following is the correspondence.*

January 4, 1975

The Editor
The New York Times
New York City

To the Editor:

Your outspoken editorial deploring the rise in cigarette smoking, especially among teen-age girls, and placing much of the blame on advertising, would be commendable were it not for the fact that the *New York Times* is one of the worst offenders in this respect.

Anyone who understands *The Times'* long tradition of independence of Editorial and Advertising from each other, and who understands the necessity for such a policy if there is to be a free press, can accept (though occasionally with revulsion) the publication of advertisements for even the most repugnant of political philosophies.

But does the printing of an advertisement for a commercial product known to be harmful to health fall into the same category? If someone wished to run an advertisement for candy bars containing cyanide capsules, would *The Times* accept it? In the name of Freedom of the Press?

I suggest that a review of your commercial advertising policy is in order.

Sincerely,

George F. Gitlitz, MD

January 20, 1975

Dear Doctor Gitlitz:

Since your letter of January 2 pertained to advertising, it was referred to the Advertising Acceptability Department.

The Times has published many news articles reporting developments in research and the opinions of experts who have held that cigarette smoking is harmful. Also in our editorial columns we have repeatedly set forth our position on the hazards to health involved in cigarette smoking.

In August, 1969, this newspaper established minimum stan-

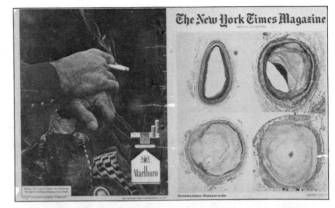

A story on coronary heart disease on the front cover, a pack of coronary risk factors on the back cover.

dards for the acceptance of cigarette advertising. In November, 1970, the cigarette package label itself was changed to read: "Warning: The Surgeon-General has determined that cigarette smoking is dangerous to your health" and our requirements were modified accordingly. In March, 1972, the Federal Trade Commission established regulations whereby all print advertisements for cigarettes must contain health warning statements set forth in a clear and conspicuous manner. Since then, all advertisements for cigarettes published in The Times have complied with these requirements.

As you can see, we have made an earnest effort to protect our readers. However, until Congress decides, if ever, that a total ban is both necessary and enforceable, adults who have been thoroughly informed on the dangers of cigarette smoking will have to decide for themselves whether they want to accept the risks involved.

*Thank you for writing and for your interest in this newspaper.**

Sincerely,

Robert P. Smith
Manager
Advertising Acceptability

January 24, 1975

The New York Times
229 West 43rd Street
New York, N.Y. 10036

To the Editor: (Not For Publication)

I respectfully but strongly object to the manner in which you handled my letter commenting on your editorial on smoking.

Obviously, I do not expect every letter I write to *The Times* to

---

Address correspondence to Dr Gitlitz, 33 Mitchell Avenue, Binghamton, NY 13903.

* A decade ago (March 19, 1973), the present editor of the *Journal* received an identical letter in reply to criticism of *The Times'* acceptance of cigarette advertising.

be published, especially if the literary quality does not merit publication.

But I do feel that the thoughts expressed therein are appropriate to your Letters-to-the-Editor section (whether in my words or someone else's), and should not be hidden from the eyes of your readers behind the smoke screen of the very polite but all too private Public-Relations-type reply.

Certainly, your advertising policy is your own business. But you allow your readers to throw brickbats at *The Times* on other matters, and I am confident *The Times* could survive a public discussion of this matter on your Editorial page.

I take the trouble of writing this because of similar experiences I have had in the past. I have had a number of letters-to-the-editor on the subject of smoking accepted by various papers (including *The Times* 8/11/69, and *Times Magazine* 2/24/74). But whenever the subject of a letter has been a criticism of that publication's acceptance of cigarette advertising, the letter is never published, but a personal reply from an ad man is always forthcoming.

The arguments which Mr. Smith uses are the party line of the Tobacco Institute. Indeed, the part about informed adults deciding for themselves whether or not to smoke is lifted almost verbatim from those horrible ads for Vantage cigarettes! Such reasoning is specious, and you know as well as I do that such reasoning, combined with the slick multi-colored ads in the Magazine, is likely to tip your 13-year-old daughter into becoming a smoker.

And thus I feel that, despite your occasional commendable editorial comments on the subject of smoking, *The Times* does a terrible disservice to a gullible public by advertising cigarettes.

It would be most interesting if you were to publish Mr. Smith's letter, or the gist of it, as an editorial, and see what your readers had to say about it.

Sincerely,
George F. Gitlitz, MD

No reply.

*   *   *

May 12, 1975

Letters to the Editor
The New York Times
New York City

To the Editor:

I would like to raise strong objections to misleading assertions which are made in current advertisements for "Saratoga 120's" cigarettes, ads which are carried in the *N.Y. Times.*

The ads state that the cigarettes are "longer (120 mm. vs. 100 mm.) and slimmer than 100's, so you enjoy extra smoking time . . . without smoking more cigarettes." And that one can smoke "longer without smoking more."

Leaving aside the faulty geometry of the suggestion that a cigarette will last longer because it is "slimmer," let's assume that the more significant alteration is indeed the increase in length, and thus that their main contention, that there are "more puffs than 100's," is essentially correct.

It is the implication that one can smoke "more puffs . . . without smoking more cigarettes," and therefore "without smoking more," that is misleading and pernicious.

The statistics which comprise publications such as the Surgeon General's reports were gathered during the decades when a "cigarette" was a "cigarette," and when "number of cigarettes per day" was a reasonably stable yardstick by which to measure the relative risk to which smokers were exposed.

But now that manufacturers have begun to play games with the cigarette's dimensions, risk can only be related to "puffs per

day" (silly though it may sound) or, less reliably (because of the "slimness" factor), to "mm. per day."

For the smoker, the whole thing is Russian Roulette, and obviously the safest course is not to smoke. But failing this, the smoker should be aware that, other things being equal—or being unproven (such as tar, nicotine, filters, etc.)—more puffs mean more trouble.

And advertisements which assert anything to the contrary, even to a readership who should know better, are objectionable.

Sincerely,
George F. Gitlitz, MD

No reply.

*   *   *

December 10, 1975

To the Editor
The New Times
New York City

To the Editor:

You have previously informed me, in great detail, of *The Times'* policy regarding cigarette advertising.

I would again respectfully urge you to make this policy public, on your Editorial Page, and invite comments on it from your readers.

If our freedoms, including Freedom of the Press, are worth anything, they should be subject to the light of healthy debate.

Your particular contention—that you continue to advertise cigarettes because as yet there is no law against it—is only a single viewpoint. Many of us feel that cigarette advertising, from a public health standpoint, is no less pernicious an activity than incitement-to-riot; and that the only difference is that the Law has not yet caught up with Twentieth Century Medicine!

In any case, I'd be interested in comments from readers of *The Times.*

Sincerely,
George F. Gitlitz, MD

December 22, 1975

Dear Dr. Gitlitz:

Your recent letter to the Editor on the apparent contradiction between our editorial position on cigarette smoking and our advertising stance has been referred to me.

The point that you make is one that has been frequently discussed at The Times. *You may recall that in mid-1969,* The Times *established its own standards for acceptance of cigarette advertising. We required a warning with respect to the risks of smoking cigarettes, and in addition, a disclosure of the tar and nicotine content. As a result of the adoption of these standards, the cigarette companies withdrew their advertising from* The Times. *Obviously, this action on our part, resulted in a reduction in advertising revenue. During this period, editorials and news stories frequently pointed out the hazards of cigarette smoking.*

In 1971, Congress banned cigarette advertising on T.V., and in 1972, the Federal Trade Commission imposed requirements on cigarette advertising in media similar to the ones that we had established in 1969.

Since 1972, some of the cigarette companies—confronted with the universal application of the above mentioned print advertising requirements and the T.V. ban—resumed advertising in The Times.

In summary, the question we face is whether against the background I have described, we should bar cigarette advertis-

ing when cigarettes are not illegal; when the advertising meets legal requirements and includes a specific warning; and when, we must presume, our readers are fully aware of the risks of smoking cigarettes.

Our conclusion has been, and still is, that our readers should make that decision for themselves. We have considerable difficulty embracing the idea that the way to curb harmful or potentially harmful products is by banning advertising for them.

This is a very difficult and somewhat controversial subject, and we very much appreciate your own view of the matter.

Sincerely,

John J. McCabe
Assistant to the Publisher

December 24, 1975

John J. McCabe
Senior Vice President
The New York Times
New York City

Dear Mr. McCabe:

I greatly appreciate your taking the trouble to write me regarding *The Times'* position on cigarette advertising.

Without belaboring the point, however, I would be much happier if *The Times* were to state this policy publicly, editorially—and thereby evoke comments on it from your readers.

Because *The Times* does consistently discuss the great moral issues of the day, it's difficult for me to accept your reticence about airing this particular one. Indeed, you have yourself given the best possible reason for doing so: because "This is a very difficult and somewhat controversial subject." If *The Times* can't deal forthrightly with such material—who can?

Having made a similar suggestion in the past, and having received a similar response, I have the uncomfortable feeling of facing a paper curtain—a polite but impenetrable "omerta." It's one thing to have a Letter-to-the-Editor rejected—but quite another to receive a lengthy personal reply from a Senior Vice President of the newspaper. Perhaps I should be flattered, but I can't help thinking that this relieves you of the less attractive task of defending your stance before your whole readership.

And finally, quite honestly, much as I respect *The Times*, it's hard to believe that your reluctance to open the matter publicly isn't influenced to some degree by economic considerations. "Say it ain't so, *Times!*"

Seriously, I think such a debate would be in the public interest, and that there's a responsibility here that *The Times* ought to meet.

Thank you for your attention,

George F. Gitlitz, MD

No reply.

*   *   *

June 9, 1976

Letters to the Editor
The New York Times
New York City

To the Editor:

The hypocrisy of *The New York Times* is astounding.

You run a self-righteous editorial criticizing the Reserve Mining Company for dumping cancer-producing asbestos wastes into Lake Superior. "Should people in the area develop cancer fifteen years from now," the editorial says, "they will (not) forgive the unconscionable reluctance of the Reserve Mining Company to allow considerations of public safety to cut into its profits."

And in the same issue of the newspaper you run advertisements for cigarettes. And you keep the money.

Sincerely,

George F. Gitlitz, MD

No reply.

*   *   *

October 13, 1976

Fred M. Hechinger, Assistant Editor
Editorial Page, *The New York Times*
New York City

Dear Dr. Hechinger:

Though I've had letters-to-the-editor on the subject of smoking and health printed in *The Times* (8/11/69) and *The Times Magazine* (2/24/74), I've been totally unsuccessful with a number of letters I've submitted on the subject of the *Times'* own policy of advertising cigarettes.

The letters are not merely rejected. Rather, I've received long personal replies, wih extended explanations of your policy, from your "Manager of Advertising Acceptability," Mr. Smith (1/20/75), and from none less than Mr. McCabe, the Senior Vice President (12/22/75).

Really, I have little interest in such privately expressed apologias, but prefer, instead, to have the issue brought to the attention of your readers.

Please, then, be so kind as to give me honest answers to two simple questions:

1. Is there any chance of having a letter on this topic printed in *The Times?* Or, if the stumbling block is merely some deficiency in my personal literary style:

2. Is there any chance of *The Times'* setting forth and justifying its cigarette advertising policy in an editorial of its own? And lest there be any misunderstanding: not an editorial on cigarettes, but on cigarette *advertising*, *your* cigarette advertising.

I know that you have many important things to write editorials about, like Lassa fever, and I certainly wouldn't want you to choke your Editorial Page in trivia, especially after your stout denunciation of it in the presidential campaign. But the 1975 edition of the Surgeon General's Report does say that "cigarette smoking remains the largest single unnecessary and preventable cause of illness and early death."

I'm enclosing a copy of yet another letter-to-the-editor, but I confess that I have little serious hope of penetrating your paper curtain. Green paper, that is.

Sincerely,
George F. Gitlitz, MD

Letters to the Editor
The New York Times
New York City

To the Editor:

Re: Editorial, October 12 (on Lassa fever and Legionnaire's disease)

The Times' concern over the "mysterious diseases" certainly is touching. These scares will be useful, says *The Times*, "if they discourage complacency and induce stepped-up medical research into their mysteries."

Bravo, *Times!* Always keeping us on the alert; urging research into "diseases medical science does not know"; diseases which have "taken as many as 230 lives in Zaire and Uganda." Or about two dozen in Philadelphia. Or one at Fort Dix.

Meanwhile, *The Times* advertises cigarettes, perfectly well known to be virtually the only cause for 75,000 deaths per year from lung cancer (in this country alone!), and known to be one of the three main factors, if not *the* main factor, in 600,000 deaths per year from heart attacks.

And *The Times* muses, wistfully, that there are "diseases medical science ... knows but cannot do much if anything

Headlines on the back page sometimes seem more important than those on page 1. *Times* sports writers or TV critics seldom question the sponsorship of televised sports events by cigarette companies.

about."

Of course we can't! And you're one of the reasons!

George F. Gitlitz, MD

No reply.

* * *

An article on cigarette advertising was sent to Arthur Ochs Sulzberger, President and Publisher of *The Times*.

May 2, 1977

Dear Dr. Gitlitz:

Thank you for your letter of April 23 and its enclosures.
We are, as of this moment, rethinking many of our advertising acceptability standards, so your letter is, indeed, most timely.

Sincerely,
Arthur Ochs Sulzberger

* * *

Arthur Ochs Sulzberger
President and Publisher
The New York Times
New York City

Dear Mr. Sulzberger:

It was with great disappointment that I learned that a change in the *Times'* policy of advertising cigarettes—at which you had hinted in your letter to me of May 2—was not to occur; and that the *Times'* "rethinking" of its standards for advertising acceptability had brought forth only a curtailment in the advertising of pornographic movies.

My understanding of the *Times'* policy, if I read correctly the news story and the editorial in the June 21 edition, is that the issue turns not on any question of potential harm to the consumer of a product (assuming that commerce in the product is legal), but solely on the taste or propriety of the ad itself.

Thus *The Times* sharply limits advertisements for pornography, a product whose harmfulness is at worst a matter of controversy; and carries ads by the page-ful for a product undisputed as being the number one threat to health in the country. Because,

A department store white sale advertisement also promotes a cigarette-sponsored jazz festival (L). Gimbels, Kool cigarettes, and Saks Fifth Avenue are all owned by BATUS (British American Tobacco). In 1982 approximately $25 million in cigarette advertising was invested in the three New York City daily newspapers, and more than six times that amount was placed by department stores.

says *The Times*, the ads for the former are a "blight in print."

It would be superfluous to suggest to you that those of us who amputate legs which have become gangrenous from smoking, or who daily see smokers dead in their 40's from heart attacks and cancer—might regard cigarette advertisements as a "blight in print." Each of us has his own personal threshold for what turns the stomach. For this surgeon, it's advertisements for cigarettes. *The Times* has its own reasons for deciding what's "fit to print," and I don't presume to debate them.

However *The Times* occasionally does remind us that it's not unaware that smoking is harmful. Unfortunately, at such moments the apparent obliviousness of the editorial staff to the facts of life on the business side of the paper can try the patience of a person who ordinarily regards the Editorial Page as a forum for serious ideas.

Consider the "topics" item on July 12: Terrible things, cigarettes, it tells us. New studies show that they're even worse than we thought they were ... People, now even women, dying in droves ... Terrible ... Must save these victims ... How ... So *The Times* proposes a solution—a massive informational campaign!

"Surely it is time for a large-scale Federal campaign to impress the dismal data on the smoking public, particularly the young."

Mr. Sulzberger, where in the world has your editorial writer been? Does he think that this information is *not* already available to the public? Does he think that no effort has been made to disseminate it?

Over the years I, like countless other doctors, have knocked myself out lecturing to stop-smoking clinics for adults, working with smoking-prevention programs aimed at school children, writing articles and letters-to-editors, and pestering my own patients. Abundant literature is available from the Cancer Society, the Heart Association, the Lung Association, and many other organizations. There's a warning message on every cigarette package and in every ad. And let's not forget the not infrequent news items and editorials in *The Times* and other papers.

But all of this is a teaspoonful compared to the Niagara that pours out of the cigarette advertising agencies. In the same July 12 *Times* that carried those 4½ inches of one editorial column discussing the harmfulness of cigarettes, an ad for Merit cigarettes occupied two full pages, and one for Kent ⅚ of a full page. Similar amounts of space are so occupied day after day, and far be it for *me* to tell *you* what happens on Sunday.

For whatever it's worth, the principle of "equal time," whether in political campaigns or college debating, seems to many to have some validity. The principle holds that people's minds are influenced not just by the soundness of an argument, but by the amount of time or page-space devoted to presenting it. Obviously, modern advertising techniques are a logical extrapolation of this principle. Snow 'em and spare no expense.

Knowing this (or I assume that he knows it!) does your editorial writer seriously believe that any new "large-scale Federal campaign" is going to be able to compete with the cigarette advertisers? Who would pay for all that "equal" space in *The Times*—for the art work, the glossy photos, the models, the copy? Would the Federal Government pay for it? Private contributors? The health insurance industry? Or perhaps *The Times*—out of a sense of public duty?

And even if such a campaign *could* be mounted, what a wasteful confrontation there would be. And perhaps the end result would be even more confusion than exists now.

There must be a better way. If *The Times* really believes that an effect can ensue from the impressing of "data on the smoking public," then a much more logical first step would be to halt the flood of *negative* "data," data which misinforms and misleads, data which is not data at all, false data which leads people to harm themselves—cigarette advertising.

In the present political climate, I see little likelihood that the Federal Government will force such a step. If it's to be done at all, it would have to be started voluntarily by a few influential institutions of the stature of *The Times*, doing it alone, urging

other publications to follow suit.

I feel strongly that *The Times* should cease the advertising of cigarettes.

But if *The Times* can't see its way clear to taking such a courageous step, at least spare those of us who respect the newspaper and its Editorial Page—and who already *are* trying to talk people out of killing themselves—the kind of silly and unhelpful suggestion which appeared in that July 12 editorial.

Sincerely,
George F. Gitlitz, MD

No reply.

*   *   *

January 13, 1978

The Editor
The New York Times
New York City

To the Editor:

Re: "In Defense of Smoking"
     by Ross Milhiser, Jr., President,
     Philip Morris, Inc.

Go ahead, everyone out there in Patient Country. You think the place to learn about smoking is from the president of Philip Morris?

You think cigarettes don't cause heart attacks, and lung cancer, and blocked arteries in the legs? Go ahead, then, smoke!

Just remember that we're waiting for you, with our scalpels.

George F. Gitlitz, MD

No reply.

*   *   *

November 9, 1978

Letters to the Editor
The New York Times
New York City

To the Editor:

The observation by Michael T Craig, of The Tobacco Institute, that marijuana use is high among youngsters despite the fact that it is not advertised—and the conclusion he then draws, modestly deprecating the importance of tobacco advertising—represent a facile and superficial comparison of two industries which do have some things in common, but differ in others.

But let's not labor too hard to dispel the illusion he harbors. Perhaps he'll see this as a reason for recommending to his constituents that they stop cigarette advertising. Think of the money they'd save!

George F. Gitlitz, MD

No reply.

*   *   *

John Oakes, Editorial Page Editor of *The Times*, addressed a breakfast meeting of about 300 members of the Harpur Forum of SUNY Binghamton on "Crises in today's world."

October 16, 1980

John B. Oakes
The New York Times
New York

Dear Mr. Oakes:

I regret that a last-minute emergency forced me to miss your address to the Harpur Forum this morning. Friends tell me that it was an excellent meeting.

I was particularly disappointed because I had intended, during the Question-and-Answer period, to raise the subject of a "crisis" which I presume was not covered in your talk: the health problem caused by cigarette smoking, and *The New York Times'* contribution to that problem because of its policy of advertising cigarettes.

To be sure, one person's definition of a "crisis" will differ from another's, but to put this one in perspective a reasonable estimate is that 12–14% of all deaths which occur in the U.S. can be blamed directly on cigarettes. These deaths are all, of course, unnecessarily premature. (The basic arithmetic is this: approximately 1.9 million deaths are recorded per year; approximately 150–200,000 of the 600,000 coronary heart disease deaths, and 75,000 of the 90–100,000 lung cancer deaths, are attributed by statisticians to smoking. Actually, 12–14% is probably conservative, in that it doesn't take into account cigarettes' contribution to deaths other than in those two major categories. But it's close enough.)

Physicians consider that that number of unnecessary deaths from a single source qualifies as a crisis. The Dept. of HHS considers it a crisis, and on a global scale the WHO considers it a crisis. All agree that it's the number one health problem in both developed and underdeveloped countries.

Physicians at present have little hope that *The Times* will do what it should do—stop advertising cigarettes—but those of us who otherwise admire *The Times* continue to hope that at least there might be a public explanation of the present policy.

I had intended to request, therefore (understanding that you are retired and are perhaps no longer in communication with those who set *Times* policy), that you carry back to *The Times* this challenge:

1. That *The Times* write and publish an editorial entitled "Why *The New York Times* Advertises Cigarettes," and after a suitable period publish a representative sampling of your readers' comments on the editorial; and

2. That *The Times* include in that editorial a succinct, but adequate and informative, "financial disclosure," so that its readers may know what part revenues from cigarette advertising play in the economic life of *The Times*.

Having previously put this idea in writing, but having been repeatedly put off by polite, personal communications from Mr. Smith, Mr. McCabe, and even Mr. Sulzberger himself; and believing that such private communications are not in the public interest, but rather, that *The Times* philosophy—on anything—belongs on its Editorial Page, I had hoped to voice this challenge directly to you, in public, aloud.

The circumstance which prevented my doing so was in itself ironic: As I was finishing my rounds and was about to leave for the meeting, I became involved in a lengthy, and ultimately unsuccessful, attempt to resuscitate a man who had suffered a massive coronary at about 7 AM. He was a smoker.

Sincerely,
George F. Gitlitz, MD

The sports editor of *The Times* has replied to one physician: "Please correct me, but it seems you are saying that we should not write about life on the cigarette sponsored tennis circuit while people die of cigarette caused diseases. Perhaps we should stop reporting anything until people stop dying." In Canada, where the Canadian Ski Association has accepted a multi-million-dollar sponsorship deal from the Canadian subsidiary of RJ Reynolds, the Canadian Cancer Society and the Canadian Council on Smoking & Health have denounced the arrangement: "Any fitness organization that is prepared to walk hand in hand with the tobacco industry in the 1980s has lost sight of its responsibility to all young Canadians and is out of touch with public opinion."

Acknowledgment of receipt of letter from Mr. Oakes' secretary; no reply.

* * *

September 1, 1981

John B. Oaks
The New York Times
New York, N.Y.

Dear Mr. Oakes:

I could not help being struck by your remark about the conflict between "health and profit" in yesterday's column.

You may recall my writing you on Oct. 16, 1980, suggesting that in pursuing its policy of advertising cigarettes, *The New York Times* makes precisely the choice—profit over health—which you (and I!) find so distasteful in the Reagan administration and the "predators" of the business community.

You are correct: "deaths from cancer and heart and lung disease will inevitably rise" as pollution increases. But right now, as I pointed out in my letter, deaths from those diseases are coming from cigarettes: approximately 274,000 deaths, or about 14 out of every 100 deaths in America each year, are directly attributable to cigarettes' contribution to the very diseases you've mentioned.

That's what *The New York Times* is selling, for profit.

I would repeat the challenge I made in that letter:

1. That *The Times* write and publish an editorial entitled "Why *The New York Times* Advertises Cigarettes," and after a suitable period publish a representative sampling of your readers' comments on the editorial; and

2. That *The Times* include in that editorial a succinct, but adequate and informative, "financial disclosure," so that its readers may know what part revenues from cigarette advertising play in the economic life of *The Times*.

Sincerely,
George F. Gitlitz, MD

October 5, 1981

Dear Dr. Gitlitz:

Your letter of September 1, addressed to Mr. John B. Oakes was referred to this department.

We have frequently considered whether we should ban all cigarette advertising from the paper. We always come to the same conclusion; that is, that we should not.

In our view, The Times *should keep its columns as open as possible—even to those with whom we may disagree. This does not mean that we abrogate our responsibility for good taste or fairness. It does mean, however, that we accept advertising in a wide range of categories where the message may be in conflict with the editorial opinion of the paper.*

Thank you for writing.

Sincerely,
Robert P. Smith
Advertising Acceptability

* * *

June 24, 1982

"Topics" Editors
Editorial Page
The New York Times
New York

Gentlemen:

Re: "Puff Huff"
(a *Times* comment on misleading promotions
for low-tar cigarettes)

For years, in countless letters, I have tried to persuade *The New York Times* to discuss on the Editorial Page its own policy of advertising cigarettes. I have long since given up.

The letters were always shunted to the "Manager of Advertising Acceptability," and I was repeatedly sent the standard form explaining *The Times'* stout devotion to such principles as 1) if a product is legal, *The Times* sees no reason not to advertise it; 2) well-informed adults should be able to make important decisions; e.g., to smoke or not to smoke, by themselves; 3) *The Times* was in the forefront of publishing health warnings in its ads even before the FTC required them—and other such self-serving apologies. But never in print.

And on one occasion—May, 1975—I pointed out that ads running in *The Times*, for "Saratoga 120's," were blatantly misleading, and I detailed the reasons why. No reply.

And now *The Times* looks down its Topical nose at the cigarette-makers—who, like *The Times*, are only trying to turn an honest dollar—for "deceptive advertising"!

Come, Gentlemen, isn't *all* cigarette advertising deceptive? Isn't the difference quantitative, not qualitative? Wouldn't honest men differ in the way they define "rip-off"? My definition, for example, would include photos of beautiful girls and handsome men smoking and engaging in "healthful" activities, the implication being that smoking is compatible with beauty and health—which it ain't.

Gentlemen, *you* market that product. *You* participate in all those deaths. And you talk about laughing?

George F. Gitlitz, MD

No reply.

* * *

On May 25, 1983, after reading a front-page article in The Times *headlined "Health Chief Calls AIDS Battle 'No. 1 Priority,'" Dr. Gitlitz wrote a letter to the editor of* The Times *pointing out the enormous attention paid by the media (and the Department of Health and Human Services) to AIDS, Legionnaire's disease, and certain other outbreaks of illness, in contrast to the veritable absence of coverage of the far more devastating epidemic of cigarette-caused diseases and deaths. The letter concluded with a quote from* A History of Public Health in New York City 1866-1966 *by John Duffy:*

In glancing back over the history of any city's health, one cannot help being struck by the disparity between the diseases which aroused the greatest fear and drew most attention and those familiar disorders which were responsible for the major share of morbidity and mortality.

Tuberculosis, pneumonia, and other respiratory disorders were the chief cause of death in New York City, and enteric or diarrheal diseases, the prime source of infant mortality, a close second. But they were constantly present, and their insidious ravages were accepted as the normal order.

The letter was not published, and no reply was received.

"Precious baby"

MARY ANN CROMER, MD

> You've become accustomed to seeing magazine and newspaper articles that say that smoking can harm your unborn child. Studies do show that smoking mothers, on the average, have slightly lighter weight babies. Yet with more women reportedly smoking, infant mortality rates keep reaching historic lows. Some studies have shown that the lighter babies of smoking mothers actually have better survival rates than similar weight babies of nonsmokers.
>
> —from *The Cigarette Controversy*, a pamphlet distributed by The Tobacco Institute, 1776 K Street NW, Washington, DC 20006

"PRECIOUS BABY," read the T-shirt of the very pregnant young woman in the Newark, New Jersey, airport. Yet there she sat dragging luxuriously on a Virginia Slims, supplying herself and her desired child-to-be with a dose of nicotine, carbon monoxide, hydrogen cyanide, DDT, and benzopyrene. No one screamed, "Stop!" or "Please don't!" No one murmured, "Disgusting!" or "How Sad." No one was discussing the contradiction between her chosen wearing apparel and her cigarette. In fact, I appeared to be the only one shaking my head in dismay at this remarkably ironic behavior. Could I have been the only one who noticed or wondered, "Does this woman have a doctor?"

It is naive to suggest that smoking by a pregnant woman in 1985 is a choice made by an informed adult, when every effort is being made by cigarette companies to undermine knowledge about the adverse effects of smoking on the fetus and on the mother herself. Indeed, surveys[1-5] have repeatedly demonstrated that when compared with those who have never smoked or who formerly smoked, persons who smoke are ignorant of the probability and severity of cigarette-caused damage. The media, especially magazines directed to women, have done little to educate. While purporting to promote the status of women, these publications contribute to their ignorance by censoring articles that would inform readers about the disproportionate health problems caused by smoking. Perhaps the most striking example is *Ms.* magazine, published by Gloria Steinem. Its May 1983 issue was devoted entirely to the topic of women's health—but without a clear emphasis on the leading cause of preventable disease and death in women: cigarettes. In its 13-year existence, *Ms.* has never published an article on smoking, but has carried hundreds of pages of cigarette advertising.

In a similar vein, athletes like Billy Jean King, Martina Navratilova, and Renee Richards, MD—who could be doing so much to encourage healthier lifestyles among teenage girls—may be assisting Philip Morris' efforts to "liberate" women by promoting cigarette dependence. They participate in tennis matches promoted with the demeaning slogan, "Virginia Slims. You've come a long way, baby."

For too long, the tobacco industry has gone unchallenged by women with its exploitation of the misconception that slimness allegedly due to smoking is preferable to a non-smoking lifestyle. Alton Ochsner, MD, used to comment, "Who wants to be a svelte corpse?" but his quote never made the billboards at the tennis matches.

It is small wonder why cigarette companies fear the growing number of nonsmokers' rights groups led by GASP (Group Against Smoking Pollution) and ASH (Action on Smoking and Health). In the long run, the social unacceptability of smoking, which is implicit in these groups' objectives, will succeed in cutting cigarette sales. (A memorandum distributed to tobacco executives during a clean indoor-air referendum in California in 1978 made note of the fact that if every individual who smokes were to smoke just one less cigarette per day, R.J. Reynolds alone would lose $92 million in sales each year.[6]) In addition, the high visibility and increasing involvement of women in nonsmokers' rights groups provide hope that magazine publishers who unite with cigarette companies to exploit women will see fewer and fewer women buying their publications.

To this end, organizations such as the American Medical Women's Association, NOW (National Organization of Women), the American College of Obstetrics and Gynecology, the American Academy of Pediatrics, national and local PTAs (Parent-Teacher Associations), and women's religious and civic organizations must do more—far more—than they have done to stop the assault on girls and women by cigarette advertisers.

REFERENCES

1. Shekelle RB, Liu SC: Public beliefs about causes and prevention of heart attacks. *JAMA* 1978; 240:756–758.
2. Ashton WD: Cigarette smoking and associated disease. *J Roy Coll Gen Pract* 1979; 29:229–233.
3. Aho WR: Smoking, dieting, and exercise. Age differences in attitudes and behavior relevant to selected health belief model variables. *RI Med J* 1979; 62: 85–92.
4. Weinberger M, Greene JY, Manlin JJ, Jevin MJ: Health beliefs and smoking behavior. *Am J Public Health* 1981; 71:1253–1255.
5. Arch PJ, Carpenter D, Webster JH, Chant AD: Smoking, ignorance, and peripheral vascular disease. *Arch Surg* 1982; 117:1062–1065.
6. MacDougall AK: California no-smoking vote gets tobacco firms all hot. *Miami Herald*, September 13, 1978.

Dr. Cromer is a pediatrician.
Address correspondence to Dr Cromer, Somerville Hospital, Somerville, MA 02143.

Anacin claims trimmed

WASHINGTON—A Federal Trade Commission order issued last week requiring American Home Products to have rigorous scientific support behind claims for Anacin and its other analgesics is FTC's first major tactical move in the proprietary drug area since withdrawing from plans for industrywide regulation.

The same order also requires that ads for Anacin, Arthritis Pain Formula or any other AHP analgesic containing aspirin disclose that aspirin is the pain-reliever whenever performance claims are made. That would end blind references to "the pain reliever most recommended by doctors."

The FTC commissioners, however, rejected an administrative law judge's recommendation—made in 1978—that AHP include a corrective disclaimer in more than $20,000,000 of future Anacin ads stating that the product is not a "tension reliever." FTC noted that the claim had been dropped in 1973 and was not likely to "endure (Continued on Page 88)

Luckies tries as low tar

Women top cig target

By JOHN J. O'CONNOR

New product frenzy in the cigaret market shows no sign of abating, and there is compelling evidence to suggest that the nation's major cigaret marketers will be stepping up development of brands directed exclusively toward women in 1982.

In an interview, Gerald H. Long, recently named president-chief executive officer of R. J. Reynolds Tobacco, noted that in the first eight months of this year, the industry produced some two dozen new brands or line extensions to make 1981, in his opinion, "the most competitive year in the history of the business."

Mr. Long, promoted from exec vp of the nation's largest cigaret company, also listed three trends to which RJR and its five rivals are responding in their new product development: Continued growth of low tars; the booming success of 100mm cigarets, and women as a percentage of the total smoking population.

Even American Tobacco is about to succumb to new product fever. Having doted mainly on its successful ultralow-tar Carlton line for the last five years, American will attempt to revive its long-neglected and declining Lucky Strike brand. According to sources, American will move into two markets Nov. 9 with a reformulated and repackaged Lucky (Continued on Page 93)

highlights

line. See Page 4.

INTERNATIONAL

his hand at the new at Warner Amex

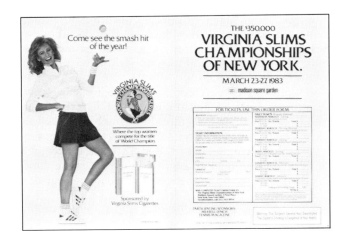

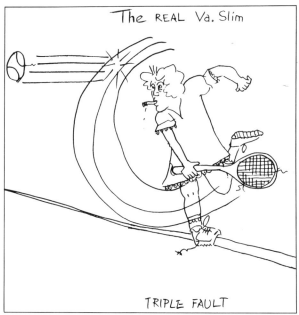

"Women top cig target" reads the headline in *Advertising Age*, September 28, 1981 (top R) and the message is clear: cigarette makers will go to great lengths to create imagery that glorifies the woman who smokes. An advertisement in the *United States Tobacco Journal* (middle L) lacks the health warning, as do many advertisements in store displays. The advertisement for the Virginia Slims Ginny Jogger suit (middle R) may be the only fitness ad ever with a health warning at the bottom. While Philip Morris touts its Virginia Slims tennis tournament at $20 a ticket (bottom L) a group of medical students at the University of Miami protested the tournament in 1978 and created a poster (bottom R) of the *real* Va. Slim. Yes, Virginia, there is a lung cancer.

Doctors who smoke

RICHARD C. BATES, MD

It is to the credit of the medical profession that physicians as a group smoke at only about half the rate for the general population; it is to the individual doctor's discredit that he smokes at all. That discredit has medical, moral and philosophic components.

In the psychiatric, medical mode, it is healthy to like oneself: to "feel good" or "I'm OK" about oneself; to have a positive self-image. Psychiatrists were once called "alienists" because they treated people who were alienated—not only from the rest of the world but from themselves. Indeed, those two cannot be separated. As Eric Fromm pointed out, one can only love others to the degree and depth that one loves oneself.

The doctor-smoker cannot approve of himself as a smoker. Well, perhaps there *are* three ways out of that certainty, but all incompatible with being capable of medical practice: (1) He might be ignorant of the effects of smoking on health, (2) He might deny that preservation of health is important, or, (3) He might be psychotic or brain-damaged. Otherwise, he is alienated within himself. He carries out an act that he, as a proper physician, must disapprove.

Philosophically, the smoking physician doesn't fare very well, either. As a person who belongs to a profession, he is a "professor," ie, one who professes to have certain knowledge and skills. Physicians originally professed to be able to heal the sick; in quite recent times they have been additionally burdened with responsibility for *preventing* illness. Even radiologists and pathologists, who only detect illness, in so doing, profess to stand between a patient and a greater degree of illness.

"Professing" is a dignified word for "selling." Doctors sell themselves as health experts and as being able to bring a desirable product to their customers. Recently, some of them have even placed advertisements to that effect in telephone books and news media.

Philosophically, then, a physician who smokes is marketing a product, health preservation, that he does not buy and use himself. He is in the position of a policeman who breaks the law; a clergyman who sins; an accountant who over-draws his checking account; a banker who goes bankrupt, or a Ford dealer who drives Chevrolets.

Dr Bates is an internist.
Address correspondence to Dr Bates, 2909 East Grand River Ave, Lansing, MI 48912.

Then there's that touchy subject, morality. Theologically, our bodies are sacred. That being the case, anyone who willfully damages his body, sins. More than that, it is immoral for a physician, a parent, or anyone else to carry out a negative act that influences others to do the same. As physicians, we enjoy the privileges of being exemplars: admired, significant pacesetters for society. How many times have we all been chided by laymen at social functions for eating saturated fats, drinking alcoholic beverages or being corpulent? These tiresome gibes, tasteless attempts at humor though they may be, express a common belief that, when it comes to health preservation, a physician is obligated to "set the pace." A physician who breaks health rules tells laymen either that the rules aren't important, or the physician is a mere, frail mortal and not a god at all. The belief that physicians are specially anointed people is the same for the smoking layman's silliest rationalization: "You doctors smoke." To the extent that physicians are more influential, their misbehavior is more damaging to others.

Given such devastating arguments against smoking, how can so many otherwise reasonable, admirable members of our ranks continue it? As with any other behavioral disease, the person who continues to perform a self-damaging act derives more pleasure from that act than pain from its consequences. This is most likely if one can avoid reality by dodging behind an array of psychologic mechanisms: denial, projection, rationalization, to name the common ones.

But underlying all health-threatening behaviors is the one defense dangerously attractive to physicians: a magical belief in one's omnipotence. That's what any driver displays when he doesn't fasten his seat belt; what the physician-pilot feels before his plane crashes in bad weather; what youngsters believe when they inject street drugs; what the cigarette smoker rationalizes: "Cigarettes cause emphysema, heart attacks and cancer—but only in other people, *not me*."

How often have we all seen that emotion in our suddenly sick patients: surprise! "But, doctor, I didn't think this could ever happen to *me*." Or, "I thought that only happened to other people." What a special surprise it is to physicians to discover that cigarettes, storms, heart attacks, cancer and the laws of probability all apply to us in exactly the same ways, with no respect whatsoever for our medical degrees.

Meanwhile, how are the rest of us to reply when our patients say, "But you doctors smoke"?

Looking ahead, medical school admissions committees could snuff out smoking among future doctors by rejecting premedical students who smoke. As long as we're turning away hundreds of well-qualified medical school applicants every year, there's a certain justification in favoring those who husband their health.

—RICHARD C. BATES
Smokers shouldn't be admitted to med school
Medical Economics 1975;52(10):80–90.

Are physicians to blame if patients smoke?

SHELDON B. COHEN, MD

In working with patients, studying the smoking behavior of health professionals, and attempting to influence medical organizations and institutions, the preponderant attitude I have found is one of ambivalence. For some patients, stopping smoking, despite obvious gains in health and a sense of accomplishment, remains tinged with feelings of resentment and deprivation.

Similarly, although the treatment of patients who stop smoking and shift to a healthier lifestyle is a gratifying professional achievement, the attitudes of physicians in medical societies are sometimes more ambivalent than those of patients. On the surface, all physicians acknowledge that nonsmoking is desirable, but they may be indifferent about taking responsibility for smoking, whether in their patients' lives, their offices, or in meetings of their professional societies.

I have attempted to influence medical organizations to which I belong by suggesting that they put into practice their knowledge of preventive medicine and make offices, hospitals, and meetings smoke-free. These organizations frequently do not know how to handle the matter; they may refer it from committee to committee or may respond that preaching may be tolerable only so long as it does not interfere with "smokers' rights." Some hospital administrators have even bemoaned the loss of income from the sale of cigarettes.

Why are physicians, who themselves have given up smoking more dramatically than any other group, often apathetic or downright hostile to the concept of promoting nonsmoking? The underpinnings of the attitudes of each physician toward smoking are rooted in the matrix of significant, unique early-life experiences. Among the crucial factors that determine involvement in discouraging smoking may be the physician's own smoking habits, other drug dependencies, or a serious disease or death from a smoking-related illness in a close friend or a relative.

Most relevant to the pervasive passivity of all too many physicians are the attitudes and behaviors that derive from society at large. Although we may pride ourselves on being more altruistic and self-sacrificing than ordinary mortals, our similarities with the rest of humanity outweigh our differences. The resistance of medical organizations and institutions to change from an illness orientation is not really surprising. Nor is this phenomenon unique to medicine. In all fields, success is directly related to the size of the problems confronted and "solved." Thus, generals seek larger armies and more weapons, lawyers look for more cases to litigate, and accountants are wont to make financial matters more complicated. Medicine's critics might well believe the conspiratorial theory that in a time of a physician surplus the only way for physicians to maintain a proper share of patients is to increase the number of people they diagnose as ill! Although this is nonsense, such indeed may be the case unintentionally in those physicians who focus on the performance of intricate, technical maneuvers and ingenious diagnostic tests at the expense of trying to understand the overall patient. They may perfunctorily tell patients they should not smoke but do not consider it part of their duties as physicians to assist them to stop smoking or to refer them for help "unless they ask for it." Most physicians appreciate the intellectual stimulation of rare diseases and complex diagnoses. And beating one's colleagues into print with a report of some new finding does give one a feeling of pride. Why is that zeal lacking when it comes to the health education of patients? Insurance companies pay surgeons and hospitals princely sums for procedures to bypass clogged coronary arteries, but how many of the same companies are willing to pay a fraction of the cost of surgery to the physician who teaches the patient how to modify lifestyles?

We do need to reassure our patients that we realize that smoking may have many complicated origins and that it may be difficult to stop. But we can most assuredly add that ending their dependence on cigarettes may be one of the most rewarding accomplishments of their lives. Similarly, the onus for creating smoke-free hospitals should not be on physicians concerned about smoking to explain the cost effectiveness and improved quality of the environment, but rather on those who administer the organizations to explain why they have done so little.

One might wonder why a psychiatrist should be particularly concerned about the prevention of smoking-related diseases, while some mental health care facilities still use cigarettes as rewards for appropriate behavior. For one thing, it is neither pleasant nor healthful to breathe the tobacco smoke of others. For another, the treatment of physically well and highly motivated patients is much less stressful and enervating than that of individuals preoccupied with the ravages of physical illnesses. Consider the case of a colleague who provided a lengthy but ultimately successful treatment for a man with a serious mental illness, only to watch him die shortly thereafter from lung cancer. This therapist eliminated smoking in his office as a first step in a more prevention-oriented practice, for he had been convinced that in no way could he further facilitate self-destructive behavior by his patients.

Dr Cohen is a psychoanalyst and past vice-president of the American Society of Clinical Hypnosis.

Address correspondence to Dr Cohen, 401 Peachtree Street, NE, Atlanta, GA 30308.

Cigarettes and fire deaths

Andrew McGuire

According to the United States Fire Administration, fires caused by cigarettes kill over 2,300 men, women and children—and burn over 5,000 others—each year in the United States.[1]

In 1981 there were 65,000 fires caused by cigarettes, resulting in $300 million in property damage. Local, state, and national fire data all list cigarette-caused fires as the leading cause of fire fatalities. In one study of 530 fire fatalities in Maryland between 1971 and 1977, 45% of fatalities occurred in fires caused by cigarettes; the next highest category occurred as the result of heating equipment (8% of fatalities).[2]

There are three ways to prevent fires caused by cigarettes. First, persons who smoke can be warned against smoking in bed and reminded to dispose of cigarette butts properly. Since half of all victims of cigarette fires are intoxicated, warnings may not be heeded.

The second approach, favored by the tobacco industry, would be to make the environment more resistant to fire from a smoldering cigarette. By adding chemicals to fabrics and by changing the construction of furniture, some progress has been made in reducing the likelihood of cigarette fires. However, the existing furniture, carpets, mattresses, and bedding will be in use for the next two or three decades and thus cannot be rendered cigarette-resistant. Also, a tremendous cost would be passed on to the consumer: furniture industry estimates are between $1 billion and $2 billion. Even then, the mutagenic and carcinogenic potential of the chemicals used in fire-proofing has become a cause for concern.

The third method would be to modify the source of ignition, the cigarette, which the tobacco industry claims is not possible.

There have been four studies that have shown the feasibility of a fire-safe cigarette. The first was conducted by Arthur D. Little, Inc., Cambridge, MA, in 1974.[3] The conclusion of the report suggested that if cigarettes were manufactured to self-extinguish within 10 minutes of being placed on furniture, then ignition would most likely not occur. In 1981, the National Bureau of Standards issued a report on the initial work for developing a fire performance standard for cigarettes.[4] Three brands were shown to have less potential for igniting furniture: Carlton (American Brands), More (R.J. Reynolds), and Sherman's (Nat Sherman). In contrast, Pall Mall (American Brands) and Viceroy (Brown and Williamson/BAT) consistently ignited the furniture. In another study, the US Testing Company found that More and Sherman's did not ignite the mock-up furniture, yet Benson and Hedges Menthols (Philip Morris) ignited over half the mock-ups tested.[5]

There have been over 95 patents issued worldwide for methods claiming to render a cigarette fire-safe or self-extinguishing.[6] One of these patents has been tested for fire-safety properties by the California Bureau of Home Furnishings in the State Department of Consumer Affairs. This report concluded that an American patent caused cigarettes to self-extinguish.[7]

There is no question that a fire-safe cigarette is a technically feasible product. There are two brands, More and Sherman's, that are currently sold nationwide and that have been shown to be more fire-safe than all other brands tested. In short, what the tobacco industry says it can't do, it is already doing.

According to documents from P. Lorillard (Loews) and Philip Morris Research Centers, manufacturers maintain the continuous burning of a cigarette even when it is not being inhaled by adding citrate and phosphate compounds or calcium carbonate to the paper or wrapper.[8] Thus, the intentional addition of burn-promoting chemicals, along with other factors, causes cigarettes to burn like a fuse (Fig 1).

FIGURE 1. **Conclusion of Researchers at National Bureau of Standards**

"Our preliminary work indicates that the following cigarette construction parameters may reduce ignition propensity:
- low diameter (less contact with the substrate);
- low packing density (low fuel load);
- filter (no increase in airflow at the butt end and, consequently, no increase in heat flux);
- paper with low citrate content, but not necessarily low porosity;
- high burning rate (short contact of heat source and substrate).

Cigarettes with one or more of these construction parameters are already in production. According to our best information, producers do not even know that some of their cigarettes have lower ignition propensity."

(*Letter to Deputy Director, Division of Cancer Cause and Prevention, National Cancer Institute, from John Krasny, Product Flammability Research, Fire Performance Evaluation Division, Center for Fire Research, National Bureau of Standards, U.S. Department of Commerce, May 9, 1980*)

A concern for preventing forest fires led Representative Edith Nourse Rogers (R, Massachusetts) to raise the issue of a self-extinguishing cigarette in Congress in the late 1920s. Legislation to this end was first introduced by Senator Phil Hart (D, Michigan) in 1974. In 1979 an investigative journalist, Becky O'Malley, funded by the Oakland, CA, firefighters union wrote an article for *Mother Jones*, entitled "Cigarettes & Sofas." [8] The article became the touchstone for the first widely supported campaign for a fire-safe cigarette.

Prompted by media publicity and a cigarette-caused fire in his home district in which a family of seven was burned

Address correspondence to Mr McGuire, Executive Director, Trauma Center Foundation, San Francisco General Hospital, San Francisco, CA 94110.

to death, Representative Joseph Moakley (D, Massachusetts) introduced legislation in 1979 calling for a fire-safe cigarette. The same year, after a lobbying effort by the Junior Leagues of California, Senator Alan Cranston (D, California) introduced a companion bill in the Senate. The first hearing of the House bill occurred on March 21, 1983, and the bill is awaiting further action in the Subcommittee on Health and the Environment. The first hearing in the Senate was on July 28, 1983, in the Special Committee on Aging, chaired by Senator John Heinz (R, Pennsylvania). In 1984, the tobacco industry agreed to permit a two-year government study of the feasibility of a fire-safe cigarette.

There have been legislative efforts on the state level. In 1980 Oregon became the first state to act. The Oregon bill, which called for fire-safe cigarettes to be sold in the state three years after passage of the bill, passed the Senate but was killed in a House committee. Since then eight states, including California and New York, have introduced fire-safe cigarette legislation. In 1983, the bill passed the New York Assembly 123 to 13, only to die in the Senate. A similar sequence of events took place in Connecticut.

In May 1979, the American Burn Association asked cigarette manufacturers for their views on fire-safe cigarettes. The Board of the American Burn Association wanted to know the official stand of the companies before the Association would support a fire-safe cigarette campaign. There was no response from any company (but see Fig 2).

FIGURE 2. In 1939 RJ Reynolds was proud to advertise its slow-burning cigarette. In 1985 the tobacco industry denies it can come up with a cigarette that will burn out when unattended, even though Reynolds' MORE brand has been shown to do just that. Neither cigars nor pipes nor cigarettes will keep burning while unattended. Selling cigarettes that burn continuously makes for higher sales—and higher costs to society for fires and burn deaths and injuries. (Photograph courtesy, DOC Archive)

The only document on fire-safe cigarettes produced by the Tobacco Institute was delivered by A. W. Spears, PhD, Executive Vice President, P. Lorillard, as testimony during Congressional hearings on March 21, 1983.[6] The document states that there is no science available to render cigarettes fire-safe. It also concludes that:

> . . . cigarettes made with low porosity paper (7 CORESTA units) produced a mainstream smoke condensate which was more tumorigenic on mouse skin than that produced from cigarettes with paper porosities greater than 25 CORESTA units.

All tobacco industry arguments presented in the media and in state hearings have been based on the Spears work.

The success of the tobacco industry thus far in thwarting legislation for the fire-safe cigarette has not prevented the Tobacco Institute and individual companies like Philip Morris from contributing money and equipment to various fire-service organizations through the United States, most often in states that are considering passage of measures prohibiting tobacco manufacturers from continuing to add burn-enhancing chemicals to cigarettes. The Tobacco Institute has given nine fire departments between $5,000 and $10,000 worth of supplies apiece for fire prevention efforts. In testimony before the Subcommittee on Health and Environment in March 1983, Horace Kornegay, Chairman of the Board of the Tobacco Institute, named New York City, Seattle, Des Moines, Boston, Milwaukee, Chicago, Detroit, Baltimore, and Portland, Oregon as recipients of money from tobacco interests.[9] In addition, the National Volunteer Fire Council has received materials that were developed by the New York public relations firm of Burson-Marsteller, and the Foundation for Fire Safety (a Virginia-based, tobacco-funded organization) was given $50,000 to develop a high school fire safety curriculum in the State of New York. The Tobacco Institute has donated $640,000 to the National Fire Protection Association, the organization that sets fire codes, for a smoke detector program.[10] In December 1982, *Firehouse* reported that "For its service and commitment to fire safety, Philip Morris USA has received the Fire Department of New York City's Fire Prevention 1982 Award, presented annually to corporations which have helped foster and underwrite the department's fire prevention efforts." In April 1983 *Firehouse* noted another award:

> In appreciation for his corporation's ongoing financial and technical support of the Fire Department of New York, Shepard Pollack, president of Philip Morris USA, was recently named a deputy chief of the department.

There are three areas of activity that are being pursued around the country. First, there will be an expansion of the coalition that will lobby state capitals and Washington, DC. Second, the fire-safe cigarette campaign will emerge in other countries and will become an international campaign. Third, there will be personal-injury and product-liability suits filed on the behalf of victims.

Mierley and Baker[11] have noted that during a three-year period 39% of all cigarette-fire deaths in urban residences were innocent victims. This is the one nagging problem for cigarette manufacturers: the entire population, especially infants, children, disabled people, and the elderly, is at risk because of the carefully "planned obsolescence" of the American-made cigarette. A fire started by an apartment dweller, a houseguest, a hospital patient or employee, or a hotel guest can burn or suffocate neighbors who are asleep or incapacitated, or who live on high floors. When the tobacco industry refuses to change its product to stop deaths and burn injuries, it expands a credibility gap that cannot be bridged by claims that "more research is required." The industry is withholding a solution to a grave public health problem, and no longer is this being excused by members of state legislatures and Congress in the name of free enterprise.

Acknowledgment. Organizations that support the Cigarette Safety Act include the American Burn Association, the American Medical Association, the American Public Health Association, the International Association of Fire Chiefs, the International Association of Fire Fighters (AFL-CIO), the Junior Leagues of California, the National Fire Protection Association, the Phoenix Society, and numerous fire departments.

Note: *Mr McGuire has produced two films on the tragedy of burn injuries,* Here's Looking at You, Kid *and* Heroic Measures. *He also aided the production of* Sleeping Death, *a documentary for KRON-TV (San Francisco) on the subject of cigarette-caused fires.*

A highly acclaimed film on the subject, Hospitals Don't Burn, *is available for showing from Pyramid Films, PO Box 1048, Santa Monica, CA 90406.*

REFERENCES

1. 1981 National Fire Incidence Reporting System (NFIRS) & Federal Emergency Management Agency (FEMA) analysis of National Fire Protection Association (NFPA) survey data, available from FEMA, US Fire Administration.
2. Birky MM, Halpin BM, Caplan YH, et al: Fire fatality study. *Fire Materials* 1979; 3:211–217.
3. Arthur D. Little, Inc, report, in: *Potential Flammability Hazards of Upholstered Furniture—Progress Report on Industry Activities to the Consumer Product Safety Commission,* edited and published by Furniture Flammability Committee. May 9, 1974, pp 1–6.
4. Krasny JF, Allen PJ, Maldonado AM, et al: *Development of a Candidate Test Method for the Measurement of the Propensity of Cigarettes to Cause Smoldering Ignition of Upholstered Furniture and Mattresses: Final Report,* (NBSIR) 81-2363. US Dept of Commerce, National Bureau of Standards, 1981, pp 1–37.
5. Macaluso C: *Cigarette Ignition Studies, Report of Test for The Burn Council,* San Francisco General Hospital, by United States Testing Company, Inc, 5555 Telegraph Road, Los Angeles, CA 90040; September 23, 1982, pp 1–7.
6. Spears AW: *A Technical Analysis of the Problems Relating to Upholstered Furniture and Mattress Fires Relative to Proposed Cigarette Legislation Including a Review of Relevant Patents;* submitted to the Subcommittee on Health and the Environment of the Committee on Energy and Commerce for its hearing on H.R. 1880, March 21, 1983, pp 1–46.
7. McCormack JA, Damant GH: *Self Extinguishing Cigarette Study;* Laboratory Reports Nos. 2442-2479 and 2443-2479, Bureau of Home Furnishings, Department of Consumer Affairs, State of California, November 13, 1979, pp 1–3.
8. O'Malley B: Cigarettes & Sofas. *Mother Jones* 1979; 4(6):54–60.
9. Kornegay HR: *Statement on H.R. 1880 before the Subcommittee on Health and the Environment of the Committee on Energy and Commerce,* March 21, 1983, pp 9–11.
10. The Washington connection; fighting fire with firemen. *Fortune* 1983; 108:52.
11. Mierley MC, Baker SP: Fatal house fires in an urban population. *JAMA* 1983; 249:1466–1468.

CIGARETTE FIRES ON AIRPLANES

Citing three fires in 1983 aboard commercial aircraft which were caused by smoldering cigarettes and which resulted in numerous fatalities, the Air Travelers Safety Association has urged the Civil Aeronautics Board (CAB) to ban smoking on airliners. A bill in Congress (HR 3847) calling for such action has been introduced by Rep. Bob Traxler (D, Michigan).

The Association, headed by William Plymat, Sr, chairman emeritus of Preferred Risk Mutual Insurance Company and a member of the Presidential Commission on Drunk Driving, is also urging support for a return to the two-drink limit aboard commercial aircraft as a means of curbing careless smoking by intoxicated persons which may lead to fires. A bill to prohibit airlines from offering free drinks (HR 54) has been introduced by Rep Charles E. Bennett (D, Florida).

Further information may be obtained by writing the Air Travelers Safety Association, 2908 Patricia Drive, Des Moines, IA 50322.

The New York Cigarette Fire Safety Act

Hon. Alexander B. Grannis

An 11-year old girl whose six-year old sister was killed by a fire in their Stony Brook, Long Island, home early Wednesday morning, died yesterday . . . . The girls were asleep in their home when smoke and heat—the result of a fire that started with a smoldering cigarette in a downstairs den—billowed up the stairway to their bedrooms . . . .

Newsday, May 14, 1982

The deaths of the children who lost their lives in this fire become even more senseless when viewed in light of the fact that this tragedy and other fires like it could have been prevented.

Despite the tobacco industry's claim that no such cigarette exists in a form that the public would want to smoke, there is strong evidence that cigarettes, the leading cause of residential fire deaths in the United States, can be made fire-safe.

The tobacco lobby continues to obfuscate the facts regarding the feasibility of a fire-safe cigarette. It is interesting to note that the same industry that insists cigarettes, regardless of tar and nicotine level, do not pose any health risks, expresses its concern that a fire-safe cigarette will lead to increased tar and nicotine. The National Bureau of Standards has shown no correlation between a cigarette's level of tar and nicotine and its propensity to ignite furniture.

Nothing in the actions and attitudes of the tobacco industry suggests it is capable of voluntarily acting in the public interest. It is for this reason that Senators Ralph Marino (R-C, Nassau), Emanuel Gold (D-L, Queens), and I have introduced the Cigarette Fire Safety Act (A3814/S3059), a bill that will require the New York State Office of Fire Prevention and Control to set fire safety standards for cigarettes sold in New York State. The standards would ensure either that cigarettes go out in a few minutes when not puffed or that they meet some other performance standard to limit the risk of igniting mattresses or other household furnishings.

The Cigarette Fire Safety Act has received support from every major professional and volunteer firefighter organization across the State, as well as burn surgeons and burn victims, the State PTA, the Secretary of State, the Commissioner of Environmental Conservation, and many others. The Tobacco Institute, the public relations arm of the six major tobacco companies, is the only opponent of this legislation, but its power should not be underestimated. It is one of the richest and most aggressive lobbies in the country, and it opposes any effort to regulate its clients in any way.

The tobacco companies' vehement opposition to any form of regulation is also apparent in their efforts to stop another proposed measure, Assembly Bill 939, which would require manufacturers of cigarettes to provide the Commissioner of Health with a list of chemical substances used in the manufacture of their products.

Unlike the manufacturers of other consumer goods, cigarette manufacturers are not required by any state or federal regulatory agency to disclose what is in their products. The tobacco industry has managed to exclude cigarettes from classification as a food, drug, or hazardous substance. According to the most recent US Surgeon General's report, there are a startling number of chemical components in both the gas and particulate phases of cigarette smoke, such as toluene, a narcotic affecting the central nervous system, and vinyl chloride, a known liver carcinogen.

The Tobacco Institute claims that state legislation is unnecessary because the six major cigarette manufacturers have made available to representatives of the US Department of Health and Human Services (HHS) a list of all ingredients commonly used in cigarettes. However, the agreement with HHS specifies that the manufacturers disclose only those ingredients that are added by three or more manufacturers or by any single manufacturer in a substantial amount. It is left to the manufacturer to determine what exactly will be considered a "substantial" amount.

I do not believe that it should be the responsibility of public or private health agencies to struggle through complicated testing procedures in an attempt to identify the chemical additives in cigarettes. The public has the right to know about the toxic effects of the chemicals they encounter as a result of their exposure to cigarette smoke, and the cigarette companies have a responsibility to provide the necessary information.

Address correspondence to Assemblyman Alexander B. Grannis, Room 522, Legislative Office Building, Albany, NY 12248.

HOSPITAL FIRE TRAPS THREE

Dade Hospital Is Hit By Fire; 46 Patients Taken Out Unhurt

Newspaper headlines. Cigarette-caused fires hurt the most vulnerable members of society.

The Minnesota Clean Indoor Air Act
A model for New York and other states

Hon. Phyllis L. Kahn

In my ten years in the Minnesota legislature, the issue which has received the most attention from both the press and public has been the 1975 Minnesota Clean Indoor Air Act, of which I was the chief sponsor. This was not the first law to attempt to control smoking in public places, but it was the first one to use the comprehensive approach of saying that smoking would be prohibited everywhere unless it was specifically permitted. How did Minnesota come to pass a law which has been lauded by health professionals but criticized by the tobacco lobby as restrictive and confusing and the first step in the total destruction of personal freedoms?

The first reason was the work of a persistent and devoted (although small and new) organization, the Association for Non-Smokers' Rights (ANSR). Its activities included helping to write the bill, getting witnesses before committees, writing letters, and maintaining visibility in the legislative process at every stage. ANSR was supported by organizations such as the American Lung Association and the American Cancer Society, and most other health bodies in the state. One of the important jobs performed by the American Lung Association was the publication of a popular pamphlet translating part of a report of the Surgeon General into words that even legislators could understand. A former Surgeon General, Jesse Steinfeld, MD, testified before the legislature a year before passage. Charles Mayo, MD, a local physician and a descendant of the famous medical family, gave further testimony. Without the support of these and other physicians the bill may well have failed.

Another help was a dramatic change in the composition of the Minnesota legislature from older individuals who smoked to younger nonsmoking members (the nonsmoking majority has increased at each election). Also, there is no sizeable tobacco industry in the state, in contrast to neighboring Wisconsin where a small tobacco industry has blocked similar legislation. Perhaps the most important reason for passage of the law is its reasonableness: it doesn't prevent anyone from smoking but requires certain easily adopted protective measures such as dividing restaurant dining areas, meeting rooms, and working areas. (If such measures do not result in a smoke-free atmosphere for the nonsmoker, then the entire area must be made non-smoking.)

The law was backed up by a clear set of regulations written by the Minnesota Department of Health, again with the advocacy and assistance of volunteer groups. People have said that the law might be useless because of a lack of enforcement, but one of the major difficulties in enforcement has turned out to be the major strength of the law. Certain other states have listed a greater or lesser number of places where smoking is prohibited. The Minnesota law takes the step of forbidding smoking everywhere unless it is specifically allowed, but this step is psychologically far more difficult for people to understand. This single line in state law required a massive change in cultural attitudes. Yet the very existence of the law, and the attendant publicity, is important. Few people continue to smoke when it is pointed out to them that it is against the law. Despite the complaints and some inadequate compliance, most restaurants initially had small but definite smoke-free areas. By a more recent revision of the rules, they are now required to have a minimum of 30% of their seats designated nonsmoking. In this respect, the voluntary groups took the lead in education and in the insistence on the right to a smoke-free environment.

Although this measure was not aimed at individual smoking deterrence, but rather at protection of clean indoor air, it has had an interesting effect on those who continue to smoke. This is probably why the tobacco industry became so interested in it, albeit belatedly in Minnesota. It turns out that as smoking is considered socially and legally unacceptable, and also as it becomes more difficult to smoke, people smoke far less. Legislators who smoke have told me that with the passage of the nonsmoking rule on the floor of the Minnesota House, their cigarette consumption has gone way down just because of the additional effort it takes to go someplace else to smoke. I also believe the bill passed in part because it was not taken very seriously by its opponents. They thought it was such a completely ridiculous thing to do that they kept laughing at it all the way to the governor's office. Only after it was signed (unlike in Illinois and Maine, where the tobacco lobby has succeeded in obtaining gubernatorial vetoes of similar legislation) did they start complaining about curtailment of rights.

In a Roper Organization poll prepared for The Tobacco Institute, A Study of Public Attitudes Toward Cigarette Smoking and the Tobacco Industry in 1978, the conclusion was reached that the nonsmokers' rights movement is "the most dangerous development to the viability of the tobacco industry that has yet occurred." The economic effect of reduced smoking will also be formidable. From the *Tobacco Observer*, September 18, 1980, one learns that if each American smokes one less cigarette each day, the resultant loss to the tobacco industry is $500 million a year.

Specific funding for enforcement has never been appropriated, since the added workload in the implementation of this Act has been absorbed by the State department of

Based on a presentation delivered at the Fifth World Conference on Smoking and Health, Winnipeg, Canada, July 11, 1983.

Address correspondence to Ms Kahn, Member, Minnesota Legislature, District 58B, 100 Malcom Av., SE, Minneapolis, MN 55414.

health. This includes establishing and modifying appropriate rules, answering complaints, and adding compliance with the Act to the list of items in health inspections. The average cost to the department has been about $4,600 per year for the past three years. The placement of signs is a responsibility of the supervising authority or proprietor of any public place and is a minimal cost. (In Michigan, where legislation was also passed requiring nonsmoking areas in restaurants, the signs were in many cases provided by the Michigan Lung Association or the American Cancer Society.) Although there is a penalty section in the law, there have been few formal summonses issued. Inasmuch as any law can be, this one is self-enforcing. Persons irritated by smoke expect to find a no-smoking section and have become more assertive in establishing their rights to such a space. Others look for smoking sections before lighting up and mistakes are generally taken care of by simple reminders. The law effectively works to simplify and reinforce rules of common courtesy.

There is a public acceptance of restrictions on smoking.

In 1980, the Minnesota Poll, a public opinion survey conducted by the *Minneapolis Tribune* since 1944, found that 92% of nonsmokers and 87% of heavy (two pack a day) smokers favored the law. The Act has also been politically popular. It passed in 1975 with a good bipartisan majority, and some legislators who voted against it have become ardent supporters after conversations with constituents.

The establishment of legislation protecting nonsmokers deserves serious consideration world-wide as a useful tool in limiting smoking. As Jesse Steinfeld, MD, said in testimony before the Minnesota legislature in 1974:

> There is no doubt in my mind that in some future time a healthier group of humans will look back with horror and amazement on these three or four centuries when people voluntarily committed a slow form of suicide through smoking, and foisted a noxious environment upon their nonsmoking companions. These future citizens will regard ours as a primitive, unhealthy, unintelligent era, inexplicable except for the greed of those who manufacture cigarettes and of the governments which derive revenue from taxation thereof.

ORGANIZATIONS WORKING ACTIVELY IN BEHALF OF NONSMOKERS' RIGHTS

Alaska Council on Smoking or Health   PO Box 3-3868, Anchorage, AK 99501

Smoking and Health Action Coalition   7 S Fluorite, Tucson, AZ 85745

Californians for Nonsmokers' Rights   PO Box 668, Berkeley, CA 94708

GASP (Group Against Smoking Pollution) of Colorado   Box 39692, Denver, CO 80239

Wichita GASP   PO Box 17602, Wichita, KS 67217

Bowie (MD) GASP   PO Box 863, Bowie, MD 20715

GASP of Massachusetts   PO Box 242, Brookline, MA 02146

Association for Nonsmokers' Rights   1829 Portland Ave S, Minneapolis, MN 55404

New Jersey GASP   105 Mountain Ave, Summit, NJ 07901

New Mexico Nonsmoker Protection Projects   PO Box 657, Los Alamos, NM 87544

GASP of New York   7 Maxine Ave, Plainview, NY 11803

FANS (Fresh Air for Nonsmokers)   PO Box 24052, Seattle, WA 98124

NATIONAL ORGANIZATIONS

ASH (Action on Smoking and Health)   2013 H St NW, Washington, DC 20006

Non-Smokers' Rights Association   455 Spadina Ave at College, Suite 201, Toronto, Ontario M5S 2G8 Canada

—compiled by Regina Carlson, New Jersey GASP

A physician-led referendum for cleaner air in Florida

CHARLES FRANKLIN TATE, JR., MD

By 1970, after 20 years of writing articles and letters to the editor and speaking at schools, churches, and medical meetings in Dade County, Florida (population 1,000,000), concerning the importance of clean indoor air in public places and in the working environment, the effort was beginning to pay off. Smoking had been banned in 1972, the last cigarette machine at the 1,250-bed, tax-supported Jackson Memorial Hospital was removed, and the sale of all tobacco products on the premises was stopped. Other progressive measures soon followed in the community at large.

As with most successful health legislation efforts that are fought by vested interests, the various clean indoor air measures adopted in Dade County (affecting department stores, supermarkets, and elevators) were sponsored by a forceful elected representative who could not be bullied or bought by the tobacco lobby. When this man, Commissioner (and former United States Senator) Harry Cain, died, in 1979, all subsequent action at the County Commission ceased.

After repeated futile attempts to get the Commission to pass a Clean Indoor Air Act to cover all public places, I decided to try getting the issue directly before the public on a referendum.

Much to my dismay, none of the major health charities (American Lung Association, American Heart Association, American Cancer Society) would offer any assistance. Therefore, I turned to the local chapter of GASP (Group Against Smoking Pollution). Not only did the two leaders of this organization aid in obtaining the thousands of signatures required to get the measure on the ballot, but they worked virtually nonstop for weeks on end as Referendum Day approached.

Although as a past president of the Dade County Medical Association, I was able to get the Association to go on record in favor of the ordinance (which placed restrictions on smoking in physicians' offices), there was no appreciable support from the medical community. Many physicians openly derided our efforts, feeling that there was no way to beat the tobacco industry, which, it would later be revealed, spent more than $1 million in mass media advertising—a national record for a county referendum—to our $5,000. Less than $1,000 of our opponents' money was contributed by Dade County citizens; $297,000 came from R.J. Reynolds Tobacco Company and $225,000 from Philip Morris.

Typical of the tactics of the tobacco industry-supported opposition group Dade Voters for Free Choice, was the slogan, designed with a heavily Jewish population in mind, "DON'T LET IT HAPPEN HERE!" Incredibly, too, the local president of the Fraternal Order of Police was depicted in ads condemning the proposed ordinance. Donations were made by the tobacco companies to the Fraternal Order of Police at the time of the referendum.

On May 8, 1979, more than 192,000 voters went to the polls. The ordinance was defeated by just 820 votes—the closest election in County history. Many who had ridiculed GASP and opposed the ordinance—such as the *Miami Herald* and the *Miami News*, prime beneficiaries of tobacco company advertising dollars—begrudgingly admitted their admiration for our efforts and began supporting several of the very changes we had proposed. Had even a single health charity lent support to our effort, there is little doubt that we would have felled Goliath.

As it turned out, many restaurants and retail establishments saw in the vote that good business was not synonymous with obeisance to cigarette companies. Nonsmoking areas began to be established in many public places.

Unfortunately, there was little impact on the workplace, so in 1980 we went through the same battle, sure that this time the voluntary agencies and the medical community and the media editorialists would join in. They did not, and a less-restrictive ordinance was defeated by a wider margin than the 1979 vote. The tobacco companies, calling themselves FAIR (Floridians Against Increased Regulation), pumped in $600,000, only $185 of which was contributed by Floridians. We raised $3,200 and were unable to compete with or challenge the legality of ads by FAIR which suggested the law would deal no differently with smokers than with murderers and rapists.

As a professor of medicine and pulmonary diseases for many years, I have witnessed the suffering of thousands of victims of cigarette smoking. Cases of squamous cell carcinoma of the lung in individuals who never smoked can be counted on the fingers of one hand,—except possibly for the spouses of persons who smoke. From the workplace, countless patients, nonsmoker and former smoker alike, are pleading for relief from fetid, allergenic air caused by tobacco smoke.

Although the American Medical Association has written up a model for clean indoor air legislation, by and large organized medicine has stood back or spoken with restraint. Ironically, as other groups challenge the medical profession's leadership role, physicians and medical societies that do not actively support such legislation are losing out on a prime opportunity to enhance their positive health image and to prove their commitment to lowering the cost of medical care in their communities.

Dr Tate is Professor Emeritus—Medicine and Pulmonary Diseases, University of Miami School of Medicine.
Address correspondence to Dr Tate, 1150 NW 14th Street, Suite 302, Miami, FL 33136.

Clean indoor-air legislation: the Illinois experience

LUKE L. BURCHARD, MD

Illinois would seem to be the ideal state for passage of clean indoor-air legislation; it does not grow tobacco, and no tobacco companies are headquartered there. It has one of the best systems of community-based medical education in the country and a trend-setting city that is home to the world's largest medical, dental, and hospital associations. Its governor, James Thompson, is the son of a surgeon and the standard-bearer of the political party of Illinois' most famous citizen, Abraham Lincoln.

It would be expected that opposition to restrictions on smoking in public places or on cigarette advertising would be led by the tobacco lobby and Illinois tobacco and candy distributors. But the state is also home to the advertising agency (Leo Burnett USA) with the world's largest cigarette account (Philip Morris' Marlboro, Merit, and other brands), to one of the Midwest's largest department store chains (Marshall Field, owned by British American Tobacco), to billboard companies which receive much of their income from cigarette advertising (and on whom politicians rely during election campaigns), and to a number of sports teams and entertainment centers that receive substantial cigarette company money. The influence of the tobacco lobby over the Chicago City Council has been such as to block attempts to pass clean indoor-air measures and even to kill attempts at prohibiting free distribution of cigarettes on public avenues and at city-sponsored events.

My personal involvement with clean indoor-air legislation began in Missouri in 1982, when as a member of Doctors Ought to Care (DOC) I testified in favor of the Missouri Clean Indoor Air Act. Physician-aided efforts there resulted in a unanimous recommendation in favor of the passage of the bill by the Public Health Committee of the Missouri House of Representatives, but the measure was never brought to the full House for consideration. After I moved to Illinois, it was a simple matter to research previous efforts at clean indoor-air legislation. The first such measure was passed by the General Assembly in 1974 but was vetoed by then Gov. Dan Walker, who claimed there was no provision for enforcement. A measure that included such a provision was passed in 1978, only to be vetoed by Governor Thompson, within minutes after meeting with cigarette

company lobbyists. In 1980 the bill was stopped due to surprise opposition from the Department of Public Health which claimed that enforcement of the bill would be too costly.

I rewrote the 1983 Illinois Clean Indoor Air Act to take into account previously stated objections, especially in regard to cost and enforcement. Three State senators sponsored the measure, and we were encouraged by the initial support.

We anticipated the attempts of the president of the Senate to kill the bill, but were unprepared for the level of opposition from black and female legislators. One of the saddest ironies of the effort to pass legislation aimed at curtailing cigarette smoking and improving public health is that some of the most ardent opponents have included women and members of ethnic minorities—currently the leading targets of cigarette advertising and the fastest growing market for cigarette sales. With one exception (a paid tobacco lobbyist) all witnesses against the bill were from out of state, and all were paid by the tobacco industry. In contrast, those testifying in support of the bill came on their own time and at their own expense. They included physicians from three medical schools, members of DOC, and representatives of the Chicago Heart Association and the American Lung Association. The Coles County Medical Society officially endorsed the act, but support from the Illinois State Medical Society was minimal. The bill was sent to a subcommittee composed entirely of senators opposed to the legislation.

The complexities of health care financing have preoccupied organized medicine. It remains to be seen whether state and national medical associations will accord greater legislative priority to preventive medicine issues.

Many physicians in my county took advantage of an opportunity to expand their public health role by becoming involved in an important piece of legislation. In spite of our initial political naïveté, much has been learned from this effort, and the groundwork has been laid for future legislative successes. Public concern over both the irritant and unhealthful long-term effects of second-hand smoke, especially to children, is such that the media no longer mock or ignore the importance of clean indoor-air legislation. The grassroots public support is growing, and we shall be more savvy in translating public approval into passage of the measure.

Dr Burchard is a family physician and president of the Illinois chapter of DOC.

Address correspondence to Dr Burchard, 1810 Charleston Ave, Mattoon, IL 61938.

On November 8, 1983 voters in San Francisco approved a ballot proposition that protects the right of employees to a workplace free of tobacco smoke. Cigarette companies contributed $1.3 million to defeat the measure, while proponents raised $85,000 mostly in small donations from local citizens.

Preventing tomorrow's epidemic

The control of smoking and tobacco production in developing countries

MIKE MULLER

Consider the case of one African country where health authorities announced their intention to introduce legislation to control the promotion of smoking. They had submitted a draft law to the attorney general's office for a final version to be prepared, but there it had stayed for nearly two years. The draft had been submitted to the agriculture ministry for comment since it dealt with a crop produced in the country; the ministry had stopped the process in its tracks by the simple expedient of not replying to the letter. "The permanent secretary just sees red. He refuses to talk to me about it," complained one health ministry source. The laws that had been passed about tobacco provided for compensation to be paid, from public funds, to the country's handful of tobacco farmers should their crops be damaged by bad weather.

This case is not atypical, and certainly shows the need for proponents of smoking control to come to grips with the agricultural and industrial aspects of tobacco if they wish to control its use. The agriculture lobby is, in many countries, far stronger than the health lobby. And those who wish to promote smoking control in developing countries will have to deal with a tobacco lobby in which the farmers will play an increasingly important part.

The environmental damage done by tobacco growing, particularly in developing countries, and the limited scope for tobacco exports from Third World countries in the future are two issues on which the tobacco growers and manufacturers can legitimately be challenged. This article will focus on three more: (1) the competition between tobacco and other crops, (2) the organization of tobacco growing and manufacture—advantages and disadvantages of state monopolies for tobacco, and (3) the future of the cigarette—"safe" cigarette technologies and the interests of the Third World farmer, the manufacturer and the economy.

TOBACCO VERSUS FOOD

The most immediate of these issues is the question of the competition between tobacco and other crops, often portrayed as a competition between tobacco and food. The points that have received the most attention have been the

use of land for tobacco that could be used to grow other crops, particularly food crops; and the interference of tobacco in the production of other crops because of its high labor demand at particular stages of cultivation and processing.

In some developing countries, neither land nor labor is in short supply, and there are no markets for other crops that could offer comparable returns for the farmers.

In the case of each country, it is necessary to seek the principal constraints placed on agricultural production. There are usually six such determinants in developing countries:

Land. Not just the absolute available areas are involved, but so are the areas available to farmers within the local political context. In the case of tobacco, the land required to grow fuelwood for curing should not be forgotten.

Labor. Help may be hired or may be provided by the farmer and his family. For tobacco, the labor force must be available during short periods of peak demand and must be willing to do the manual work required for the minimum wage rates essential if the crop is to be produced at competitive prices.

Capital. In Third World agriculture, the principal problem is not the availability of cash but the existence of institutions that effectively lend it to all farmers on a short- and medium-term basis.

Technical support. The availability of technical support and the institutional backup needed to make it effective may make all the difference to the viability of a crop.

Markets. Farmers will not produce crops unless they have a market for them. What is often not appreciated outside of agriculture is that it is not just the price that matters but the guarantee that the crop will be bought, the time from delivery to receipt of payment, and the location of the point of sale. The existence or prospect of a foreign market will often transform the market conditions in the many countries where foreign exchange is short. It should also be noted that although the presence of hungry people may indicate a need for food, it does not necessarily show the existence of a market for it.

Energy. A unique constraint on the production of tobacco is the energy requirement for its curing.

The questions of land, labor, and energy availability and the resultant impact of tobacco on the rural economy are easily analyzed. In a sparsely populated country like Tanzania, it will be found that tobacco growing does compete with food-crop production for labor, to the detriment of food

Based on a presentation delivered at the Fifth World Conference on Smoking and Health, Winnipeg, Canada, July 12, 1983.
Mr Muller is a civil engineer.
Address correspondence to Mr Muller, CP 119, Beira, Mozambique, Africa.

yields. The same is not true in those parts of India where the large pool of landless laborers means that labor is not an important constraint. Similarly, in Malaysia, situated as it is in the tropical forest belt, it is not surprising to find that wood for curing is not yet a major constraint on tobacco production, but it is in the long-established tobacco-producing areas of Southern Brazil as well as in the arid fringes of Pakistan, Kenya, and Nigeria. Less well appreciated and more difficult to analyze are the questions of credit and technical and marketing support. In these areas the competition between tobacco growing and other agricultural activities is often acute.

Consider the data quoted for tobacco production in Costa Rica in the Economist Intelligence Unit (EIU) report *Leaf Tobacco—Its Contribution to the Economic and Social Development of the Third World.*[1] This purports to show the superior profitability of tobacco as a cash crop in the Parrita Valley and suggests that tobacco is respectively four and five times more profitable than the alternatives, sorghum and rice. However, the comparison is based on the assumption that equal areas of land are planted to each crop. But, because tobacco needs far more labor (4.5 times more than rice, 3.7 times more than sorghum), the comparison is only valid if land is the limiting factor on cultivation in that area. Since the average farm size in Parrita is around 25 hectares (ha) if the plantations of the United Fruit Company are excluded, the constraints that limit farmers' choice of crops are more likely to be the availability of capital on the one hand and labor on the other. A comparison of the profitability of rice, sorghum, and tobacco using either the same labor input for each or the same financial investment for each reveals a completely different picture and suggests that sorghum offers a better return than tobacco (see Table).

SUPPORT FOR THE FARMER—THE MAJOR CONSTRAINT

Even if tobacco is not the most profitable crop, farmers may still opt to grow it. In developing countries, the choice is determined by the support available to overcome the specific constraints on each crop rather than its absolute profitability. Indeed, in the Costa Rican case, the EIU cites a farmer who chose to grow sorghum "to compare the re-

sults with his usual tobacco crop. The income was very good, he claims, but he quickly reverted to tobacco and has not considered sorghum again, a telling comment on the relative profitability of each crop." More likely, the reality is that he also wanted the financial and technical support available through the local subsidiary of British American Tobacco (BAT).

Thus, in Nigeria, "no other crop in the savanna zone of Western Nigeria receives such a highly coordinated package of assistance" wrote one commentator.[2] Kenya, where for many years tobacco production was minimal, achieved virtual self-sufficiency in just a couple of seasons when BAT (Kenya) started to support growers and finance them through company-administered Agricultural Finance Corporation loans.[3] The EIU report paints the same picture for other countries. Referring to company support for Costa Rican tobacco growers, it concludes "Probably no other crop in the Parrita area receives such careful attention as tobacco." In Karnataka State, in India, "compared with the cultivation of other dry crops, this support at field level and the orderly marketing mechanism in tobacco are in fairly dramatic contrast."

NATIONAL RESOURCES

What is sometimes not obvious is that the resources used to support tobacco growers are principally those of the country itself. Company backing for farmers is usually sufficient to ensure that local banks will lend them money. Bankers do not, in general, care to lend funds to small borrowers in high-risk activities like agriculture, particularly when they have little or nothing to offer in the way of security. Thus, tobacco helps them to meet their political commitments to the smaller borrower at the least risk. To quote the EIU report again: "Companies prefer to leave the provision of investment capital to commercial or state banks . . . . The banks are prepared to extend credit to farmers who wish to grow tobacco in Karnataka only if such farmers are sponsored by a tobacco company . . . ." In Costa Rica, "Banks' attitudes to tobacco growing are influenced strongly by the backing which farmers still receive from the companies."

The support involved is substantial. In Karnataka, the 300 million rupees (approximately US$37.5 million) ad-

Costa Rica. Costs and Income From Tobacco,* Rice and Sorghum Under Varying Constraints[1†]

Limit	Crop	Labor Costs	Other Costs	Total Costs	Income	Profit	Area (ha)**
Land (1 ha)	Tobacco	6,180	9,390	15,570	17,845	2,275††	1
	Rice	1,370	2,140	3,510	3,960	450	1
	Sorghum	1,670	1,000	2,670	3,250	580	1
Labor ₡6,180	Tobacco	6,180	9,390	15,570	17,845	2,275††	1
	Rice	6,180	9,653	15,833	17,863	2,030	4.5
	Sorghum	6,180	3,701	9,881	12,027	2,146	3.7
Cash ₡15,570	Tobacco	6,180	9,390	15,570	17,845	2,275	1
	Rice	6,077	9,493	15,570	17,566	1,996	4.4
	Sorghum	9,739	5,831	15,570	18,952	3,382††	5.8

* Data refer to burley tobacco; flue-cured costs are higher.
† Monetary unit: 1 ₡ (colon) = US $43.35 (free float).
** Average farm size in the sample area is 25 ha excluding plantations of the United Fruit Company.
†† Most profitable crop.

65

vanced to a relative handful of farmers (less than 8,000) in 1978 represented a full 15% of state agricultural credit in that state.[1] The amount involved is far greater in Brazil where seasonal credit alone (not including finance for barn building, for instance) came to approximately US$150 million, or 875 million cruzeiros in 1979.

The picture is the same in technical support. In Kenya, 190 BAT extension workers support 8,000 farmers, one to 46 farmers.[4] An estimated 2,000 technicians support the 75,000 small tobacco farmers in Brazil's Rio Grande de Sul.[1] Even if the task of the juniors among them is merely to help farmers fill in the application forms for Banco do Brazil loans, the ratio of less than 1 to 400 is remarkable. The ratio in a pioneer area like Parrita is even more dramatic, with four technicians for fewer than 80 farmers.

The first question, then, that needs to be posed in the developing tobacco-growing countries is not "How can alternative crops be encouraged?" but "Why is tobacco so favored?" and "What would be the effect of a redeployment of the resources used to promote tobacco?" In a Third World country with no shortage of capital, no shortage of skilled agricultural extension workers, and adequate price support and marketing arrangements for other crops, redeployment would make little difference. But such countries are few and far between.

What this means for smoking control will be familiar to those who follow the activities of the World Health Organization (WHO) and the exhortations of its director general. International action is helpful but it is national action that is crucial. The WHO may have been successful in persuading the Food and Agriculture Organization (FAO) and the World Bank to give less support to tobacco pro-

duction, but this support was minimal from the start. Tobacco production is expanded by tobacco companies—and they use national resources to do the job. So the question must now be asked in each country: "How much government support, how much national investment is going to tobacco, directly or indirectly, and why?" If agricultural banks, agricultural schools, and agriculture ministries were to stop using national resources to support tobacco, the efficiency of the corporate support system would be reduced and alternative crops would benefit from their redeployment and hence become more attractive.

And there are alternative crops. The tobacco journals document their variety—in Korea, it is red peppers,[5] in Thailand, peanuts and and mung beans,[5] in Syria, vegetables,[5] in Brazil soya beans, and in Costa Rica, sorghum and rice.[11] What these alternatives usually lack is the consistent technical, financial, and market support that tobacco enjoys.

MULTINATIONALS OR MONOPOLIES?

The best-developed support systems for the Third World tobacco farmer are those of the major international tobacco companies. What would happen if these multinationals were to be excluded? The question is not an academic one—there is ample precedent for the control of tobacco production and marketing by state monopolies rather than by private industry, a practice commendable in that it makes more visible the basic fiscal function of tobacco. Nor does there appear to be any stigma attached to this kind of state control which is practiced in such unashamedly capitalist countries as Japan, Italy, France, Spain, Korea, and Taiwan.

It may be that there are countries in which this choice has

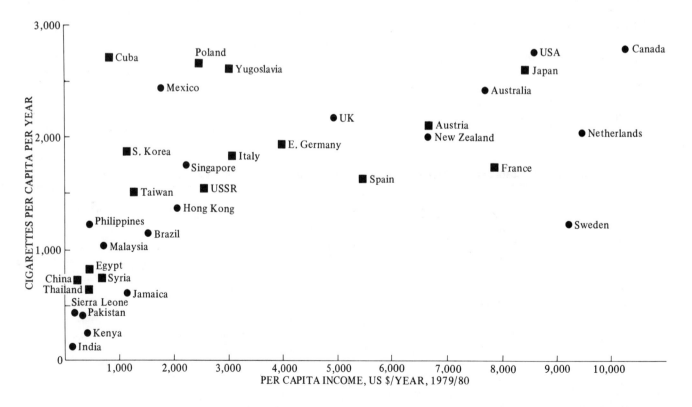

Figure.   Cigarette consumption v national income; monopolies v private industry. ●: private industry; ■ monopoly/state company.

66

not yet been made or in which it will be raised; therefore, it would be useful to look briefly at the implications. Corporate propaganda, backed by empirical evidence, suggests that without the technical and organizational support of one of the major companies, tobacco growing will invariably be less efficient. This is likely since tobacco would then be treated more like any other crop. There is also strong evidence that the multinationals, the major international tobacco users, tend not to buy from countries whose cigarette markets are closed to them by national monopolies and hence export prospects are penalized.

The inefficiency of the enterprise may be a positive disadvantage, however, when it comes to smoking control. The private tobacco companies aim to maximize their income and profits. They do this essentially by selling as many cigarettes as possible at whatever profit margin they succeed in negotiating with the government. The objective of monopolies, on the other hand, is to provide revenue for the state. Theoretically, they can maximize this revenue by raising prices until consumption falls so fast that their total income and return are reduced. In practice, however, it appears that the monopolies are not notably efficient in this regard. The Japanese Tobacco and Salt Monopoly recently raised prices by over 10% which cut consumption by only 3%, suggesting that the Monopoly could be earning far more for the state than it is.[6] In Egypt, cigarette prices are fixed and, because of shortages, street prices are 30% higher than the legal price—a margin that could be earned by the state rather than by blackmarket speculators.[7] And, in general, there is no clear difference between per capita consumption in countries with monopolies and in those where the cigarette industry is in private hands. Indeed, in a number of countries where there are monopolies, consumption is higher than would be predicted in terms of national income—the socialist countries are particularly depressing in this regard (see Figure).[7] (Caution should be used in interpreting these figures since there are complicating factors that make such comparisons difficult. Countries with monopolies may be those where income inequalities are less acute, with higher consumer purchasing power as a consequence; where there are historical reasons for high consumption; or where other consumer goods are in short supply.)

On the basis of this evidence, only if tobacco monopolies can be relied on to maximize revenue for the state by increasing prices should their establishment be encouraged by smoking control advocates, although from the perspective of tobacco production they are less likely to lure farmers from other crops and also less likely to win the export markets that might encourage domestic tobacco production and use in parallel.

THE HAZARDS OF "SAFE" SMOKING TECHNOLOGIES

The third issue that raises important questions about tobacco in developing countries is that of the new technologies being introduced in the industry. There is considerable, if understandable, confusion about the techniques used to produce the "low-tar" cigarettes that the rich world-tobacco industry has been introducing in response to the health criticisms made against its products. These techniques may have a very important bearing on both tobacco growing and cigarette manufacturing. Within the

new technologies lie the seeds of an expensive continued dependence of Third World countries on the multinationals for their cigarette technology and of a serious loss of competitiveness for Third World tobacco exporters.

To understand this, it is first necessary to appreciate that a "low-tar" cigarette does not necessarily contain more or less "tars." Rather, it is a cigarette which, when smoked at the rate, say, of one standard puff per minute, yields less particulate matter in the "inhaled" smoke. Imperial Tobacco's then research director, Dr Herbert Bentley, explained some years ago one simple way of making a low-tar cigarette: "If you're not worried about nicotine and if you assume the smoker does not change his smoking habit, one way is to make the cigarette burn faster. To do this, you use more porous paper; the rate of burn is faster, there are fewer puffs." Tar yield can also be reduced by ventilating the filter that dilutes the smoke taken in by each fixed volume puff of the smoking machine. Filters, too, can directly reduce the yield of particulate matter virtually to zero.[8]

One problem faced by the industry in designing a consumer-acceptable product is that these techniques tended to reduce the nicotine delivery and dilute the flavor to an unacceptable extent. A more far-reaching approach is to extract from the tobacco itself some of the substances that are precursors of undesirable particulate matter. One approach to this is to reduce the cured tobacco leaf to a pulp and reconstitute it as a paper, a process long used to salvage waste tobacco within the industry. The tar yields of reconstituted tobacco sheet are usually substantially lower than those of the original leaf. Further, once the tobacco is in a slurry, other components can be removed (particular focus has been on nitrates, precursors of noxious products like acetonitrile), nicotine content can be adjusted up or down, and flavor components removed or reinforced. Recent reviews of industry practice suggest that all of these methods are already in use to a greater or lesser extent.[9]

NEW TECHNOLOGY ON THE FARM

The last-mentioned technique dovetails with new farming methods being developed in the United States. These are intended to enable the US tobacco industry to continue to compete with low-wage Third World competitors in export markets—the price of tobacco on the world markets varies remarkably, but US leaf is consistently and disproportionately more expensive than the products of its competitors. One commentator recently quoted the US average price for flue-cured tobacco at $1.66 per pound compared with $1.12 in Zimbabwe, 91¢ in Malawi, 79¢ in Thailand, 48¢ in India, and 45¢ in Brazil.[10] The major obstacle to cost cutting in tobacco growing has been the labor-intensive business of harvesting and curing which involves a series of hand operations not easily mechanized on small farms. In response, easily packed bulk barns that can receive machine-harvested leaf have been introduced. In a more far-reaching effort, the US Department of Agriculture and the tobacco companies have been investigating prospects for a mechanical harvesting and curing system that would further simplify the process; the machine-harvested tobacco leaf is reduced to a slurry in which the fermentation reactions of curing take place more efficiently than in an expensively heated and ventilated barn. The slurry is then reconstituted. By enabling the tobacco to be produced on an entirely mechanized basis, the competitive position of American farmers would be transformed—at the expense of Third World exporters.[3,8,11]

The technique of homogenized leaf curing (as it is known) has an added public relations boon for the industry in that it allows undesirable components to be subtracted at an early stage; among these are leaf proteins. The result has been optimistic claims that tobacco may soon become a major source of protein. Even the FAO, which should know better, has suggested that it is possible that "tobacco leaf may in time become one of the world's principal sources of protein for human consumption and livestock feed."[12] In fact, there are other, more productive plants from which to extract leaf protein, and, even if all the flue-cured tobacco produced worldwide were to be so processed, protein yield per year would only be of the order of 500,000 tons—insignificant in food terms when compared with the production of oilseeds which in the 1970s was already 55,000,000 tons of protein equivalent.[13]

FAO strays farther from the track when it recommends that member countries might choose to produce mild tobacco leaves for the manufacture of less hazardous products. The trend seems to be back to intrinsically higher tar and nicotine, more "flavored" tobacco, which presumably provides a better processing starting point, rather than the mild, low-nicotine leaves that were briefly the vogue in the mid-1970s.[1,9]

In India, export buyer preference apparently switched rapidly from "flavored" strong tobaccos to mild-leaf and then back again[9]; in Brazil, the switch was from mild "filler" leaf to higher nicotine "flavored" leaf.[1]

The panorama must be depressing for Third World countries. If they follow the trend to low-tar cigarettes, they will require the complex new technology and carefully quality-controlled raw materials. This will mean a continued dependence on the multinational cigarette companies and will raise the foreign exchange cost of domestic smoking. The export market for tobacco will become less attractive when quality becomes less important as its control moves from unpredictable fields to the factory and farm prices fall. The introduction of a new technology is a political decision and the tobacco companies have shown themselves to be expert political operators. Thus, it would be rash to predict that the full burden will fall immediately on the developing countries. The industry will time the introduction of the new technologies to minimize the impact and also to avoid upsetting the farm lobbies in their home countries, particularly in the United States where the smaller farmers will also be adversely affected. The trends are clear, however, and they are not in the Third World's favor.

THE BROADER CONTEXT

The smoking-control advocates can thus challenge the apparent attractions of tobacco growing on a number of fronts, whether on the questionable future for tobacco exports, or the cost of the support that makes tobacco appear such an attractive crop, and the future dependence on multinationals for tobacco-manufacturing technology. It would be wrong to suggest, though, that tobacco does not remain a viable crop, particularly for small-scale peasant farmers who invest principally their own labor in its production. It would also be wrong to ignore the transfer of resources implied in tobacco growing and manufacturing from the better-off strata of society, who consume it, to the poorer groups either directly through the sale of tobacco or indirectly through taxation.

Thus, the focus on cutting the demand for tobacco must remain paramount. While there is still a demand for tobacco, it will continue to be grown. This article will draw, from an understanding of the production of tobacco and tobacco products, some lessons for those who seek to reduce the demand for them.

On this front, the first point to be made is that cigarette manufacturing is an expensive way to collect taxes. The cost of establishing a tobacco-processing plant and cigarette factory is high, and in the case of most Third World countries, it is paid mainly in foreign currency. Egypt, for example, is budgeting over $100 million to build a cigarette factory, which will then enable the state-owned Eastern Tobacco Company to meet projected consumption increases of 30 billion cigarettes per year by 1990. The project has been delayed because of cash shortages—the government was hoping to use some of the $300 million promised by the United States for food-industry projects as part of the Camp David peace agreement and is also exploring a deal with South African-based Rothmans to set up a joint venture.[7] In Kenya, $20 million is to be spent to modernize BAT's cigarette factory and upgrade its leaf tobacco plant.[5] In Nigeria, BAT subsidiary Nigerian Tobacco Company is to spend $15 million on a green-leaf processing factory alone.[9] Thailand, which in 1978 spent 720 million baht (about $40 million) to build a big new factory with a capacity of 24 billion cigarettes a year (doubling the Thailand Tobacco Monopoly's capacity) is now faced with the need to build yet another to meet ever-increasing demand.[14]

All the countries mentioned currently face severe economic problems, with investments in many sectors held up for lack of foreign exchange. One commentator recently put the prospects for the 1980s as follows: "For the small, low-income countries, there is no choice but to cut. The options are nationally planned cuts, externally imposed cuts, and the random cuts of unmanaged economic disintegration."[15]

In the face of these harsh realities, the only reason that the tobacco industry receives investment funds is its importance as a tax collector. But governments can maintain or increase their revenue without raising cigarette consumption (by tax rises) and thus avoid production investment. They need to be helped to make cigarette price rises respectable—a health promotion exercise rather than revenue raising. The practice of maintaining low cigarette prices as part of anti-inflation price controls—as in Egypt for instance—must be challenged. More fundamentally, it may be possible to use the present financial crisis to switch tax collection away from tobacco and alcohol to sources that do not require expensive investments and that do not pose hazards to health. (Alcohol must be included here, for its fiscal function is the same as that of tobacco and its health and economic impact are far more immediate.)

CONCLUSION

To look only at tobacco growing is to see only one side of the picture. There is a need to find alternative sources of revenue to cigarettes as well as alternative crops to tobacco. When both are identified, the smoking control advocates will have a case to present that no government can ignore, particularly not a developing country government facing the economic rigors of the 1980s.

REFERENCES

1. Economist Intelligence Unit: *Leaf Tobacco—Its Contribution to the Economic and Social Development of the Third World.* 1982, pp 173, 210, 69, 70.
2. Kolawole: *Savanna.* 1975; 4:13–22.
3. Muller M: *Tomorrow's Epidemic?* War on Want. London, 1978.
4. British American Tobacco Company (Kenya): *Annual Report* (suppl), 1981.
5. *Tobacco International.* Nov 26, Aug 20, June 6, July 7, 1982.
6. *Japan Times.* Apr 7, 1983.
7. Naguib MR: *Tobacco International.* Feb 19, 1982; May 5, 1979; Feb 14, July 23, Sept 17, 1982.
8. Muller M: *New Scientist.* May 18, 1978, pp 434–436.
9. Baskevitch N: *World Tobacco.* Mar 1982, p 69, Dec 1981, July 1982.
10. Wayne, K: *Tobacco International.* Apr 2, 1982.
11. US patents 4 308 877, 4 302 308, and 4 267 847: Recent examples of specific techniques.
12. World Health Organization: *SMO.81.3* Appendix 1. Food and Agriculture Position on WHO Smoking and Health Programme, 1981.
13. Berg A: *The Nutrition Factor.* Brookings Institution, 1973.
14. *Nation Review*, Bangkok, Mar 10, 1978.
15. Green: *Third World Quarterly.* 1983; 5:72–94.

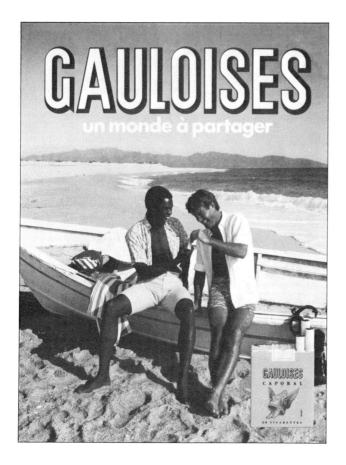 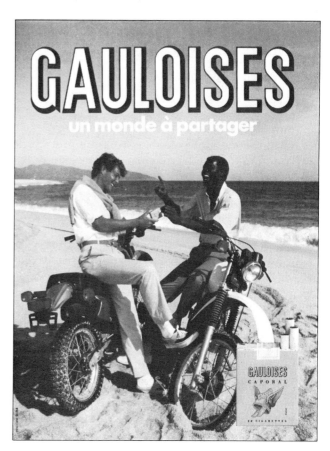

"A world to share" is the theme of one cigarette advertising campaign in the magazine *Jeune Afrique.* Africans are becoming a prime target of American, British, French, and South African cigarette companies.

The environmental impact of tobacco production in developing countries

JOHN MADELEY

Most people believe tobacco kills because use of it can result in cancers, heart disease, and emphysema. But there is a far less well-known way in which tobacco is a major global killer: to grow tobacco is to destroy the trees—and land. Tobacco curing, the process of making it fit for cigarette production, requires an enormous amount of wood. The unheralded scandal of the tobacco industry is the damage to land in developing nations. The United States Global Report 2000 (Report to the President, London, Penguin Books, 1982) identifies deforestation as the most serious environmental problem now facing the Third World.

Just how much damage is tobacco production doing? Almost 100 developing countries have become involved in growing tobacco, most of which is grown by peasant farmers on small farms. Typically a farmer will grow tobacco on half a hectare ([ha] 1 ha = 2.47 acres) of a four-hectare farm. Worldwide production of tobacco in 1981 was 5.6 million tons. Curing is done in different ways, the most common of which are flue, burley (open air), and oriental sun dried. In 1981, according to the Commonwealth Secretariat, the Worldwide breakdown of tobacco curing was

Flue cured	2.81 million tons
Burley	0.63 million tons
Oriental sun dried	0.83 million tons
Other types	1.39 million tons

About half the curing was done in flues or barns. In this process, tobacco leaf is placed in the barns and slowly dried by burning wood. In a few countries, coal is used, but around 2.5 million tons of tobacco is flue-cured each year with wood, a large volume of which is needed to cure comparatively small amounts of tobacco. Peasant farmers use between two to three ha of trees to cure one ton of tobacco. In Tanzania, as in most parts of Africa, the curing of tobacco is done by farmers on their own premises, each with his own curing barn, each having to find his own wood.

Other tobacco-producing countries seem likely to have much the same requirements as Tanzania for the amount of wood needed in the curing process. Tobacco manufacturers do claim to be introducing the more efficient curing barns that need considerably less wood. But even an estimate favorable to the tobacco industry would still mean that 2.5 million ha of trees have to be axed each year to cure 2.5 million tons of tobacco. According to the Global 2000 report, between 18 and 20 million ha of trees are being axed each year for all purposes. Maybe one out of every eight trees cut down is used for curing tobacco. In countries such as Kenya, which lies near the Equator, much of the land has

lost its protection due to deforestation, and food production is threatened—all because the economic incentives provided by the tobacco companies make tobacco an irresistibly profitable commodity. Where tobacco is grown in hilly areas such as the Himalayas, it can cause severe soil erosion. In other circumstances, it can cause havoc, as in Sri Lanka. There the combination of treeless hillsides and heavy rains portends disaster for a series of dams currently being built, which are in danger of being filled with silt. Another problem of denuding the land is the resultant change in climate.

Tobacco growing also poses problems for the rural dweller who does not grow tobacco but who needs trees for cooking fuel. If tobacco farmers are axing trees for their tobacco, then those who do not grow tobacco have to walk farther each day in search of wood fuel, thereby adversely affecting production time and income.

The very growing of tobacco has a direct effect on health, since a great deal of insecticide has to be used in the early stages of tobacco growth. An internal document of a British tobacco company that operates in Africa reveals that farmers are employed on contract and are supplied with different pesticides. According to the accompanying instructions, in the month before planting and in the three months after planting, no fewer than 16 applications of insecticide have to be made. It would take a Western farmer with a degree in agriculture to be able to follow these instructions, which an African farmer would find difficult to understand. One of the insecticides on the list is Aldrin (Shell Oil Company), which is banned or restricted in most Western countries. In the Third World, most farmers can not afford protective clothing. Precautions on most chemicals generally inform the user of the need to avoid pouring them into rivers and streams, to wash with soap and water after use, and to consult a physician immediately in the event of symptoms of poisoning. Yet chemical runoff into streams does occur; soap is often unavailable, and in rural areas access to medical care may not exist. It is plainly preferable that tobacco not be grown at all, but if it continues to be grown then tobacco companies must be compelled to promote other ways of curing it. In some countries, tobacco leaf is collected from the small farmers and then cured centrally, which is far less demanding in the use of trees. Also, alternative methods such as solar units are available to cure tobacco. On the other hand, it is difficult to think of a way around the risks posed by pesticides. Maybe this problem is nature's way of telling us that tobacco is a thoroughly antisocial crop.

Farmers need to be encouraged to substitute other crops for tobacco. The World Health Organization (WHO) has identified a number of alternatives: cereals, legumes, most vegetables, sugarcane, bananas, coconut, pineapple, and cotton. The telling question is whether or not the governments of tobacco-producing countries are prepared to help

Based on a presentation delivered at the Fifth World Conference on Smoking and Health, Winnipeg, Canada, July 12, 1983.
Mr Madeley is a freelance journalist who contributes to the *London Observer*. Address correspondence to Mr Madeley, 19 Woodford Close, Caversham, Reading, United Kingdom

70

farmers switch from tobacco to other crops. The WHO ought to have the backing of the United Nations Food and Agricultural Organization (FAO) in this task. One of the mandates of the FAO is "to secure improvements in the efficiency of the production and distribution of all food and agricultural products from farms, forests and fisheries, and to better the conditions of country dwellers" (Basic Facts About the UN, New York, 1975).

A recent FAO document, *The Struggle for Food Security* (Rome 1979), stated

The world's forests play an important part in the protection of agriculture and their progressive destruction poses a serious haz-ard to future production. The forest is a whole ecosystem: it protects soil from erosion and produces food itself.

Those in the FAO who defend the tobacco industry may be seeing the issue only in the short term. Since the FAO is interested in helping farmers in countries with increasing their food production on a sustained basis, it seems senseless for it to support tobacco production. More research is needed on the subject of deforestation for tobacco production in developing countries. But it is clear that, over and above the devastating health consequences, the environmental costs of tobacco production are high. An enormous amount of destruction is taking place, and what is it all for?

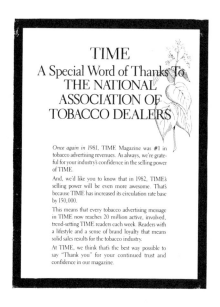

Many of the publications that blame the medical profession for the problem of rising health care costs are covetous of cigarette advertising revenue. *TIME* and *The New York Times* have thanked cigarette companies in the pages of *The United States Tobacco Journal*, while Booth newspapers, *Rolling Stone*, *The St. Petersburg Times*, *The St. Louis Post-Dispatch*, and the *Milwaukee Journal*, among others, have sought cigarette ads in *Advertising Age*.

Aspects of smoking in developing countries in Africa

D. FEMI-PEARSE, MD

Tobacco was introduced into Egypt and Asia by the Turks in the 14th century. Cultivation of tobacco in East, West, and South Africa is attributable to the explorers of the 16th century who on graduating from the School of Prince Henry the Navigator sailed to all parts of the world. The explorer Crowley may have been the first to report on smoking in Africa. Calling at Sierra Leone on his way to the West Indies in 1607 he saw "tobacco growing in small patches and natives smoking it."[1]

Still, tobacco growing was not a major crop until recent years. In Nigeria in 1934 just 86 acres of land were cultivated for tobacco. But in the same year a pilot cigarette factory was established, and a second one was built in 1937. In 1982 the first green-leaf thresher was installed, capable of handling 6,000 kg of green leaf per hour. In peak season it employs 480 persons on two shifts.

Today cigarettes reach developing countries by importation (eg, Ethiopia and Sudan) or by local cultivation of tobacco and manufacture of cigarettes (eg, Zimbabwe, Nigeria).

AGRICULTURE

The cultivation of tobacco in Africa has been encouraged in recent years by multinational companies, especially British American Tobacco and Rothmans, thus avoiding import duty on raw materials and conservation of scarce foreign exchange.

In Nigeria 60,000 farmers now grow tobacco on 120,000 acres. The three major deleterious effects of cultivating tobacco are:

1. Competition with cultivation of staple food crops, such as rice, millet, cassava, and guinea corn.
2. Displacement of necessary cash crops, such as cotton.
3. Loss of timber through tree felling and bush fires due to ignited cigarette stubs and promotion of erosion and sahelian migration in areas with already sparse vegetation.

In the Sokoto region of Nigeria, tobacco thrives in the flood plains where rice would normally be expected to grow. Because tobacco provides ready cash, rice is a second choice for cultivation. The net result of such displacement of staple food crops is that rice is now imported into Nigeria. Any development economist would rather cultivate rice than tobacco. Forest reserve has been lost from clearing bush to promote cultivation of tobacco and using wood fuel in flue-curing of tobacco. The ecologic consequences in areas bordering on the desert are disastrous.

Yet the spinoffs to the grower of tobacco cannot be dismissed. Most obvious is that cash returns for cultivating tobacco are better than for food crops. In the Sokoto area of Nigeria, crop value in 1977 to 1979 was N4,270,682 or US$6,406,023—providing an annual income per head of N153 or US$230. If other crops are also cultivated, the farmer can earn more income. Tobacco farmers thus have a generally higher status than do food growers. Because tobacco growers are relatively prosperous, they tend to stay on during periods of drought whereas other food growers tend to migrate to the urban areas.

The acquisition of modern skills is associated with growing tobacco. The multinational tobacco companies take pains to teach local farmers modern methods of land preparation, ploughing, harrowing, germination of seeds, planting, and usage of fertilizer. Scholarships are provided as incentives for the children of tobacco growers. The traditional business sector is exposed to new marketing strategies and international business practices. Tobacco companies provide long-term and short-term credits for development of farms.

Despite the apparent economic improvement generated by tobacco companies, the subservient role of women, particularly in the farming villages of the Third World, has remained unchanged. Women are still the "beasts of burden" through whom the tobacco companies and male farmers become prosperous.

It is obvious that in the hungry countries of the Third World, governments must employ the strategies of tobacco companies to sustain the growth of food crops—and do much more than they in preparation of land, ploughing, distribution of germinated seeds and fertilizer, and provision of stable economic prices for food crops through cooperative societies. Credit facilities should also be available to bona fide farmers.

The fight against cultivation of tobacco can be won not by rhetoric, but by planned action. Recently, tobacco companies have introduced programs such as block farms among tobacco growers. Farmers are now encouraged to grow not only tobacco but other crops, especially those related to food, in small land holdings. Several acres of such land are demarcated for growing a food crop such as cassava. In 1978 the Nigerian Tobacco Company set up a block farm for the cultivation of a new high-yielding and disease-resistant cassava obtained through the International Institute of Tropical Agriculture in Ibadan. Farmers were encouraged to plant the cassava in rotation with their tobacco. This cassava matures in 11 to 12 months instead of the normal 15 to 18 months and yields up to 25 to 30 tons of tubers per hectare (2.47 acres), compared with the traditional 5 to 7 tons. The *Annual Report* for 1979 of the Nigerian Tobacco Company stated:

When the harvest was in, net earnings on this block farm averaged N1000 or US$1500 per hectare from tobacco and N1000 or US$1500 per hectare for cassava. Since each farmer has 3 hectares—one each for tobacco and cassava and one for rota-

Based on a presentation delivered at the Fifth World Conference on Smoking and Health, Winnipeg, Canada, July 11, 1983.
Address correspondence to Dr Femi-Pearse, Provost, College of Medicine, University of Lagos, PMB 12003, Lagos, Nigeria.

tion—a farmer and his family were able to net N2,000 or US$3,000 per annum, after providing food for themselves from their cassava . . . . With farmers' earnings reaching such dimensions, the drift from rural to urban areas may not only be halted eventually, but may even be reversed.

In the past five years the tobacco industry has begun active reforestation programs since 3.5% of wood-fuel consumption is devoted to flue-curing of tobacco. It is hoped that reforestation will prevent erosion and desert encroachment, and provide wood pulp for the paper industry.

ECONOMICS

Governments in the Third World have been slow to arrest the tobacco-smoking habit because of large government revenues derivable from sales and manufacture of cigarettes. In Nigeria, revenue of about US$25 million was collected in 1965. The figures for 1980 are quoted from the Nigerian Tobacco Company's *Annual Report*:

During the Company's financial year ended 30th September 1980, out of a gross annual revenue of N95 million (or US$143 million) about N34.36 million or US$51.5 million was due to government in cigarette excise, import duties on materials and in company tax. During the same period, N5.0 million (US$7.5 million) (5.3%) is being distributed to stockholders, with N2.8 million (US$4.2 million) (2.9%) retained in the business.

The consumption of cigarettes is underestimated in government or commercial statistics because smuggling accounts for 25% of total cigarette consumption, and in Nigeria loss to government in revenue is about N40 million or US$60 million.

When the income from tobacco (excise duty, import duty, profit tax, dividend tax) is totalled against the expenditure on importation of food crops (eg, rice) displaced by tobacco growing and costs of treating cigarette-induced diseases, promotion of tobacco sales ceases to be profitable.

Although adults are the main consumers of tobacco—at least 41% of the men in Lagos, Nigeria smoke—smoking nevertheless begins between the ages of 10 and 17 years.[2] A 1973 survey in Lagos, Nigeria, found that 17.5% of the boys and 2.7% of the girls were regularly smoking, figures which have surely increased. Smoking by children assumes enormous importance with the realization that the risk of lung cancer is greater among those who start the habit early.

It may be argued that students smoke because of ignorance of the dangers of smoking. Senah,[3] analyzing data from Ghana, reported that only 8.5% of 12,516 survey respondents had knowledge of the product as a drug of dependence. Perhaps greater awareness of the dangers will reduce the number of regular smokers. In this study only 16.3% of 705 school teachers indicated tobacco as a drug of dependence in a list that included alcoholic beverages, marijuana, dexamphetamine, black coffee, opium, hashish, heroin, and cola. The score for marijuana was highest at 28.4%. Senah asked teachers to name two drugs which they used regularly; 140 out 450 (31.1%) admitted to being cigarette smokers. Among 331 parents only 12.1% were aware of tobacco as a drug of dependence and addiction. Forty percent (99) of 233 parents were regular smokers.

Another study showed that in Nigeria parental objection to school children smoking is quite high (75% of fathers and 95% of mothers for boys and 85% of fathers and 97% of mothers for girls).[2] Most parents of medical students also objected. Why, then, is there defiance? Although the number of experimental smokers may not diminish appreciably it may be possible through drug education to teach young people to make the right choices.

In the Dakar study[4] 55% and 28% of school children were offered their first cigarette by friends and parents, respectively. When asked "Why did you start to smoke?" the responses were: To look like an actor or sportsman, 45%; To be like a friend or parent, 18%; For curiosity, 23%.

Cigarette smoking has a strong influence in provoking the usage of other drugs of addiction. Haworth[5] in Zambia found that the smoking of tobacco and cannabis were related: of 15% of males and 37% of females who had never used alcohol or tobacco, only 2% had used cannabis, whereas 35% of those who had smoked tobacco, 13% of those who had taken alcohol, and 55% of those who had used both tobacco and alcohol used cannabis. All the known pathologic consequences of cigarette smoking occurring in Europe and North America are now occurring in the Third World. Yet in most African countries at least one third of practicing physicians smoke, thus reducing their credibility as role models. All nations of the Third World must examine critically the relevance and desirability of imported lifestyles such as cigarette smoking. The material and social costs of the pandemic of cigarette smoking cannot be justified.

REFERENCES

1. Taha A, Ball K: Smoking and Africa: the coming epidemic. *Br Med J* 1980; 2:991–993.
2. Elegbeleye, Femi-Pearse: Incidence and variables contributing to onset of cigarette smoking among secondary school children and medical students in Lagos, Nigeria. *Br J Prev Soc Med* 1976; 30:66–70.
3. Senah AK: *A Study of Problems Associated with the Use of Drugs and Drug Education in Ghana.* UNESCO Distribution Limited, 1980.
4. Wone I, Koate, Pand de Lauture H: La lutte contre le tabagisme dans une optique de sante de communaute. *Medicine d'Afrique Noire* 1980; 27:573–579.
5. Haworth A: Study of smoking among students in Zambia. Paper presented to a national seminar on Cardiovascular Diseases, Lusaka, Zambia, October 16–17, 1981.

"A RESPONSIBLE TOBACCO INDUSTRY PREVAILS"

We recognized early that ours is a global business and built markets around the world. Our future is particularly bright in developing areas, where income and population are growing.

—from an address by Joseph Cullman III,
Chairman, executive committee, Philip Morris, Inc.,
to the annual meeting of the Tobacco Merchants Association
of the US, Hotel Pierre, New York, NY, May 19, 1983

Smoking or health: the Brazilian option

FERNANDO L. LOKSCHIN, MD, FERNANDO C. BARROS, MD

In Brazil, tobacco plays a key role in both disease and the economy. About 135 billion cigarettes were smoked in the country in 1981,[1] and cigarette-related diseases far outnumber infections as the leading cause of death.[2] At the same time, Brazil is the fourth world producer and the second exporter of tobacco. Two and a half million people (2.1% of the total population) are maintained by tobacco-related activities. Cigarette sales taxes provide 11.6% of the country's total taxes.[1] Involved in a deep economic crisis, the Brazilian government relies on this revenue and has not introduced a single measure to control or counteract the high-pressure marketing of cigarette manufacturers.

In this article we discuss the present influence of tobacco on both the health and economy of the country and also the current policies—or lack of them.

THE DEATH TOLL

Ischemic heart disease is the leading cause of death in Brazil, taking 90,000 lives in 1979.[2] Using the estimates of the World Health Organization,[3] at least 25% of these deaths could be ascribed to smoking.

Surprisingly, for a developing country with a very large young population, cancer rivals infectious diseases as the second largest cause of death. In 1979, there were 60,000 deaths due to cancer (10% of these deaths caused by lung cancer). Accepting the estimate of Doll and Peto[4] that 30% of the cancer deaths are provoked by smoking, we are left with more than 20,000 deaths caused by tobacco. In Brazil, lung cancer is the second highest cause of death from cancer in men, and ranks third in women.[2]

Besides these well-known causes of death, smoking also influences mortality in other ways. For example, smoking is definitely associated with low birth weight,[5] and this is the most important single predictive factor of perinatal and infant mortality. In a study in Pelotas, Southern Brazil, smoking during pregnancy has been found to double the rate of low-birth-weight babies, even when maternal nutrition and family income are controlled (F. C. Barros et al, unpublished data). Smoking is the main etiologic factor responsible for more than 20% of all low-birth-weight babies of the city.

Another effect of tobacco on infant health was signaled by Victora and Blank[6] who showed that in the district of Santa Cruz do Sul, located in the southernmost state, Rio Grande do Sul, the decline in infant mortality rate was 30% less than expected. The Secretary of Health also found that the infant mortality rate was not decreasing at the same pace as the rest of the state. In this district is the large cigarette factory of Souza Cruz (British American Tobacco Co. subsidiary); and 71% of the population of 99,600 inhabitants get their salaries from the tobacco industry, whether from manufacture or from agriculture.[1] It is probable that the bad record on child health was due to the fact that the rural workers gave up subsistence crops in order to grow tobacco.[6]

Another important point is that in low-income populations expenditures for cigarettes often wreak havoc on the family budget, with less money being made available for essential goods. Silveira Lima et al,[7] studying a fringe population of Sao Paulo, found that expenditures for cigarettes ranged from 3.1% to 14.6% (mean 9.8%) of the family income. This was higher than expenditures for transportation (5.8%) and milk (8.3%).

EFFECTS OF SMOKING ON THE ECONOMY

The most important taxpayer in Brazil is the cigarette industry, which contributes 37% to 40% of the total amount collected by the Industrialized Products Taxation.[1] The second most important payer is the car industry, with alcoholic beverages ranking third.[1] During the first five months of 1983 the government collected more than $500 million from the tax on cigarette sales (Banco de Brazil, unpublished data). Of the consumer price, 75.2% goes to the government; this is the highest taxation in the world, twice that found in the United States.[1]

As a result of the high tax rate and the enormous number of cigarettes sold every day (almost 370 million cigarettes per day in 1981), 11.6% of all the country's revenue comes from the tobacco industry. This percentage is almost twice that found in Britain (6%)[8] and shows the dependence of the government on cigarette manufacturers.

The Brazilian Association of Tobacco Industries (ABIFUMO) has been trying to link cigarette sales to the social development of the country. In a recent publication it is claimed that revenues from smoking taxation are large enough to: (1) pay all expenses of national and public defense during two years, (2) pay all expenses for medical care in the country, including drugs and hospitalization, and (3) pay 40% of all social benefits in the country.[1]

What is not said is how much the country is spending and losing from all disease, disability, and early death provoked by smoking. There are also no data about the ecologic consequences of tobacco growing and its influence on food production.

In spite of paying such large taxes, cigarette companies are far from destitute. Souza Cruz returned BAT in Britain well in excess of $100 million during the ten years 1965 to 1975 on a total external investment of less than $5 million in the last 60 years.[9] In only the first six months of 1983, Souza Cruz declared a net profit of $28 million.[10]

POLICIES OF SMOKING CONTROL

Governments worldwide have traditionally adopted an

From the Department of Social Medicine, Universidade Federal de Pelotas (Dr Lokschin), and the Department of Material and Child Health, Universidade Católica de Pelotas (Dr Barros), RS, Brazil.

Address correspondence to Dr Barros, Assistant Professor, Department of Social Medicine, Universidade Federal de Pelotas, Caixa Postal 464, 96.100-Pelotas-RS, Brazil.

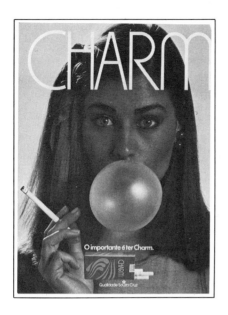

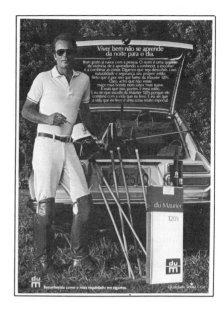

Cigarette advertisements in Brazil

ambivalent approach in dealing with the smoking problem, often discouraging individual consumption but stimulating production. In Brazil this dualistic behavior has been not seen: tobacco companies are provided with a huge market free of any constraints. In fact, the country lacks consistent smoking control policies, as the following examples show.

- There are no health warnings in cigarette packets and advertisements. Brazil is almost 20 years late in relation to the pioneer US legislation that was quickly followed by almost all countries in the developed world.[11]
- There is no legislation and also no type of voluntary agreement about advertisements of cigarettes on television, radio, or in magazines. Cigarette manufacturers are the top advertisers in the mass media, and smoking is always connected with success and achievements in sports, business, and love affairs. Sales promotions are totally uncontrolled by any official body.
- Cigarettes are freely sold to teenagers and even to children throughout the country.
- There is no product description on the packets, and the levels of tar and nicotine only recently were released to the press.

• Taxation is the only measure adopted by the government. There is no correlation between taxes and levels of nicotine and tar. Because of this, lower-tar cigarettes are the top-priced ones, available only for the better off. Taxation is usually considered an effective way of reducing smoking, but in Brazil there is a trend to introduce cheaper brands every time the price is increased.

• Cigarettes are seldom banned in public places. Only a handful of municipalities have prohibited smoking in buses or in other public places.

Recently some medical associations have urged the government to take stronger measures, but physicians are still reluctant to speak out. Specific legislation regulating cigarette sales and advertisements is badly needed.

The first task is convincing politicians and other policy-makers that aiding and abetting the cigarette companies is, in the long run, bad for the economy.

Medical institutions are in a key position to pressure the government and the tobacco industry. Physicians are expected to provide the population with the necessary health education. Neglecting to act against smoking is a kind of malpractice.

REFERENCES

1. ABIFUMO: *A Indústria do Fumo e a Economia Brasileira.* Rio de Janeiro, 1981.
2. Centro de Documentação do Ministério da Saúde: *Estatísticas de Mortalidade.* Brasília, 1983.
3. World Health Organization: *Controlling the Smoking Epidemic. Report of the WHO Expert Committee on Smoking Control.* Geneva, 1979.
4. Doll R, Peto R: *The Causes of Cancer.* Oxford, Oxford Medical Publications, 1981.
5. Meyer MB, Jonas BS, Tonascia JA: Perinatal events associated with maternal smoking during pregnancy. *Am J Epidemiol* 1976;103:464–476.
6. Victora CG, Blank N: Epidemiology of infant mortality in Rio Grande do Sul, Brazil. The influence of agricultural production. *J Trop Med Hyg* 1980;83: 177–186.
7. Silveira Lima LA, Berezin A, Guedes M, et al: Implicações médicas e socio-econômicas do tabagismo em famílias de baixa renda em São Paulo (Capital). *J Pediat (Rio)* 1982;52:325–328.
8. Wald N: Smoking as a cause of disease, in Bennett AE (Ed): *Recent Advances in Community Medicine.* London, Churchill Livingstone, 1978, pp 73–96.
9. Muller M: *Tobacco and the Third World: Tomorrow's Epidemic?* London, War on Want, 1978.
10. *Jornal do Brasil,* July 30, 1983.
11. Marks L: Policies and posture in smoking control. *Brit Med J* 1982;284: 391–395.

"Score a goal! Don't smoke." In Uruguay, although efforts to curtail smoking and restrict cigarette advertising have barely begun, an increasing number of children and soccer players alike are sporting this logo instead of buying a pack of Winston (RJ Reynolds). Reynolds has become a principal sponsor of the World Cup soccer championships and the sole sponsor of Team America, the US's would-be entry for the World Cup. In 1983 former Secretary of State Henry Kissinger lobbied the World Soccer Federation to hold the next World Cup competition in the United States, but his efforts in behalf of the US interests did not succeed.

Smoking in Malaysia

Promotion and control

SOON KEE TEOH, MB BS

The tobacco industry is unusual in Malaysia since the functions of growing, curing, and manufacturing are performed by separate groups. Because of this division of functions, the farmers are more interested in quantity than in quality.

TOBACCO CULTIVATION

Since its introduction as a cash crop by the Malaysian Tobacco Company (MTC, a subsidiary of British American Tobacco) in 1959, the flue-cured Virginia tobacco has increased steadily in hectarage and production. By 1982 12,000 hectares (ha) (30,000 acres) were cultivated, and it is expected to increase to 15,800 ha in 1985. The output had increased from 1.82 million kg in 1970 to the peak of 9.4 million kg in 1982, worth M$90 million (US $38 million).

Malaysia's population is 14 million. About 62,000 families (120,000 people) are involved in tobacco farming, and the 360 independent curers employ about 25,000 workers. Most of the farmers have small farms, about $1/2$ to 1 acre each, resulting in about US $100 to $140 income per month to each farmer. This is considered higher than that derived from fishing and rice growing.

The Minister for Primary Industries has declared that "higher tobacco prices have raised the socioeconomic standards of people in the rural areas" and the Deputy Agriculture Minister has pointed out that "the success of tobacco growing promises to raise rural living standards of the East Coast States." Tobacco is now the third largest revenue earner for the state of Kelantan. In addition, the two coastal states, Kelantan and Trengganu, have been economically backward with strong opposition political parties. The irony is that these parties are conservative, Muslim parties. In Islam, alcohol is considered "haram" (sinful); tobacco smoking is only "makroh" (discouraged).

TOBACCO MANUFACTURE

There are seven companies manufacturing cigarettes, of which the largest are multinational: Malaysian Tobacco Company, Rothmans, and RJ Reynolds. MTC itself holds 70% of the market and the increase in turnover and profits of MTC reflects closely the rise in consumption of tobacco in the country. The turnover had risen from US $73 million in 1974 to US $274 million in 1982, a rise of 270% over nine years, an average of 30% per year. The profits have also increased consistently, from US $22 million in 1978 to US $42 million in 1982, an increase of 90%. MTC is the 19th largest company in the Malaysian corporate sector.

Rothmans also increased its turnover, from US $116 million in 1979 to US $145 million in 1982 (rise of 24%), and its pretax profits rose from US $8.3 to US $11.3 million (increase of 37%).

The total turnover of all cigarettes sold in 1982 was nearly US $460 million. This figure can be compared with the US $273 million allocated to the Health Ministry for a period of five years. The government derived over US $210 million or 47% of the total turnover in various forms of taxes. This large amount influenced the government in its dealings with the issue of cigarette smoking.

The tobacco manufacturers have direct interest in the tobacco growing as revealed in 1976 when a spokesman for the industry said "to encourage tobacco growing so as to reduce costs from the increasing prices of imported tobacco." The industry, unable to deny the harmful effects of cigarette smoking, is now exploiting the economy of the tobacco farmers to justify their business and to influence the government from taking any action against smoking. They still provide technical expertise, guarantee purchase of tobacco, and provide almost 75% of the fertilizers used.

At present 60% of the tobacco required for cigarette manufacturing is locally produced and is expected to increase to 65% to 70% by 1985.

CIGARETTE ADVERTISING

Cigarettes were the leading form of product advertised in 1981 when US $9 million was spent, the only product to exceed the US $8 million mark. Until cigarette ads were banned from radio and television (both government owned), US $680,000 was spent on radio ads and US $2 to 3 million on TV in 1978. By 1982, 10% of the total revenue to Radio and TV Malaysia (RTM) was from cigarette advertisements. As elsewhere around the world, the tussle surrounding cigarette ads on TV was intriguing. In 1978, the Minister of Information declared that cigarette ads would not be banned since he believed that banning is futile in reducing smoking and would only result in greater unemployment! But by 1979, several restrictions were made at different occasions. First, the ads were not permitted to include any human prop; then they were restricted in number; and, later, ads were not allowed before 9 PM. It was then decided to add the health warning notice which was silent but later was to be voiced over. The frequent changes in rules led to complaints by the manufacturers.

In 1982 all cigarette ads on TV and radio, and in all

Based on a presentation delivered at the Fifth World Conference on Smoking and Health, Winnipeg, Canada, July 12, 1983.

Dr. Teoh is Chairman, Antismoking Committee, Malaysian Medical Association. Address correspondence to Dr. Teoh, Suite No 7, Ipoli Specialist Centre, 26 Jalan Tambun, Ipoh, Malaysia.

government publications were prohibited. By then, the new Minister said that cigarette ads formed only 10% of the revenue to RTM and could be replaced by other avenues.

The action had far-reaching implications since both radio and TV are entirely government owned. Nearly half the adults regularly listened to the radio, and there are 2.5 million TV sets (each with an average of four viewers) in a population of over 14 million.

Of course, the cigarette companies continued their promotional campaigns as they said "The ban is definitely making our advertising task difficult—new ways out of this dilemma have to be found." The newspapers offered them a suitable channel with over 50 newspapers in eight languages, and a total of over 4 million newspapers were published in the country (Chinese 1.49 million, Malay 1.47 million, and English 0.83 million); full-page multicolored ads were regularly appearing. Although the warning sign is compulsory, it is small and inconspicuously placed in one corner.

Cigarette companies also camouflaged their advertisements by using brand names to sponsor certain televised events: Benson and Hedges Golf, Football sponsored by Dunhill, or Rothmans Grand Prix. An insidious campaign by MTC in launching their new brand "Heritage" is the holding of an exhibition "Heritage of Gold" at different towns over the last two years, with the logo of "Heritage" and "Benson and Hedges" (packaged in the familiar gold box) displayed over TV. Winston (RJ Reynolds) had a campaign to associate its flying eagle symbol with the sale of prints of the "Eagle for the World Wildlife Fund." In August 1983, "Winston of America" sponsored a world badminton championship (Fig). Live football telecasts were sponsored by Dunhill of London, a cigarette company.

The Annual Malaysian Press Awards are sponsored by the Malaysian Tobacco Company.

CIGARETTE SMOKING IN MALAYSIA

The number of cigarette smokers has been increasing by about 5% to 7% over the last 10 years. In 1975, a study by a leading newspaper showed that 1.25 million or 20% of the total adult population smoked. Most of them (91%) were males. Nearly three quarters of them (74%) were in the lower socioeconomic class earning less than US $125 month; 60% of them were Malays, 31% Chinese, and 8% Indians, as compared with the population ratios of 50% Malays, 35% Chinese, and 10% Indian. The average cigarette consumption per adult aged 15 years and above had risen from 1,440 per year in 1965 to over 2,000 per year in 1978, an increase of 44%. In 1977, over 10 billion cigarettes were consumed.

Recent studies of secondary schoolchildren showed that the smoking incidence is about 20%, about half of whom were habitual smokers; about 20% of them had smoked for over three years. As for the reasons, more than half smoked for fun and 30% were influenced by friends; 20% were ignorant of the dangers of smoking. Concern had been shown for student smokers not so much due to the health dangers of cigarettes but due to close association with drug addiction; this was revealed in a study showing that almost all the young drug addicts began their habit through cigarette smoking. The Education Ministry banned smoking on

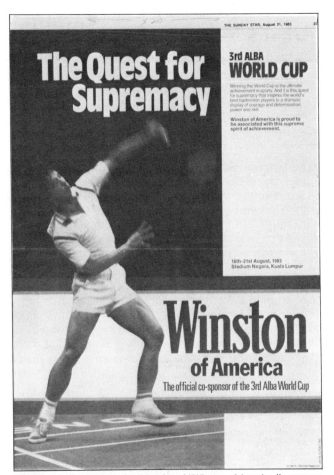

FIGURE. RJ Reynolds, under the guise of "Winston of America," sponsors championship badminton. "Winning the World Cup is the ultimate achievement in sports," says the ad copy which does not identify the product being advertised as cigarettes, much less warn of smoking's effect on athletic performance.

school premises except in the teachers' common room. Students caught smoking could be punished by warning, caning, or even suspension.

Except for elderly villagers, smoking is still uncommon in women. A recent study of women attending an obstetrics clinic showed only 3% were smoking in contrast with 41% of their husbands who smoke.

ACTION AGAINST SMOKING

Prior to 1980, action against smoking in public places in Malaysia was slow and sporadic.

The medical profession was the first to raise the issue. The Malaysian Medical Association (MMA), together with the Ministry of Health, formed a joint Antismoking Committee in 1970. After five years of lobbying against strong opposition, a breakthrough of sorts was achieved. In 1977, the Cabinet approved the proposed legislation that all cigarette packets should include the health warning in the Malay language: "Smoking is hazardous to health." Although the effects of the health warning are debatable, this action is the most definitive sign that the government acknowledges the dangers of smoking, thus making subsequent demands easier to justify.

Progress was slow partly because many of the political leaders were smokers; the Prime Minister in the early '70s even declared that he enjoyed smoking. The Speaker of the Federal Parliament was made Chairman of Rothmans (Malaysia) when he retired. Packets of Rothmans cigarettes were especially prepared and distributed free to all Members of Parliament.

In 1980 the World Health Theme on smoking proved to be a catalyst in focusing attention on the issues of smoking. The Ministry of Health in collaboration with the MMA and consumer groups such as the Consumers Association of Pemany began a campaign featuring local government personalities.

It was also opportune that the new Prime Minister, Dr. M. Mahathir, is a medical doctor and a nonsmoker. New antismoking measures were taken, culminating in a 19-point federal government directive prohibiting government employees from smoking in the offices and at meetings, and restricting cigarette promotion in government media. Unfortunately, few means of enforcement were provided. At the start, "nonsmoking" notices were not even available, and the MMA had to supply posters to many government departments.

Several town councils took action to prohibit advertising in public places, including the federal capital and the state capital of Kelantan, the largest tobacco-growing state. However, there were several loopholes. The federal act covered advertising on roads and in public buildings. Private establishments including restaurants, cinemas, and even stadiums could continue advertising.

Smoking on public transport became a burning issue, with numerous letters appearing in the press. Although the Road Transport Ordinance of 1959 prohibited smoking by bus drivers and conductors while at work and even prohibits smoking by passengers in buses that have "No smoking"

signs, implementation was not effective since it was left to the bus operators to carry it out.

Nonsmoking areas were provided in trains and ferries. The national airline in early 1983 took an unprecedented step of converting the seating to the vertical division on the grounds that smokers complained that they had always to sit at the rear. Protests made by Action on Smoking and Health (ASH) of the MMA were instrumental in persuading Malaysian Airline Systems (MAS) to change this decision to fore-aft division.

The 1982 budget increase on the excise duties on local tobacco and on the import duties on imported tobacco led to the first significant increase in the price of cigarettes. For many years, the price increase of a packet of 20 cigarettes was lower than the rate of inflation, being only US $.60 in 1980; the increase in duties led to an increase of $.30 per packet. The sudden rise in price did lead to a drop in the sales as admitted by retailers and as evidenced by figures for 1983 declared by MTC. Although the turnover in dollars rose as a result of higher-priced cigarettes, profits dropped and as MTC admitted "fewer cigarettes were sold as a result of the increase in prices."

Forthcoming action will be targeted along the following lines:

1. Banning all cigarette advertisements, or at least plugging the loopholes on cigarette advertising, such as increasing size of the warning sign and preventing pseudo adverts with the use of cigarette brand names on nontobacco products.
2. Stopping all cigarette sponsorship of sports events.
3. Publication of tar, nicotine, and carbon monoxide levels.
4. Stricter implementation of nonsmoking areas in public places.
5. Greater efforts in health education especially in the non-English language media and to youth.

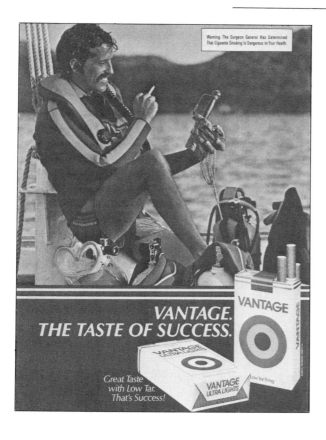

In the United States RJ Reynolds has advertised cigarette smoking in association with aerobic activities such as SCUBA diving and ballet, as well as with other risk-taking endeavors (rodeo, drag racing, motocross) nearly as dangerous as smoking. (The "AMA" in the bottom ad stands for American Motorcycle Association.)

India's shame

A war on smallpox but a welcome for cigarettes

UMA RAM NATH

WHAT PRICE TOBACCO?

"Tobacco growers, like cigarette butts, are throwaways," said a 72-year-old farmer, who has been growing the leaf for over 50 years in the state of Andhra Pradesh, one of India's major tobacco growing areas. And it is a lucrative business—that is, for the national exchequer and the industry. The farmers do not do so well. They have been protesting, with bloody and sometimes fatal results, for about three years at the low prices being paid to them for their crop. Although land under tobacco represents only 1% of total cultivated land, it fetches more than 7,500 million rupees (US $1,000 million) in excise duty and 2,000 million rupees (US $300 million) in much prized foreign exchange. Figures for central excise receipts for 1980 to 1981 showed that cigarettes topped the list of 27 commodities while the hand-made bidi (a cheap, rolled leaf cigarette) came 17th, and tea, 24th.

Tobacco is thus a valuable source of revenue in India, which puts the government in the position of seeking ways to profit from cigarette sales.

Meanwhile, the roadside signs tell the whole story, asking you to smoke A-1, Royal Pipers, and Personal Preference. These and other new brands signal a major assult by the lesser cigarette companies on a market dominated by India Tobacco Company Ltd (ITC, the Indian associate of British American Tobacco). ITC has over half the market for over 90 billion cigarettes sold annually.

Advertising is the major weapon; it is the creation of positive perceptions of smoking that reigns supreme in India. The men are rugged and virile, the women elegant and seductive. All of them have what one could naively describe as "class." They are planted in situations the ordinary Indian would shrink from in reality, but aspires to in his dreams.

HEALTH LEGISLATION

What laws have cigarette manufacturers had to observe? The Cigarettes Act of 1975 mandates that a health warning ("Statutory warning: Cigarette smoking is injurious to health") should appear on each packet of cigarettes and on any form of advertising including "visible" representation made by any means of light, sound, smoke, or gas.

Negotiations are under way for the health warning to be printed in 16 different regional languages, rather than just in English and Hindi as they are at this time. The industry claims this would be unmanageable logistically since cigarettes manufactured in one part of the country are not necessarily sold in the same area. What use is a warning printed in English when only a small section of the population is literate? It is a patently false observance of the letter of the law. And cigarettes in India, as in many developing countries, are often sold "by the stick" anyway, so what use is this minimal genuflection to health legislation when most smokers do not even see the packet?

There are regulations governing the placement of advertising signs—these may not be placed near schools, hospitals, and other public institutions. Cigarette advertising does not appear on radio or TV, but it is allowed in the cinema. There is no advertising in newspapers, but magazines carry ads. There is no control over the companies' sponsorship of sports events, cultural jamborees, or beauty contests.

A CIGARETTE IN EVERY VILLAGE

It is really by default that cigarettes are being promoted in India. It is a cynical disregard for the health of the consumer—a trading on the lack of knowledge and informed opinion—that allows cigarettes to be sold and promoted. The biggest markets are in rural areas where 70% of the population lives. The marketing and distribution organization of the cigarette manufacturers is awesome; one can find some kind of cigarette in every village store. Successful promotional gimmicks and giveaways to encourage cigarette sales penetrate the most remote areas, while standard government food distribution sometimes flounders.

For the first time this year I saw a health education film on smoking on Indian television; however, there are hundreds of millions who do not see TV. Moreover, it was made in Germany, and was obviously intended for Western audiences. Its portrayal of the "pleasures" of smoking and its damaging consequences was so far removed from the Indian context that it might as well not have been shown at all. Such is the mismanagement and lack of coordination and planning among various executive arms of the government. India has taken a progressive stance on advertising and promotion of breastmilk substitutes and, included within that, infant foods. Although doubts are still being cast on the efficacy of the restrictions on advertising, the fact is that there is some public debate; informed consumer opinion groups and physicians are involved in setting the record straight. But cigarettes are an extreme threat to health, and there is little public debate or consumer movement in this field.

The government has not shown it is ready to fight the power of the tobacco interests and ban all advertising. But it should be possible to legislate on the nature and contents

Based on a presentation delivered at the Fifth World Conference on Smoking and Health, Winnipeg, Canada, July 11, 1983. Copyright © 1983 by Uma Ram Nath.

Ms Ram Nath is the author of *Smoking—Third World Alert*, commissioned by the World Health Organization (WHO) and the Swedish International Development Authority.

Address correspondence to Ms Uma Ram Nath, Third World: EEC, 35 Cardozo Road, London, N7 9RJ England.

of cigarette advertisements and prohibit depiction of people and situations that create a false glamour for the product. If, as the industry claims, they are only seeking to increase brand share, and not promote the idea of smoking, then a reproduction of the brand packet should suffice. One could go a step further and restrict such advertising to point of sale only; that should reduce the appeal and visibility of the product. Second, promotional activities should come under scrutiny—schemes such as sending in tops of cigarette packets to obtain a free pack of cards should be banned. Sponsorship should also be examined. On Indian television brand names of cigarettes loom familiarly in broadcasts of cultural and sporting events, for the advertisers choose their sites with care. The visual element is exceedingly important, given that not all the population is literate and instant messages of this kind are very powerful.

One has to counter the ubiquitousness of the cigarette with other messages about its harmful effects. There have been only the most feeble attempts at health education. Four years ago I saw the rough drafts for a series of health education posters on smoking and health, but have yet to see even one on any public billboard. With India's fast-growing population, educators are gamely trying to design curricula that will teach young people about birth control, nutrition and other aspects of health; meanwhile, the tobacco industry is looking forward to a reservoir of advertising-indoctrinated youngsters.

Of course one would like to see statements of tar, nicotine, and carbon monoxide levels disclosed on cigarette packets. The industry itself has become aware of the threat to its business; thus ITC has tried to corner a new slice of the market. As one magazine so subtly put it, "The health-conscious smoker with Wills Lights, India's first mild cigarette."

With the help of the World Health Organization and the cooperation of the Indian people, it was possible to exterminate the dreaded smallpox. The antismallpox poster offering a reward for any report of suspected cases was very effective. Therefore, the image makers must be mobilized to do the same for smoking.

The budget for health care is severely strained—how do we assign priorities? Problems of sanitation, drinking water, immunization, and maternal and child health schemes still rank above smoking control. Therefore, the only answer is to make health professionals and workers aware that smoking is fast becoming a visible cause of disease and that we can avoid the hideous costs and consequences of the future smoking epidemic by doing something about it now.

As Halfdan Mahler, Director General of the WHO has said, health education information must be carried out fearlessly. Nowhere is that more true than on the issue of smoking with so many vested financial and government interests around the world at stake.

THE UNIQUE HARM OF CIGARETTE BILLBOARDS

There are three basic reasons why cigarette billboards are more harmful than other cigarette ads. First of all, billboards are difficult to ignore, since they are thrust upon the viewer. Secondly, young children will see the ads and will be unable to understand the severity of the health hazard created by smoking. Both of these reasons were given for the Congressionally mandated ban on television and radio cigarette ads. Finally, eliminating cigarette billboards would remove some of the visible pollution from the sides of our highways in furtherance of the goals of the Highway Beautification Act of 1965.

People do not choose to look at billboards as they choose to read magazines or newspapers. Billboards are intentionally placed on the sides of roadways and in our cities in order to attract the eyes and minds of people who are looking for something else, a street address, scenery, or whatever. These advertisements often have a short verbal message or a picture and seek to influence their audience at the first glance. Turning away from the billboard does not remove the effects of the advertisement, since the damage may have already been done.

Children are particularly susceptible to the ill effects of cigarette advertisements. Even before they can read, young children enjoy looking out of car windows at the new world around them. They are likely to be attracted and influenced by a cowboy smoking a cigarette, or by a huge, larger than life sized, adult smoking cigarettes. Our hope of reducing the amount of cigarettes consumed rests clearly on the possibility of preventing young people from getting hooked on this harmful and often deadly habit.

Removal of billboards will be beneficial to those interested in seeing an uncluttered view of our cities and countryside. If billboards are going to be eliminated, it would make sense to remove the most harmful ones first: the ones which preach for death and disease.

—from a Petition for Rulemaking in the
Matter of Advertising of Cigarettes on Billboards,
by Action on Smoking and Health, placed by Senator Frank Moss
in the *Congressional Record*, 120(22), February 26, 1974.

The transnational tobacco and alcohol conglomerates

A world oligopoly

FREDERICK F. CLAIRMONTE, DSc

If we expect a solution to the tobacco problem, it must be understood that this is a world problem. An analysis takes us into the critique of the political economy of global capitalism and its ramifications. Changes within the global corporation are political changes, and when we are talking about tobacco, we are obviously talking about politics. We are not simply talking about cancer. Cancer is a mere offshoot; the health element is, in a sense, a very minor aspect. We are talking about power—how that power is distributed among nations and for whom these profits are being made. Slogans like "Health for all by the year 2000" are created by bureaucrats, and are a dime a dozen. We have to strip such slogans of their metaphysics if we desire to come to grips with the underlying forces that are molding the world economy and which can bring to bear enormous political pressures on even the World Health Organization (WHO).

The tempo of annexation of the tobacco giants has moved apace, and to call them just tobacco giants is singularly misleading; prior to 1914, they never were tobacco companies. From the 1960s onward, the tempo of the concentration and centralization of capital had reached the stage where they had simply burst the confines of a one-product company. The United States was the pioneer of antitrust legislation in 1898, 1911, and 1914. President Franklin D. Roosevelt added such important measures as the creation of the Security and Exchange Commission. This tradition is now being dismantled by the Reagan administration.

The tobacco companies have been picturesquely called the Seven Smoking Sisters. At present, tobacco manufacturing in the developed and underdeveloped capitalistic economies is dominated by these seven giant tobacco transnational conglomerates (TTC) whose world sales exceeded $56 billion in 1979: British American Tobacco Company (BAT), with sales on the order of $16 billion, R.J. Reynolds, Imperial Tobacco, Philip Morris, the South African controlled Rupert/Rembrandt/Rothmans Group (now heavily controlled by Philip Morris with whom pricing policies are linked), smaller fish like American Brands and Gulf and Western. and, until it recently became part of the retailing giant Tchibo, the German company Reemtsma (one of the main financiers of the Third Reich). In terms of structure, they have the appearance of being independent companies, but they have really become multiproduct companies. And although endowed with formerly separate corporate structures, BAT and Imperial have always had certain common interlocks through joint ownership in several corporate bodies. They are an oligopoly, and by four major indicators—sales, total assets, net capital assets, and profits—the tobacco industry in the United States ranks second only to the automobile industry in degree of concentration.

The element of competition of which their spokesmen are very proud to extol is by no means incompatible with their policies of collusion. We cannot imagine, for instance, that cigarette brands are truly secret when BAT can annex Lorillard's international cigarette operations and take over the manufacture of such proprietary brands as Kent; or Philip Morris buying out the entire foreign cigarette operations of Liggett and Myers for $108 million and making the same Chesterfield brand produced in the United States by Liggett.

The irrepressible annexationist momentum of the tobacco conglomerates has been made possible not only due to the specifically addictive nature of the commodity, but also to the global working relations between finance capital and the industry. The TTCs cannot therefore be perceived as wholly separate entities from the larger banks—strikingly so in the case of the seven huge New York banks or the British "big four." The chairmen of the Deutsche bank and Mitsubishi are on the international advisory board of R.J. Reynolds. It is such massive financial leverage that permits R.J. Reynolds to acquire two corporations well in excess of $1 billion within a very short time span. Philip Morris equity shares held by banks topped 25% in 1971, of which three, Chase Manhattan, Citibank, and Morgan, held 13%, or over half the bank total.

Whether or not the tobacco corporations are funding research projects in the pharmaceutical industry and the WHO I am not in a position to say. If that is so, it is a tragedy. But what I do know is the enormous pressure that I have seen personally by the tobacco companies to influence the direction of research to eliminate certain kinds of research that they regard as inimical to their interests.

An increasingly significant commodity for the oligopoly in recent years has been alcohol. Philip Morris, the world's number three tobacco company, has become the world's number two producer of beer and is heavily involved in wines. The Imperial Group, the United Kingdom's number one cigarette producer, is also one of the corporate beer giants through its Courage subsidiary. The Rupert/Rembrandt/Rothman Group is a global cigarette colossus which also substantially controls the South African wine monopoly. Tchibo (through its Reemtsma subsidiary) is a major producer of beer as well as cigarettes. The overriding unifying factor of these firms is that they are oriented

Based on a presentation delivered at the Fifth World Conference on Smoking and Health, Winnipeg, Canada, July 12, 1983.

Dr Clairmonte is a staff member of the United Nations Conference on Trade and Development (UNCTAD). The views expressed by Dr Clairmonte are his own and not necessarily those of the secretariat to which he belongs.

Address correspondence to Dr Clairmonte, Commodities Division, UNCTAD, Palais des Nations, CH-1211, Geneva 10, Switzerland.

toward the global market, which determines their operational strategies. This has become even more important for tobacco and alcohol corporations, since consumption in certain developed market economies (eg, United States) has exhibited signs of stagnation in recent years. Within this framework, the conquest and further expansion of developing country markets become vital for corporate survival. Thus, the highly successful techniques of multibillion dollar mass advertising, brand proliferation, oligopolistic pricing, and collusive practices become self-reinforcing strategies in the marketing of both commodities.

In other words, one addictive commodity is now being married to another addictive commodity. Such self-reinforcing complexities must be studied at the grass roots level.

As far as R.J. Reynolds is concerned, it can be defined in almost an algebraic equation:

$$\text{tobacco (R.J. Reynolds)} = \text{bananas (Del Monte)} = \text{containerized shipping (Sea-Land)} = \text{oil (Aminoil)} = \text{alcohol (Hublein).*}$$

All of a sudden one has one of the world's largest business concerns, concentrated with vast political implications.

These corporations must be studied individually, but we must also study them within a political, economic, and social context—above all, in a context that affects our individual lives.

*In 1984, R.J. Reynolds sold Sea-Land and acquired Sunkist and Canada Dry soft drink companies, thus emulating other tobacco companies by concentrating on consumer products.—Ed.

"THE SOCIAL ACCEPTABILITY ISSUE WILL BE THE BATTLEGROUND"

(*The following is an excerpt of a memorandum written by a cigarette company executive after observing the Fourth World Conference on Smoking and Health in Stockholm, Sweden, in 1979. It was obtained and published by To-bakken og Vi, magazine of the Norwegian Association on Smoking and Health.*)

I. SITUATION

At the 4th World Conference on Smoking and Health spiritual leaders of the antismoking front were showing their vision of a smoke-free world and trying to demonstrate the road to go there.

Particularly, Dr. Halfdan Mahler, director general of the WHO, Geneva, was a powerful visionalist, recognized as such by friend and foe. His analysis—as he gave it in his speech on global efforts for better health—the role of smoking control—gives valuable indications of the topics on which the antismoking forces will concentrate.

He pointed out the central role of the social acceptability issue. In this field nothing came up which was new to us. *It was just a confirmation of our own analysis that the social acceptability issue will be the central battleground on which our case in the long run will be lost or won.*

The second "lever" which Mahler expressly proposed to use against the fortified positions of the tobacco forces was the Third World Issue. The argument goes basically to say that the imperialistic and colonialistic white man exports or at least sells death to the people in the underdeveloped countries, and at the same time robs their anyway meager economy of huge economic assets . . . .

II. ANALYSIS

By introducing the emotional and political powers of Third World countries, the antismoking forces have given the fight about the smoking issue a new dimension. If the social acceptability "lever" is designed to work in the society of *men*, the Third World agreement aims at exactly the same effect in the society of states.

For a state it shall be internationally and politically unacceptable to further and promote the growing and selling of leaf tobacco, the manufacturing and distributing of manufactured tobacco. The tools to achieve that are argumentations along the confrontations of black man–white man, the first being exploited in health and wealth by the second.

The march through the institutions has already begun. WHO has always been on the other side. For an organization which must look first for fields of action which justify its own existence (and its ample budget) the smoking issue is an ideal target . . . .

UNCTAD (United Nations Council on Trade and Development) has only recently committed itself to the other side, probably because they sense the stronger battalions there. Because they can have no rational argument against an economic branch being responsible for a substantial part of World Trade and one of the most important cash crops of developing countries, FAO (Food and Agriculture Organization)—although our natural ally—is showing signs of switching sides.

UN itself has naturally not been involved yet. But if all suborganizations agree that they have spotted mankind's foe Number One, we might by one process or the other even become object of UN attention (like drug traffic, slavery, etc.). This even more so because we would be a comfortable scapegoat on which everybody, red and free, black and white, rich and poor, could easily agree.

III. OBJECTIVE

We must try to stop the development toward a Third World commitment against tobacco.

We must try to get all or at least a substantial part of Third World countries committed to our cause.

We must try to influence official FAO and UNCTAD policy to take a *pro* tobacco stand.

We must try to mitigate the impact of WHO by pushing them into a more objective and neutral position. . . .

The business of smoking

The following are profiles of the six major American cigarette companies, three of which are headquartered in New York City. All material for these profiles was gleaned from these sources: annual reports, The Wall Street Journal, The New York Times, Advertising Age, The United States Tobacco Journal, American Medical News, *and* Everybody's Business (*Moskowitz M, Katz M, Levering R (eds), Harper & Row, 1980*).

The American Tobacco Company

(American Brands, Inc, New York, NY)

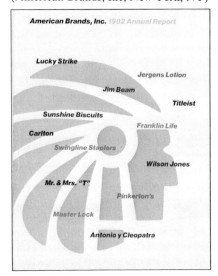

The American Tobacco Co, a subsidiary of American Brands, is the remnant of the giant tobacco company established by Buck Duke. In 1911, the Supreme Court dissolved the monopoly into R. J. Reynolds, Lorillard, Liggett & Myers, and American Tobacco.

In 1916, American introduced Lucky Strike, which caught fire among women a decade later when adman Albert Lasker coined the slogan, "To keep a slender figure, Reach for a Lucky instead of a sweet." (Lasker later helped found the American Cancer Society.) Under American Tobacco chairman George Washington Hill, Luckies became the number one brand in the country, and did not relinquish this position until 1958. Among celebrities used to promote Lucky Strike were Al Jolson, Jean Harlow, Gary Cooper, Spencer Tracey, Robert Taylor, Douglas Fairbanks, Sr., Rex Harrison, Jack Benny, Santa Claus, Miss America, and, according to one advertisement in 1930, "20,679 physicians."

In 1964, shortly after the Surgeon General's report on smoking and health

was published, American Tobacco introduced a filter cigarette, Carlton, in an effort to stem falling sales. Since 1978 the brand has sold widely as the result of the promotion of a study from the National Cancer Institute that suggested that smoking Carlton carried a substantially smaller risk for lung cancer than any other brand.

In 1969, American Tobacco changed its name to American Brands, reflecting the company's diversification into national and international consumer markets. But despite its successful diversification and its drop to fifth place among the six American cigarette makers, tobacco is still very important to American Brands. According to the 1982 annual report, tobacco is the prime performer of the corporation, with the American Tobacco Company and the tobacco division of Gallaher Ltd accounting for over $4 billion of the conglomerate's $6.5 billion in sales. American Brands is the only US cigarette company that sells more cigarettes outside the country than in it.

Since 1982 Lucky Strikes have returned in force but with a filter, and are being aimed at readers of sports pages. The slogan: "Lucky Strikes again. The moment is right for it."

Brown & Williamson Tobacco Company

(BATUS, Inc, Louisville, KY)

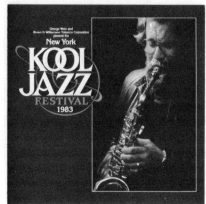

BATUS, Inc is a wholly-owned American subsidiary of BAT Industries, Public Limited Company of London, England, formerly British American Tobacco. The BAT group is the world's largest manufacturer of tobacco products, marketing over 300 brands of cigarettes and a broad range of cigars, pipe tobacco, and other tobacco products. It also sells cosmetics and owns paper and packaging, home improvements, and insurance businesses.

BAT formed BATUS, Inc in January 1980 in order to concentrate management of its US assets, including the Brown & Williamson Tobacco Corporation (B & W) of Louisville, KY, which it purchased in 1927, when B & W was a small company in North Carolina.

In addition to selling tobacco products through B & W the BATUS retail division, headquartered in New York City, owns major department stores in the United States, including Saks Fifth Avenue, Gimbels, and Marshall Field & Company, as well as the midwestern Kohls food stores, a food processing plant, a crabmeat company, and paper, packaging, and printing companies. The business strategy of BAT, according to the BAT annual report, is to concentrate on fast-moving consumer goods and services rather than on heavy industry and evolving technology.

B & W entered the cigarette market in the 1930s, and had modest success with low-cost, "economy" brands during the Depression. But the company was not successful until after World War II. Until then, its major brand was Raleigh, which B & W promoted by including coupons in each pack, redeemable for products. Viceroy was one of the first filter brands in the United States, but it was the success of Kool that moved B & W from sixth to third place in the US market between 1961 and 1968. Today, Kool is the fourth largest selling US brand, and is number one in the black community, where much of the adver-

AMERICAN BRANDS, INC.
New York, NY

Sales in 1983: $7.1 billion	No. of employees: 52,000	Advertising spending in 1983: $75.6 million (9th in magazines, 6th in billboards)	79th leading US advertiser

ORGANIZATIONAL PROFILE	US CIGARETTE BRANDS	ADVERTISING THEME	ADVERTISING AGENCIES	SPONSORSHIPS AND PROMOTIONS
The American Tobacco Company (New York, NY) Sales in 1982: $1.2 billion No. of employees: 7,250 No. of cigarettes sold in the US in 1982: 43.6 billion Share of the US market: 7% No. of adult consumers: 3.9 million	*Carlton* ” Filter ” Filter, box ” Menthol ” 100s ” 100s Menthol ” 100s Filter, box ” 120s Filter ” 120s Filter Menthol	Health		Lucky Strikes Again—American Dream Classic (bowling) Lucky Strike dart tournaments Lucky Strike salute to former National Hockey League players Sports page, *New York Times* and *New York Post*
American Cigar eg, *Sail, Flying Dutchman, Roi-Tan* James B. Beam Distilling Co. eg, *Jim Beam* bourbon Sunshine Biscuits eg, *Hydrox, HiHo, Krispy* Franklin Insurance Co.	*Lucky Strike* ” Filters ” 100s	Virility	Laurence, Charles, and Free (NY)	Women's page, *New York Times* (Carlton) Scorecard insert in *Guns and Ammo* magazine for Olympic games shooting events
	Silva Thins ” 100s ” Menthol 100s	Slimness		
Andrew Jergens Co. eg, *Jergens* lotion Swingline, Inc. eg, staplers Master Lock Co. Acushnet Co. eg, *Titlest* golf balls Pinkerton Inc. security and investigative services	*Pall Mall* ” Filter 100s ” Light 100s Low Tar Menthol ” Light 100s ” Extra Light ” Filter King	Competitiveness		Free packs of Lucky Strikes on street corners in many cities Speedboat racing events Lucky Strike frisbee giveaways
MCM Products office products, auto repair, cutlery Wilson Jones Co. microcomputers and office supplies	*Tareyton* 85s ” Lights ” Ultra Low Tar Menthol ” Long Lights ” 100s	Taste	SSC & B (NY)	Postage meter advertisements for its cigarette brands on company mail that lack the Surgeon General's warning
Acme Visible Records office products	*Herbert Tareyton*	High-Class		
	Tall 120s ” 120s Menthol	Length		

85

BATUS, INC.
Louisville, KY

Sales in 1983: $6.1 billion   No. of employees: 46,000   Advertising spending in 1983: $146 million   43rd leading US advertiser
(5th in newspapers, 4th in magazines, 3rd in billboards)

ORGANIZATIONAL PROFILE	US CIGARETTE BRANDS*	ADVERTISING THEME	ADVERTISING AGENCIES	SPONSORSHIPS AND PROMOTIONS
Brown & Williamson Tobacco Corp. Sales in 1982: $2.1 billion No. of employees: 9,000 No. of cigarettes sold in US in 1982: 83.5 billion Share of US market: 13.4% No. of adult consumers: 7.5 million	*Barclay* Belair " Filter Longs Kool " Filter Longs " Filter Box " Ultra " Lights " Mids Raleigh " Plain Ends " Filter Longs " Lights " Lights 100s Viceroy " Filter Longs " Lights " Rich Lights King " Rich Lights 100s	High-class, Health Pleasure Virility Virility	Ogilvy & Mather (NY) Cunningham & Walsh (Chicago) 1944–1984 Doyle Dane Bernbach (NY) 1984– Grey Advertising (NY) (ended 1984) Doyle Dane Bernbach (NY) 1984–	Kool Jazz Festival, Carnegie Hall and other cultural centers (TV and radio commercials); goes to cities across the US Kool SuperNights (jazz, rock, and Latin music) Raleigh Lights Rodeo New York City Opera national tour Jazz programs on National Public Radio (NPR) National Tour of Phillips Collection of Washington, DC Royal Academy (Britain) Art Tour Promotion to Hispanic community by Sosa & Assoc. (San Antonio)
BATUS retail Division (New York, NY) *Gimbels, Saks Fifth Avenue, Kohls Food Stores, Marshall Field & Co.* BATUS Paper Division				

LOEWS CORPORATION
New York, NY

Sales in 1983: $5.3 billion   Advertising spending in 1983: $135.1 million   No. of employees: 29,000   48th leading US advertiser   (11th in newspapers, 13th in magazines, 4th in billboards)

ORGANIZATION PROFILE	US CIGARETTE BRANDS	ADVERTISING THEME	ADVERTISING AGENCIES	SPONSORSHIPS AND PROMOTIONS
Lorillard (New York, NY) Sales in 1982: $1.2 billion No. of employees: not available No. of cigarettes sold in US in 1982: 54.8 billion Share of US market: 8.8% No. of adult consumers: 5 million	*Kent* " King Size " 111 " Deluxe 100s " Golden Lights " Golden Lights 100s " Golden Lights Menthol " Golden Lights 100s Menthol	Virility	Foote, Cone & Belding (NY)	Kent Golden Lights Ladies Golf Classics (in Connecticut, the proceeds go to Greenwich Hospital) Kent Sports Business (column in *Wall Street Journal* each Friday) Cigarette poster advertising in Loews Theatres
CNA Financial Insurance	*Max 120s* Newport (Red) " Lights " Menthol Kings	Fashion Pleasure		
Loews Theatres e.g., Orpheum and Paramount (NY)	*Old Gold* " Lights	Nostalgia	MCA Advertising (NY)	Newport skiing promotion at mountain resorts.
Loews Hotels e.g., Regency (NY), Summit (NY), L'Enfant Plaza (Wash., DC)	*Satin* " Menthol Triumph " Menthol	Fashion Health		
Bulova Watch Company	*True* (Blue) " Menthol " 100s Menthol	Filter	Dancer, Fitzgerald, Sample (NY)	

*New brands 1983–1984: Richland (Economy), Geer, Dubois (NY); Eli Cutter (Rugged individualism), Geer, Dubois (NY); St. James Court (Aristocratic), Ogilvy & Mather (NY). A line of generic cigarettes was introduced in 1984.

tising is directed.

B & W promotes its products through a variety of expensive campaigns and sponsorships. In late 1980, the company introduced Barclay cigarettes with a $150 million national campaign, a record amount for the introduction of a new cigarette by a tobacco company. Barclay was introduced to catch up with the trend toward low-tar cigarettes. As part of the campaign, B & W offered free cartons of Barclay through coupons in newspapers and an 800 telephone number.

As a lure to the health-conscious, the company advertised Barclay as being "99 percent tar free," and containing one milligram of tar. The Federal Trade Commission took exception to the claim and sued B & W for false advertising. A court ruling in October 1983 barred B & W from advertising that Barclay had a certain level of tar unless the figure cited came from a test approved by the FTC.

B & W's share of the US market has been steadily shrinking and now stands at only around 12%. In response, B & W has introduced Richland, a cigarette that sells in packs of 25 instead of 20.

The corporation has promoted an association between jazz musicians and Kool cigarettes. In 1981, B & W established itself as the sole sponsor of the Newport Jazz Festival, changing the name to the Kool Jazz Festival. The sponsorship is reflected in Kool's ad line: "There's only one way to play it." B & W has also sponsored other jazz festivals around the country, as well as Latin, country and western festivals, and 1960s rock music festivals.

Brown & Williamson received adverse national publicity in 1981, when the *Lexington (KY) Herald-Leader* reported that B & W had planned an advertising campaign designed to promote confusion and doubt in the minds of the public about the dangers of cigarette smoking. In addition, the newspaper reported that the corporation had the advertising company of Ted Bates & Co, New York, prepare an advertising strategy for attracting young smokers.

According to the *Herald-Leader*, the advertising company recommended that B & W present the cigarette as an initiation into the adult world, as one of the "illicit pleasures," and as being related to pot, wine, beer, and sex. The Bates report emphasized that B & W not communicate health or health-related points, according to the newspaper article.

The newspaper further reported that a secret Federal Trade Commission report stated that B & W adopted many of the advertising agency's ideas in the development of a Viceroy advertising campaign.

Both Ted Bates and B & W denied that they were trying to entice young people to smoke, and they stated that the parts of the Bates reports quoted in the newspaper article had been taken out of context.

In addition to advertising, another component of B & W's promotion of smoking is its advocacy in 1982 of reduced trade barriers affecting tobacco and tobacco products worldwide. The corporation, working with State Department and other officials, participated in negotions with Japan aimed at lowering tariffs and reducing restraints on the marketing of cigarettes manufactured in the United States.

Liggett & Myers Tobacco Company

(GrandMet USA, Montvale, NJ)

Liggett & Myers Tobacco Co. is a subsidiary of GrandMet USA (formerly Liggett Group), owned by Grand Metropolitan Public Limited Co. of Great Britain. In Great Britain, in addition to cigarettes, the conglomerate is involved in consumer-oriented products and services, including beer, wine, liquor, food, restaurants, hotels, casinos, betting houses, and medical clinics. Recent ventures have included oil and gas exploration. Similarly, in the United States, the conglomerate has a significant presence in soft drinks, pet food, alcohol, fitness equipment, and household cleaners.

Founded in 1822, Liggett & Myers became part of the American Tobacco Company monopoly in 1899. Chesterfield was the major brand allocated to Liggett & Myers after the breakup of the monopoly in 1911. Advertising for Chesterfield was the first to cultivate smoking among women ("Blow some my way").

By 1940, Liggett & Myers controlled 22% of the US cigarette market. But sales of Chesterfield began to falter with the publication of reports on smoking and health. The company's filter cigarette, L & M ("Just what the doctor ordered") has never been a major seller. Since 1962, the company has been last of the six major cigarette makers, with current sales to approximately 2.5 million Americans. Diversification into other, nontobacco products and promotion of a nontobacco corporate identity coincided with the publication of the first Surgeon General's report on smoking and health in 1964. In 1979, the company sold its foreign cigarette business to Philip Morris. Grant Metropolitan purchased Liggett in 1980.

In the past two years of the recession, Liggett has mounted an advertising campaign for its "no-frills" generic cigarettes, sold through supermarkets and convenience stores. Thus, the name "GENERICS" has become a popular advertised brand, and Liggett sales have risen by one to two total market percentage points (each point represents approximately $200 million in sales).

Liggett is one of the 15 principal corporate benefactors of Duke University. It also sponsors a Children's Cancer Classic Celebrity Golf Tournament, in Durham, NC.

Lorillard

(Loews Corporation, New York, NY)

Founded in 1760, Lorillard is the nation's oldest tobacco company. It became part of the Duke tobacco trust, and reemerged when the trust was broken up by the Supreme Court in 1911.

In the 1920s, Lorillard introduced Old Gold. By the early 1930s, Old Gold was a leading domestic brand, but Lorillard itself remained a small company.

In the 1950s Lorillard helped to launch the filter cigarette with a major advertising campaign for Kent which attracted the greatest consumer interest

GRANDMET USA
Montvale, NJ

Sales in 1983: $1.3 billion	No. of employees, 8,600	Advertising spending in 1983: $55.5 million (22nd in magazines, 13th in billboards)	97th leading US advertiser

ORGANIZATIONAL PROFILE	US CIGARETTE BRANDS	ADVERTISING THEME	ADVERTISING AGENCY	SPONSORSHIPS AND PROMOTIONS
Liggett & Myers Tobacco Company Sales in 1982: $377 million No. of employees: 1,970 No. of cigarettes sold in US in 1982: 28 billion Share of US market: 4.5% No. of adult consumers: 2.5 million	*Eve* " Lights	Fashion	The Bloom Companies (Dallas)	Children's Cancer Classic Celebrity Golf Tournament, Durham, NC Duke University Ballet performances on the Public Broadcasting System (PBS) Entertainment pavilion at New Orleans World's Fair "Official cigarette of New Orleans World's Fair"
	L&M " Flavor Lights " Long Lights	Taste		
	Chesterfield	Nostalgia		
	Lark	Filter		
	Generics (Regular, Kings, Ultra Light Kings, Ultra Light 100s, Menthols)	Economy		
The Pinkerton Tobacco Company e.g., *Red Man* chewing tobacco				
Allen Products pet food e.g., *Alpo, Liv-A-Snaps*				
International Distillers & Vintners e.g., *J&B Rare Scotch, Grand Marnier, Baileys Original Irish Cream, Absolut Vodka*				
Atlantic Soft Drink Company Pepsi Cola bottling franchise				
Pepsi Cola Bottling Co. of Fresno, CA				
Diversified Products Corp. physical fitness equipt.				
Quality Care home health care				

a new cigarette ever had up to that time. By 1968, however, the company had flagging sales. But the company did have a steady cash flow, and was purchased by Loews Theaters. The name of the company was changed to Loews Corporation, and the Lorillard cash flow was used to finance the takeover of CNA Financial Corporation, an insurance and financial services company. In 1977, Loews sold Lorillard's international tobacco brands to BAT Industries for $141 million.

In 1982, Lorillard achieved record sales and earnings for the seventh consecutive year. Part of the credit for Lorillard's performance goes to the decision in the late 1970s to enter the low-tar market.

In 1983, Lorillard introduced Satin (with an advertising budget estimated by *Advertising Age* to be $50 to 60 million), a cigarette for women that may have the most candid slogan of any brand: "Spoil yourself."

Another Lorillard advertising strategy has been to link food to smoking. The Kent logo has been symbolically extended to various gourmet delicacies, including French bread, Brie, fine wine, fish, pastry, and even ice cream.

According to the annual report, Lorillard's president, Curtis H. Judge, is current chairman of the executive committee of The Tobacco Institute, and is a leading opponent of raising cigarette excise taxes. Judge has also tried to convince manufacturers who share the tobacco industry's distribution channels, such as the candy industry, that the tobacco companies' struggle for credibility and survival is linked to theirs.

In his keynote address at the opening session of the 1982 National Association of Tobacco Distributors convention, Judge said that these industries have an important stake in the tobacco industry's ability to withstand the assaults of its opponents, who he identified as legislators seeking revenue and publicity, groups seeking the prohibition of smoking, and assorted do-gooders. What the industry needs now, he said, are "friends from outside the tobacco family, people who are willing to stand up and face down the tobacco prohibitionists; people who are fed up with what's being done to smokers; with what's being done to the tradition that is tobacco and to the important economic role that is played by tobacco . . . ."

The chairman of the board and chief executive officer of Loews Corporation is Laurence Tisch, who is also Chairman of the Board of Trustees of New York University. The president of NYU, John Brademas, is on the board of directors of Loews Corporation.

Philip Morris USA

(Philip Morris, Inc, New York, NY)

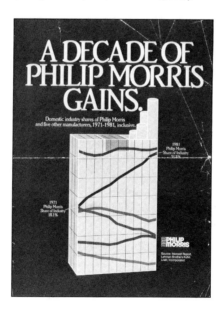

Philip Morris, Inc, headquartered in New York City, is now the largest cigarette maker in the United States. Originally a British company, Philip Morris was taken over in 1919 by its American stockholders.

The company owns nine cigarette manufacturing facilities, one of which has a daily production of 600 million cigarettes.

Over half of Philip Morris' budget for expansion of its tobacco market goes to its international market, and increasingly to Third World countries.

Until the 1950s Philip Morris' Marlboro was a woman's brand ("Ivory tips to match red lips and finger tips"), but the addition of a tattoo, a cowboy hat, a theme song from "The Magnificent Seven," and a filter made Marlboro the third largest seller by 1970; it moved into first place in 1976, and is billed by the company as the world's largest selling cigarette.

In 1976, Philip Morris headed off unfavorable publicity for Marlboro by blocking the showing in the United States of a British documentary called "Death in the West," a film made for the British Broadcasting Corporation. The film interlaces old Marlboro commercials with interviews of Philip Morris officials defending smoking and with interviews of cowboys dying from lung cancer. In September 1976, the film was shown in London to an estimated 12 million viewers. Philip Morris sued Thames Television and obtained a court order preventing the film from being shown. The company claimed that it had been deceived into allowing clips from their commercials to be used for "Death in the West." But due to the efforts of an American biostatistician, Stanton Glantz, PhD, who obtained a copy, "Death in the West" has been shown on dozens of public television stations and in schools throughout the United States. "Death in the West" curriculum may be obtained from California Nonsmokers' Rights Foundation, 2054 University Avenue, Suite 500, Berkeley, CA 94704.

In 1981, Philip Morris initiated a public opinion survey, the Merit Report, designed to gain TV exposure for the Merit brand name as a news event. Philip Morris also gains television exposure for its brands through sponsorship (by Marlboro or Virginia Slims) of many major American spectator sports.

According to its annual report, Philip Morris believes that "our business activities must make social sense, and our social activities must make business sense." In 1982, the company marked the 25th anniversary of its sponsorship of the arts by announcing a $3 million grant to help underwrite "The Vatican Collections: The Papacy and Art." Philip Morris also sponsors scholarship programs and science symposia. Philip Morris challenges assertions that there is conclusive medical proof of a cause-and-effect relationship between smoking and health. In the 1982 annual report,

PHILIP MORRIS, INC.
New York, NY

Sales in 1983: $12.97 million	No. of employees: 72,000	Advertising spending in 1983: $527 million	6th largest US advertiser (3rd in newspapers, 1st in magazines, 2nd in billboards)	
ORGANIZATIONAL PROFILE	US CIGARETTE BRANDS	ADVERTISING THEME	ADVERTISING AGENCIES	SPONSORSHIPS AND PROMOTIONS
Philip Morris USA (New York, NY) Sales in 1982: $4.3 billion No. of employees: 19,900 No. of cigarettes sold in US in 1982: 204.4 billion Share of US market: 32.8% No. of adult consumers: 18 million	*Benson & Hedges* " 100s " 100s Menthol " 100s Lights " Deluxe " Lights Menthol " Lights Ultra Lights " 100s Deluxe Ultra Lights " 100s Deluxe Ultra Lights Menthol	High-Class	Wells, Rich, Green (NY)	*Sports* Virginia Slims Tennis Circuit, televised Other tennis promotions worldwide (eg, Marlboro Australian Open) Marlboro British Grand Prix auto race; other races worldwide Marlboro Cup horserace, Belmont Park, NY, televised Billboards at key camera angles of most major league baseball and football stadiums Major advertiser in official National Football League publications, Major League Baseball, other sports magazines US Olympic Training Center Miller Hi Life Citizen Player of the Month and Game (football, baseball)
	Players	Popularity		
Philip Morris International (New York, NY) 160 brands of cigarettes in 170 countries	*Cambridge* " 100s	Health		*Cultural* Joffrey Ballet tour Music from Marlboro, 28-city chamber music tour Marlboro Country Music tour "Salute to Marlboro" (chamber music) WNCN radio, New York Art Exhibitions, 1982–84: Champions of American Sport (American Museum of Natural History, others); Buffalo Bill and the Wild West (Brooklyn Museum, others); Kandinsky (Solomon R. Guggenheim Museum, others); Grand Central Terminal (New York Historical Society); Lewis Carroll and Alice (Pierpont Morgan Library); Oom Pah Pah: the Great American Band (New York Historical Society); Edward Hopper (Whitney Museum of American Art, others); The Vatican Collections: The Papacy and Art (Metropolitan Museum of Art, others).
Miller Brewing Company *Miller High Life, Miller Lite, Lowenbrau*	*Marlboro* " Filter " Filter Box " Filter King 100s " Lights " Lights 100s " 100s " 100s box " 100s Menthol, box	Virility		
The Seven-Up Company *7-Up, Diet 7-Up*				
Philip Morris Industrial packaging	*Merit* " Kings " Kings Menthol " 100s " 100s Menthol " Ultra Lights 100s " Ultra Lights 100s Menthol " Ultra Lights Kings " Ultra Lights Kings Menthol	Taste	Leo Burnett USA (Chicago)	*Other* The Philip Morris Science Symposium (featuring Nobel prize winners in medicine) Career scholarship programs Vocational/Technical Career Scholarship Programs for high school drop-outs Grants for tobacco research (North Carolina State, University of Tennessee, University of Kentucky) Marlboro Country Store (mail order items with Marlboro logo) Virginia Slims Ginny Jogger Suit (mail order) Virginia Slims Book of Days (calendar and appointment book) Free sample distributions on major city streets, shopping centers Philip Morris Marketing/Communications Competition "Agriculture in the Twenty-First Century" (symposium)
Mission Viejo Company home building	*Saratoga* " 120s " 120s Menthol	Length		
	Virginia Slims " 100s " 100s Menthol " 100s Lights " 100s Lights Menthol	Slenderness, Independence		Public Relations Firm: Ruder & Finn (New York, NY) 1983: Opened branch of Whitney Museum at Philip Morris headquarters 1984: Sponsor of 40th Anniversary Gala, United Negro College Fund
	Parliament " King	Filter	Doyle Dane Bernbach (NY) 1982–1984 Backer & Spielvogel (NY) 1984–	

the company informed its stockholders that "no one knows what causes cancer or other chronic diseases claimed to be related to smoking." Philip Morris spends money to influence legislation affecting smoking. The company contributes to campaigns in the United States and in New York State that are aimed at defeating legislation that would restrict smoking in public places.

R. J. Reynolds Tobacco Company

(R. J. Reynolds Industries, Inc, Winston-Salem, NC)

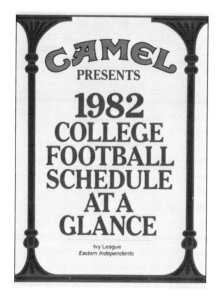

R. J. Reynolds Tobacco Company and R. J. Reynolds Tobacco International, Inc, are part of the multi-national conglomerate R. J. Reynolds Industries, or RJR. It competes with Philip Morris for the position as the leading American tobacco company. Each has roughly one third of the US market. RJR's 1982 earnings were $13.057 billion.

The world headquarters of RJR is in Winston-Salem, where the company was founded as a chewing tobacco factory in 1894. It was later a part of the American Tobacco monopoly that the Supreme Court broke up in 1911.

Reynolds entered the cigarette market with Camel in 1913. During World War I, Reynolds provided American soldiers in France with free Camel cigarettes. A decade later, about half of America's smokers smoked Camel. The company also gave free cigarettes to Cuban refugees in 1981. Camel was one of the first sponsors during the early days of radio and television.

In the 1982 annual report, J. Paul Sticht, Chairman and Chief Executive Officer, explained that the philosophy of Reynolds has been to acquire or develop businesses in the consumer products area that have a dominant or leading position in their respective industries.

Accordingly, Reynolds has acquired, among other companies, the largest processor of fruits and vegetables (Del Monte), the largest chicken restaurant chain (Kentucky Fried Chicken), the world's largest containerized shipping company (Sea-Land), and one of the largest independent petroleum exploration and production companies in the United States.*In 1982, RJR also bought Heublein Inc, the nation's second largest producer of wine and hard liquor, for $1.39 billion. Heublein's holdings include Smirnoff Vodka, Harvey's Bristol Cream, and A-1 Steak Sauce.

Reynolds Tobacco International, Inc, began exporting Winston and More to China in 1979. Since 1980, the Xiamen Cigarette Factory in China has been producing Camel filter cigarettes under contract to Reynolds Tobacco. A subsidiary of Reynolds, R.J.R. Archer, provides the technology for packaging the cigarettes.

Reynolds was the nation's fourth largest advertiser in 1982, with $530.3 million in ad spending. It is the single advertiser in *Moviegoer*, a magazine that is distributed to about 100 major markets, including hundreds of movie theaters.

The cigarette company also sponsors sports and music events. Camel cigarettes sponsors the sports scoreboard page of some newspapers, including the New York *Post*, and the company designed a collection of sportswear to emphasize what it describes as the hardy, rugged image of the Camel smoker. Camel also sponsors advertisements for rock concerts in the *Village Voice*, one of which is entitled the "Camel Sound-Board," which lists times and locations of concerts for that week. Another brand, Salem Light, sponsors the Salem Light Concert Series of rock music. Winston, which sponsors sports, backs motorcycle racing championships, and was one of the sponsors of the 1982 World Soccer Cup in Spain. Reynolds also markets its cigarette products through travel agencies, and adventure trips to Maine, Ecuador, and the Caribbean.

Reynolds supports a grassroots community projects organization, the Future Farmers of America's Building Our American Communities (BOAC) pro-

gram, which encourages high school students to address community needs. The company also supports various education programs and research at various medical research centers, including a research fellowship in biomedical sciences at Rockefeller University in New York.

The Public Policy Commitee of RJR, which is made up of members of the board of directors, includes Juanita M. Kreps, former United States Secretary of Commerce, and Vernon E. Jordan, Jr, former president of the National Urban League, Inc.

Reynolds has promoted smoking and defended the tobacco industry in several ways. It has also produced pamphlets on the economic contributions of tobacco to the United States and to southern states, and a rebuttal of medical evidence showing the health-damaging effects of smoking. The company is now building a new, two-million-square-foot cigarette manufacturing facility in Tobaccoville, North Carolina.

*In 1984, R.J. Reynolds sold Sea-Land, acquired Sunkist and Canada Dry soft drink companies.—Ed.

(concluded on following page)

R.J. REYNOLDS INDUSTRIES, INC.
Winston-Salem, NC

Sales in 1983: $13.05 billion	No. of employees: 117,000	Advertising spending in 1983: $593.4 million (1st in newspapers, 2nd in magazines, 1st in billboards)		5th leading US advertiser
ORGANIZATION PROFILE*	**US CIGARETTE BRANDS†**	**ADVERTISING THEME**	**ADVERTISING AGENCIES**	**SPONSORSHIPS AND PROMOTIONS**
R.J. Reynolds Tobacco Company Sales in 1982: $3.5 billion No. of employees: 14,815 No. of cigarettes sold in US in 1982: 208.9 billion Share of US market: 33.5% No. of adult consumers: 18 million	*Camel* " Regular " Filters " Lights " Lights Hard Pack " Lights 100s	Virility	McCann-Erickson (NY)	Camel Scoreboard (sports sections of over 100 daily newspapers) Camel Soundboard (concert schedules in newspapers) Camel Ski Days (Brodie Mt., MA and Hunter Mt., NY) Camel Expeditions (wilderness adventure) Winston Team America Series (soccer) World Cup soccer championships Western Rodeo Series International Hot Rod Association American Motorcycle Association (AMA) International Motor Sports Association
R.J. Reynolds Tobacco International, Inc. worldwide cigarette manufacturing	*Bright* " 100s	Taste	Leber Katz†† Partners (NY)	
	More " Filter 120s " Menthol 120s " Lights Filter 100s " Lights Menthol 100s	Fashion		
Del Monte Corporation eg, *Del Monte* fruits and vegetables, *Hawaiian Punch, Vermont Maid Syrup, Chun King, A-1 Steak Sauce, My-T-Fine Pudding*	*NOW* " Filter " Filter 100s " Menthol " Menthol 100s	Health		
	Vantage " Filter " 100s " Menthol " Menthol 100s " Ultra Lights " Ultra Lights 100s " Ultra Lights Menthol " Ultra Lights Menthol 100s	Success		
Heublein Spirits & Wine Company eg, *Smirnoff* vodka, *Black Velvet* Canadian whiskey, *Ingelnook* wines, *Lancers, Harveys Bristol Cream*				
Kentucky Fried Chicken Corporation eg, *Kentucky Fried Chicken, H.Salt Seafood,* and *Zantigo* Mexican restaurants	*Salem* " King " 100s " Lights " Lights 100s	Pleasure		More Filter Fashion Show Tour (shopping centers) Inter-American Festival of the Arts, Puerto Rico
Aminoil USA, Inc.** exploration and sale of oil and natural gas	*Winston* " Box " King " 100s " Lights " Lights 100s " Ultra Lights " Ultra Lights 100s " Slim Lights	Virility	William Esty Co. (NY)	National Park Service summer rhythm and blues and theatre programs Salem Spirit Street Scenes (inner city concerts) R.J. Reynolds Research Fellowship (Rockefeller University)
Sea-Land Industries Investments, Inc. containerized shipping				
R.J. Reynolds Development Corporation packaging	*Century*	Economy	Tatham-Laird & Kudner (Chicago)	*Huddle* and *Fastbreak* (regionalized, freely distributed sports publications sponsored solely by Winston)
Bear Creek Corporation fruit, garden plants				

*In March 1984, RJR acquired Canada Dry from Dr. Pepper Co. for $175 million. In October 1984, acquired Sunkist Soft Drink from General Cinema Corp. for $57 million.

**Sold in 1984.

†In 1984, RJR re-introduced Doral as a "generic" cigarette, advertised mainly in food sections of newspapers, and introduced Sterling as a "classy" brand (advertising agency: Ted Bates [NY]).

††This firm produced the public issues advertising campaign in 1984 that called for an "open debate" on smoking. The Surgeon General's warning was not included in their advertisements.

BUGA-UP (Billboard Utilizing Graffitists Against Unhealthy Promotions)

An Australian movement to end cigarette advertising

ARTHUR CHESTERFIELD-EVANS, MB BS

On national, state, and local levels, Australian health professionals are making a determined bid to eliminate all forms of cigarette advertising.[1-4]

During the past decade public awareness of cigarette smoking as a major health problem has increased, in large part due to efforts of such groups as the Victorian Anti-Cancer Council, the Australian Council on Smoking and Health, and the National Heart Foundation.

However, as in the United States, certain early successes such as the ban on televised cigarette advertising in 1975 have been undermined by stepped-up cigarette advertising in other media, combined with tobacco company promotions designed to keep a favorable image of brands of cigarettes in the public eye. A survey of Sydney teenagers showed that they smoke the most advertised brands out of proportion to the rest of the smoking population.[5]

In 1979 when even recommendations by a Senate committee for a complete ban on cigarette advertising[6] had gone unheeded, a group was formed in Sydney to mobilize greater public attention to the pervasiveness of advertising for cigarettes and other harmful products.

The group, BUGA-UP (Billboard Utilizing Graffitists Against Unhealthy Promotions), has relied on satire rather than health messages as a way of making omnipresent cigarette company trademarks such as the Marlboro man an object of ridicule. BUGA-UP's main weapon is not buttons or brochures but the spray can with which to "reface" billboard advertising and thus call attention to the original advertisement. As a BUGA-UP member explained in 1980 in its annual report,

> What we are trying to do with our graffiti is to expose the devices the advertisers are using to exploit us—demystifying their process. The advertisements use two main ways to promote their products, sexuality (both male and female) and insecurity. They do that by setting up a situation visually and verbally where the viewer is made to feel somehow insecure or inadequate, and then imply that by consuming the product they can be saved from the terrible situation in which they find themselves. The billboards say 'all you've got to do is buy this product and you'll enter this terrific fantasy.' The product can no longer exist without the fantasy.

The group has attracted hundreds of people of all ages, including physicians, journalists, teachers, and clergymen. It has also attracted the attention of the police: 38 arrests

were recorded to members of BUGA-UP between 1980 and 1983, including five physicians. But in general both the police and the courts have not been unkind to BUGA-UP. Imposing a fine of $35, one magistrate said to two defendants, "I have the utmost sympathy for you, or any person doing what he thinks can be done to remedy the situation" (*Sydney Morning Herald*, February 25, 1982). BUGA-UP's legal defense to the charge of "malicious damage" (the definition of which involves "indifference to human life and suffering") has been turned around to suggest that the billboards aren't damaged but improved. The defense of necessity has been used, whereby if one bursts into a burning house to save a child from fire but is then charged with trespassing one can be acquitted on the grounds that the crime was committed to prevent a greater evil. This defense has stimulated discussion in the legal community. One lawyer for BUGA-UP has suggested serving a Writ of Mandamus against Ministers (an action to compel persons in office to discharge a public duty) for having failed to ban cigarette advertising. Another legal authority suggests it could be an offense to conspire to encourage people to smoke: "People are allowed to kill and injure themselves, but they are not allowed to encourage others to through the use of insidiously subtle psychology."[7]

As advertisers' activities diversified into more subtle sponsorship, BUGA-UP stepped up its counterattack. In September 1981 a nationwide advertising campaign was launched by Philip Morris to find the "Marlboro man of Australia," someone, according to the entry form, with a "strong and distinctly individual masculinity." A group of Sydney health workers entered a patient who had for years smoked through a tracheostomy tube, and BUGA-UP funded the distribution of the entrant's campaign poster showing him in his wheelchair holding up a pack of Marlboro cigarettes.[8] Thousands of these posters were posted over cigarette advertisements on shops, and when BUGA-UP announced that its entrant would attend the major public presentation Philip Morris retreated and released the name of the "winner" at a private party.

In August 1982 a racing car plastered with Marlboro decals was displayed in the Art Gallery of New South Wales, as an example of technology as an art form. (A concurrent exhibition at the Gallery, "The World of Edward Hopper," originated from the Whitney Museum in New York under the sponsorship of Philip Morris.) The chaining by an artist-sympathizer of BUGA-UP to the car in the course of a public demonstration against this form of cigarette promotion resulted in the car's permanent withdrawal from the Gallery. More importantly, the action raised questions about the propriety of such sponsorship at

Based on a presentation delivered at the Fifth World Conference on Smoking and Health, Winnipeg, Canada, July 14, 1983.

Address correspondence to Dr. Chesterfield-Evans, PO Box 80, Strawberry Hills, NSW 2012, Australia.

public-supported institutions.

Other widely reported activities have included an exposé of the increasing involvement of Amatil (British American Tobacco's Australian company) in the Australian Ballet and other cultural bodies, and opposition to the proliferation of cigarette advertising at the Royal Easter Show (akin to an American State Fair), the premier children's event of the year. Along with a Melbourne-based kindred group MOP UP (Movement Opposed to the Promotion of Unhealthy Products), BUGA-UP has protested attempts to circumvent the law prohibiting cigarette advertising and sponsorship on television such as Philip Morris' Marlboro Australian Open Tennis Championships.

Far from incurring public disdain for "vandalism," as the tobacco industry and billboard companies would claim, there is no doubting that the real vandals are cigarette companies and those who defend their activities. BUGA-UP can be credited with having brought the issue of cigarette company business practices before the public eye. Physician-members of BUGA-UP, who have been hailed by the media as "The Doctors Who Fight Cancer with Spray Cans" (*Sydney Morning Herald*, February 19, 1983), have been much sought-after speakers at medical meetings and at primary and secondary schools and universities.

Even if a total ban on cigarette advertising comes about in the next couple of years, as now seems likely, BUGA-UP will not become complacent about other ways in which cigarette manufacturers may aim at children. The individuals in BUGA-UP are committed to counteracting the pervasive pushing of unhealthy products in Australia, especially the loathsome activities of the tobacco industry.

REFERENCES

1. Castleden WM: Advertising, cigarettes and young smokers. *Med J Aust* 1983; 1:196-197.
2. Woodward S: The 1982 Western Australian Smoking and Tobacco Products Advertisements Bill. *Med J Aust* 1983; 1:210-212.
3. Position statement by the Australian Medical Association on the tobacco industry and advertising. *Med J Aust* 1983; 1:225.
4. Miller C: Three doctors in the front lines. *Med J Aust* 1983; 1:238-240.
5. Chapman S, Fitzgerald B: Brand preference and advertising recall in adolescent smokers: some implications for health promotion. *Am J Pub Health* 1982; 72:491-494.
6. *Drug problems in Australia—an intoxicated society?* Report from the Senate Standing Committee on Social Welfare. Canberra, Australian Government Publishing Service, 1977.
7. Hull C: Overcoming the cancer of cigarette promotion. *Canberra Times*, April 14, 1983.
8. Bittoun R: A tracheostomy for the Marlboro man. *Med J Aust* 1982; 2:69-70.

Community-based strategies to fight smoking

Experiences from the North Karelia Project in Finland

PEKKA PUSKA, MD, PHD, KAJ KOSKELA, MD

INTRODUCTION

Since World War II a few noncommunicable diseases (NCD) have become leading public health problems in most of the industrialized world. Especially dramatic has been the increase in cardiovascular disease (CVD) rates, notably for coronary heart disease (CHD). In many countries every second premature death is due to cardiovascular disease. Thus any progress in public health, especially concerning prevention of premature mortality and disability, hinges on preventing the modern epidemic of heart disease and related noncommunicable diseases.

Extensive research has revealed that certain factors are related to CVD and other major NCDs. Although our knowledge is far from complete, it is likely that many of these factors are causal. We should also note that modification of these risk factors is safe and such changes would not only prevent specific diseases, but often promote health in general. One of the important, if not the most important, of these factors is smoking. Thus reduction in population smoking rates is a key target for control of major NCDs and for promotion of health, and thus for improvement of public health in large parts of the world.

THE NORTH KARELIA PROJECT

The toll of NCDs, especially CHD, has not been equal among all industrialized countries. In the 1960s the highest CHD mortality rates in the world were observed among men in Finland. These differences among countries were confirmed in the beginning of the 1970s by a World Health Organization (WHO) coordinated register study. Similar studies showed that there were some regional differences also within Finland, so that the highest rates were observed in Eastern Finland, especially in the county of North Karelia.

This information caused alarm about the state of public health in Finland. In 1971 the North Karelian population petitioned the Finnish Government to do something to reduce the extremely high heart disease rates in this largely rural county of 180,000 inhabitants in Eastern Finland. The North Karelia Project was formulated and launched in 1972 in close cooperation with Finnish experts and WHO. The aim of the project was to carry out a comprehensive community-based program for control of CVD and to promote health in the whole of North Karelia. This effort was considered a major national pilot program to evaluate its po-

tential for nationwide and international use. A comprehensive community-based strategy was chosen which would favorably influence these factors by promotion of healthy lifestyles in the whole community.[1]

The program has encouraged people in North Karelia to stop smoking, to change their diets, and to have their blood pressure controlled. As far as smoking is concerned, the primary objective has been cessation of smoking. Reduction in the number of cigarettes smoked has been secondary. Change to low-tar cigarettes has not been promoted. In recent years, smoking prevention among children has also been promoted.

A broad range of activities has been integrated into the local social organization and the existing service structure of the area. The activities have mainly been carried out by the community itself. The role of the project has mainly been to prepare the guidelines and necessary materials, to provide training and feedback, and to coordinate the activities. The effort to influence smoking has been based on such behavioral principles as increased health information, provision of preventive services, persuasion, teaching of practical change skills, provision of social support, environmental modifications, and community organization.[3]

During the first five years of the program the local newspapers published about 250 articles on smoking and many more about prevention of heart disease in general. The local radio broadcast several nonsmoking messages of the project. During the same period 45,000 antismoking leaflets of the project were distributed. Also other antismoking materials were used, including 150,000 copies of signs and stickers "Do not smoke here—we are in the North Karelia project." Local authorities and civic organizations were asked to promote nonsmoking areas in their facilities. Local physicians and nurses were asked to inquire about smoking, and to give advice about cessation to their patients. Specific smoking cessation courses were organized. Information on smoking was included in patient cards and files. During the same initial five-year period, 39 seminars were arranged for local health personnel for training of various education skills. Finally, a network of lay leaders was established and trained to promote nonsmoking and other healthy life styles.

Evaluation. The program evaluation in North Karelia was designed to assess the program feasibility, and its effects on health behavior, related risk factors, disease rates, and program costs. In addition, interdisciplinary research has been carried out to study various background factors and experiences associated with the activity. The coordinating center of the project is at the National Public Health Institute in Helsinki. The Institute, together with the National Board of Health, also monitors national smoking trends.

Risk factor and health behavior changes in North Karelia

From the Department of Epidemiology, National Public Health Institute (Dr Puska) and the Health Education Office, National Board of Health (Dr Koskela) Helsinki Finland.

Address correspondence to Dr Puska, Director, National Public Health Institute, Department of Epidemiology, Mannerheimintie 166, SF-00280 Helsinki 28, Finland.

have been assessed by examinations of large cross-sectional random population samples. Changes in North Karelia have been adjusted for respective changes in a matched reference area to assess the program effect ("net change" in North Karelia). Major population surveys in North Karelia and the reference area were carried out at the outset (in 1972), and five years (in 1977) and ten years (in 1982) later. Each survey included nearly 10,000 subjects. Participation rates varied between 80% and 94%. In addition, surveys of smaller population samples have been carried out annually or biannually by mail to monitor the actual change process over time. Disease rates in North Karelia have been monitored by special myocardial infarction and stroke registers in North Karelia according to WHO criteria. Mortality and disability pension have been followed through official national data.[4]

A systematic monitoring of national smoking trends was started in 1978 by annual mail surveys and using cross-sectional random national population samples (N = 5,000–6,000). In addition, national tobacco sales information and existing information of other studies are used.

Results. In North Karelia in 1972–1982, reported smoking rates among men fell about 10% during the first year and then remained constant until further reduction after 1978. Among women, changes were smaller, with some increase in the 1978–1980 period.

Table 1 shows the amount of reported daily smoking (daily number of cigarettes, cigars and pipefuls per subject) in North Karelia and the reference area, as given by the three major surveys in 1972, 1977, and 1982. Among men, smoking clearly declined in North Karelia; among women smoking increased somewhat. When the net change was calculated, during 1972–1977 a net reduction in North Karelia in smoking was observed for both men (13%, p <0.01) and for women (8%, n.s.). From 1977 to 1982 a further reduction took place among men, more so again in North Karelia than in the reference area. Thus the net reduction in North Karelia from 1972 to 1982 was 28% (p <0.001). Among women, smoking increased from 1977 to 1982 in both areas, but again more in the reference area. Thus the net reduction in North Karelia among women from 1972 to 1982 was 14% (p <0.05).

To validate the self-reported smoking data, thiocyanate was determined in all serum samples of the 1982 survey. The age-adjusted partial correlation between reported daily amount of smoking and serum thiocyanate was 0.72 among men in North Karelia and 0.67 in the reference area. Among women it was 0.69 and 0.70, respectively.

According to available national data, smoking declined in the 1960s and 1970s gradually in the whole country. The smoking trends for the whole country and for North Karelia are shown in Table 2 from 1978 to 1982, during which period comparable national data are available. During the last two years of this observation smoking among men was for the first time less common on average in North Karelia than in Finland.

Table 3 shows the net reduction in North Karelia (ie, those adjusted for changes in the general reference area) in the levels of all the three main risk factors during the 10-year period from 1972 to 1982 for both men and women. As a whole, the net reductions obtained in 1972–1977 were

TABLE 1. Mean Amount of Reported Daily Smoking in North Karelia and the Reference Area in Independent Baseline (1972), 5-year (1977) and 10-year (1982) Follow-up Survey Samples.

Year	Men		Women	
	North Karelia	Reference Area	North Karelia	Reference Area
1972	10.0	8.5	1.1	1.2
1977	8.5	8.5	1.1	1.3
1982	6.6	7.8	1.7	1.9
% net change in North Karelia				
1972–1977	13**		8	...
1972–1982	28***		14	...

** p = <0.01
*** p = <0.001

TABLE 2. Prevalence of Smoking in North Karelia and the Whole of Finland Among Men and Women According to Similar Surveys of Random Population Samples Aged 15–64.

Year	Men		Women	
	North Karelia	Whole of Finland	North Karelia	Whole of Finland
1978	44	39	18	19
1979	37	37	16	20
1980	38	38	15	18
1981	36	38	16	21
1982	31*	35	16*	19

* Preliminary data

TABLE 3. Relative Net Reductions in the Risk Factor Means Among Men and Women Aged 30–59 Years in 1972–1977 and 1972–1982.

Risk Factor	Net reduction, %[†]			
	Men		Women	
	1972–77	1972–82	1972–77	1972–82
Daily smoking	14 ± 10**	28 ± 11***	8 ± 27	14 ± 38
S-cholesterol	4 ± 1***	3 ± 2***	1 ± 2	1 ± 2
Systolic BP	3 ± 1***	3 ± 1***	5 ± 1***	5 ± 1***

† (North Karelia, 1982/77–1972)–(Reference area, 1982/77–1972)/North Karelia 1972 with 95% confidence interval. Statistical significance based on two-way ANCOVA with covariance adjustment for age.
** p = <0.01
*** p = <0.001

maintained during the subsequent follow-up.

During the period from 1969 to 1979 CHD mortality among the middle-aged male population declined 24% in North Karelia. Most of the decrease in North Karelia took place during the last six years of the period (ie, after the initiation of the program). Thus for the 1974–1979 period the reduction in age-standardized male CHD mortality was 22% in North Karelia. During this same period the respective reduction was 12% in the reference area and 11% in all Finland (less North Karelia) (p <0.05) when compared with North Karelia. CHD mortality also decreased among women in North Karelia: 51% among the middle-aged female population from 1969 to 1979. This decline among women in North Karelia was significantly greater than for the rest of the country. Because the actual number of CHD deaths was much smaller among women, the decline in deaths was much greater among men.

DISCUSSION

Influencing people's smoking is not an easy task. Even if the health hazards of smoking are well known, many activities to fight smoking have met with limited success. We consider the results and experiences presented here as an encouraging indication that, at least in favorable conditions, a comprehensive, determined and well-planned activity can indeed lead to substantially reduced smoking rates. The evaluation in North Karelia has further demonstrated that this development, together with other favorable risk-factor changes, has led to reduced cardiovascular disease rates.

The magnitude of the disease problem and the awareness of the population, especially in North Karelia but also in the whole of Finland, has been an important factor for the positive results. It might also be speculated that certain cultural factors and a well-organized primary health care system have contributed to the results. On the other hand great concern was expressed in the planning stage because the area was rural, and was of low social economic status with high unemployment and few medical resources. The baseline findings showed that the risk factors, including smoking, were clearly associated with rural living, low education and income.[5] In health and socioeconomic development, North Karelia was the worst of the Finnish counties.

Smoking and other CHD risk factors are closely connected with general lifestyle. Thus the intervention program was directed at the whole community. The aim was to introduce a general community action, using the service structure as a backbone. The role of the project was to catalyze and promote activities that would enable people themselves to make the necessary changes in their habits. The project team, in close contact with the community, outlined the different activities and provided materials and training. It was realized from the very beginning that mere provision of information about the health hazards of smoking would not be enough. Teaching people practical skills to stop smoking was emphasized. Various methods of persuasion were applied; people were asked to comply, not necessarily to reduce their own disease risk, but as part of a common action and of county pride. A community program can also promote such changes in the environment that favor nonsmoking and increase social support in favour of smoking cessation and nonsmoking. Since smoking is ultimately a community problem, the North Karelia project used community organization, ie, involving all segments of the community as much as possible, to achieve the set goals.

Independent random sample surveys were used to assess the magnitude of changes in the whole population, since follow-up of a cohort would not have been able to distinguish intervention effect from evaluation effect. Strictly standardized and similar questionnaires were used on large samples in both areas for the three surveys. The participa-

tion rates were also relatively high. The validity of smoking history could be reduced by incorrect self-reporting. The results of the serum thiocyanate analysis showed no major differences between the two areas in the validity of self-reported smoking.

Results of the surveys in North Karelia show the magnitude of smoking changes in the area. Because the change may partly or totally be due to "national" or "spontaneous" change, similar information from the reference area was used. The effect of the program was considered the change in North Karelia minus the change in the reference area. This estimate is a conservative one, because it is likely that the project influenced the development also in the reference area and nationally, as will be discussed later.

The results show that smoking among the North Karelian male population decline considerably during this 10-year period. In the 25–29 age group 52% of the men were smoking at the outset of the project. In 1982 only 32% of the male population smoked. Thus, nearly every second man who smoked in 1972 had permanently stopped smoking by 1982. The trend analysis showed that the initial campaigns of the project were associated with a considerable reduction in smoking. After that the new level was maintained. After 1978 a further substantial reduction took place, possibly due to the intensified field activities in North Karelia carried out in connection with the project's national TV health education programs.[2,9] Smoking among women showed a slight increase toward the end of the period, which was expected, since younger women cohorts who had learned the habit of smoking grew older. Still, the increase in female smoking in North Karelia was smaller than that in the reference area.

When the reference area changes were taken into account the net reductions in North Karelia during the first five-year period were 13% for men and 8% for women. This was due to both reduced prevalence and somewhat reduced number of cigarettes smoked by each individual. During the second five-year period the difference between North Karelia and the reference area further increased: the net reduction for the whole period 1972–1982 in North Karelia was 28% for men and 14% for women. This was largely due to reduction in the prevalence of smoking.

It is difficult to compare smoking rates in North Karelia with the national rates before 1978 due to lack of comparable data. It is likely, though, that in the 1960s and at the outset of the program, North Karelian men smoked more than in the rest of the country. During the last few years of the program the North Karelian men smoked less than men in the rest of Finland for the first time. The length of the follow-up and the shape of the trend curve indicate that a permanent change has taken place, and is not a short-time campaign effect.

Separate studies have shown that the reduction in smoking and the effect of the program have not been associated with particular socioeconomic groups or initial risk level.[7,8] Thus, unlike the national development, smoking has declined in North Karelia at least as much in lower socioeconomic groups as among higher ones. This all indicates that the effect of the program has had a true community impact. Thus, in accordance with the original program objectives, it has been possible to introduce general lifestyle changes in the entire community.

Coronary heart disease rates started to decrease in North Karelia during the first five years of the project. The latest results show that during the period from 1974 to 1979 (when the impact of risk factor reduction could start to show) the reduction in age-standardized male CHD mortality was 22% in North Karelia, 12% in the reference area, and 11% in the whole country, excluding North Karelia. Thus the reduction in coronary mortality among North Karelian men has not only been substantial but is also double that in the reference area and the rest of the country.

It not possible to state which factors of the intervention package have caused the reduced disease rates. However, since the greatest changes occurred in smoking, the finding supports the hypothesis that clear reduction in smoking rates can indeed lead to reduced coronary mortality rates in the community. In the future changes in cancer rates will also be assessed. So far this has not been meaningful, because of the much smaller number of cancer deaths compared with those of heart disease. But during the first five-year period it was found that changes in cough symptom prevalence in certain subgroups were associated with respective changes in smoking rates.[9]

Before 1977 it was the policy of the project not to promote respective changes in the reference area or nationally. However, during this period the project had much positive national publicity. And because of the encouraging results already during the first five-year period, by 1977 the project team had to be involved in national applications. The project experiences were considered by a government health education committee that recommended intensified national health education activities, including establishment of a new office for health education in the National Board of Health. The project health education materials have been prepared and distributed nationwide. A major national activity has been a series of health education programs on Finnish television carried out by the project since 1978. Evaluation of these activities in the whole country and in North Karelia has shown a direct and indirect impact of these programs.[10,11]

A major national action to fight smoking was the introduction of the antismoking legislation in 1977. Among other things, the North Karelian experience was used to justify the legislation. The central issues in the law are the following:

- prohibition of all tobacco advertising in the country
- maximum levels of the harmful substances in the smoke of the tobacco products
- labelling and health warnings on the packages
- prohibition of selling tobacco to anybody under 16 years of age
- smoking prohibition in public indoor places where children have free access
- responsibility for health authorities to carry out and coordinate antismoking activities

- 0.5% of tobacco tax income goes for antismoking education and research.

Attention has also been paid to the tobacco price policy. Although several price increases have occurred for health reasons, the real prices of tobacco products decreased from 1965 to 1975. Thereafter a slight increase has taken place.[12] The number of Finnish men who smoke has declined since the 1960s, a decline most pronounced in North Karelia. Sales statistics show that the national tobacco sales started to decrease only after 1975.[12] Associated with the reduction in national smoking rates is a favorable development concerning cardiovascular disease in the country. The coronary heart disease mortality of Finnish men, which used to be highest in the world, has decreased nationwide (although the decline in North Karelia has been greater).

Based on our results and experiences, we feel that a determined and comprehensive national policy can reduce smoking rates. The extensive pilot program in North Karelia has demonstrated that a well-conceived, systematic, and intensive community-based program can be effective in reducing smoking and other risk factors and that this development indeed leads to reduced disease rates. Furthermore, use of such a major pilot program can have a favorable influence on national development of a program through providing tested field methods, demonstration, training, and a visible national example.

REFERENCES

1. Puska P, Tuomilehto J, Salonen J, Nissinen A, Virtamo J, Björkqvist S, et al: *The North Karelia Project: evaluation of a comprehensive community programme for control of cardiovascular diseases in North Karelia*, Finland 1972-1977. WHO/EURO Copenhagen, 1981.

2. Puska P, Koskela K, McAlister A, Pallonen U, Vartiainen E, Homan K: A comprehensive television smoking cessation programme in Finland. *Int J Health Educ* 1979; 12:1-29.

3. McAlister A, Puska P, Salonen JT, Tuomilehto J, Koskela K: Theory and action for health promotion. Illustrations from the North Karelia Project. *Am J Public Health* 1982; 72:43-50.

4. Salonen J, Puska P, Kottke T, Tuomilehto J, Nissinen A: Decline in mortality in Finland from coronary heart disease from 1969 to 1979—a cross-area analysis. *Br Med J* 1983; 286:1857 to 1860.

5. Tuomilehto J, Puska P, Virtamo J, Neittaanmaki, L, Koskela K: Coronary risk factors and socioeconomic status in Eastern Finland. *Prev Med* 1978; 7:539-549.

6. Rimpelä M: Aikuisväestön tupakointitapojen muutosten seuranta—katsaus Suomen Gallup Oy:n toteuttamien kyselytutkimusten tuloksiin ja seurantajärjestelmän kehittämiseen. *Sos lääket Aikakl* 1978; 15:112-123.

7. Koskela K: *A community-based antismoking programme as a part of a comprehensive cardiovascular programme (The North Karelia Project)*. Publications of the University of Kuopio. Community health. Series original reports 3/1981.

8. Salonen J, Puska P, Kottke T, Tuomilehto J: Changes in smoking, serum cholesterol and blood pressure levels during a community-based cardiovascular disease prevention programme—The North Karelia project. *Am J Epidemiol* 1981; 114:81-94.

9. Koskela K, Puska P: An evaluation of a community-based antismoking programme as a part of a comprehensive cardiovascular programme (the North Karelia Project). *Health Educ Monographs* :28-88, 1982.

10. Puska P, Vartiainen E, Pallonen U, Routsalainen P, Tuomilehto J, Koskela K, et al: The North Karelia Youth Project: a community-based intervention study on CVD risk factors among 13- to 15-year-old children: study design and preliminary findings. *Prev Med* 1981; 10:133-148.

11. Puska P, McAlister A, Pekkola J, Koskela K: Television in health promotion: evaluation of a national programme in Finland. *Int J Health Educ* 1981; 14:2-14.

12. Kurkela R: Tupakkatuotteiden kulutus ja tulevaisuudennäkymät Suomessa. *Ympäristö ja Terveys* 1983; 16:1-2.

Medical associations step up activities to counter smoking

In June 1983, the Editor wrote to the secretaries-general of medical associations in 45 countries to solicit commentaries on each association's effort to combat the promotion and use of cigarettes. Nine associations replied, seven of whose commentaries appear in this section. Although expressing support for this issue of the Journal, *the secretaries-general in France and Hong Kong were unable to prepare commentaries in time for publication.*

The British Medical Association and smoking

The British Medical Association (BMA) is committed to the eradication of smoking both by challenging the public's attitude through health education programs and by calling for more strict controls on the advertisement and sale of tobacco products.

The BMA's policy is derived from a statement on smoking adopted in 1971 which said that smoking plays a major part in development of many diseases, causes physical disability, and increases mortality from vascular and respiratory causes. A survey published in June 1983 by the UK Office of Population, Censuses and Surveys shows that smokers are now in a minority in every social group and that since 1980 there has been a drop in the number of smokers in every age group except for women aged between 20 and 24 where the number is said to be the same. We believe that smoking is no longer socially acceptable and therefore it is made much harder to smoke in public places. Cinemas, theaters, and some restaurants have restrictions on smoking.

The BMA's existing policy is to ban advertisements of tobacco products except at point of sale. As the audience reached by cigarette advertising has been progressively eroded by restrictions on the type of advertisement and by the imposition of government health warnings on cigarette packets, so the tobacco industry has increased its efforts in the overt sponsorship of sporting and cultural events. Despite this, the BMA is concerned that government health warnings are not as clear as they are in certain other countries. The tobacco industry's sponsorship of sporting and cultural events is a major cause for concern as it fosters a long-term financial dependence on the tobacco industry, legitimizes the industry's role in society, and enhances its prestige. The "image" created by the tobacco industry's association with sporting events is particularly powerful among young people. Lately, the industry has diversified into the field of sponsoring holiday tour operators. The voluntary agreements between the government and the tobacco industry which are supposed to control the advertising of cigarettes and the sponsorship of sport do not go far enough. They are easily broken as shown by the fact that for the last two years a player* sponsored by British American Tobacco has worn a tennis dress bearing the distinctive house colors of a certain brand of cigarette during televised matches from the Wimbledon Lawn Tennis Championships. This happened again in 1983 despite the apologies made and the assurances received from British American Tobacco after a similar infringement in 1982. The BMA will continue to press for stricter controls on the sponsorship of sporting and cultural events.

Although the Association has concentrated on reducing advertisements and sponsorship, it has also been active in other areas. In our evidence to the Royal Commission on the National Health Service in 1977 (*Br Med J* 1977;1:299) we stated that

the encouragement of a non-smoking community is probably the single most urgent task now facing preventative medicine and the community which it serves. All the conditions in which cigarette smoking is implicated cost the National Health Service a vast amount of money to investigate and treat, not to mention the cost to the exchequer in sickness pay and pensions. It is, in fact, estimated that the total care of smoking-related disease costs far more than the revenue collected from the tobacco tax. From the medical point of view, a severe-

ly differential tax between cigarettes on the one hand, and cigars and pipe tobacco on the other, would encourage a reduction in cigarette smoking and so reduce the incidence of lung cancer as well as coronary arterial disease, strokes and bronchitis.

Since that date we have continued to urge the government to increase the excise duty on cigarettes.

The Association has always worked in conjunction with the Medical Royal Colleges and Faculties and bodies such as Action on Smoking and Health and the Health Education Council. Such unity is one of the major strengths of our campaign.

MARYSE BARWOOD
Secretary
Board of Science and Education
British Medical Association
Tavistock Square
London WC1H 9JP, England

* *The player is Martina Navratilova, and the cigarette brand is Kim.*

Germany: A bankrupt health policy toward smoking

The World Health Organization and five world conferences on smoking and health have left no doubt that more human lives could be saved and more disease prevented by a marked lowering of cigarette consumption than by any other single measure. In Germany (population 61,000,000), the government has estimated the number of German citizens who die prematurely each year because of smoking at 140,000 (Federal Parliament document 7/2070).

Forty percent of all cancer conditions in men could also be avoided by not smoking (press release, Federal Minister for Health and Family Affairs 38/

39—1978). Bronchial carcinoma, which is the most frequent form of cancer (amounting to almost 30% of all male cancer deaths), has reached a new record in Germany with around 27,000 deaths.

Virtually nothing has been done in Germany to tackle this problem so far. Although the federal government has declared smoking as "absolutely damaging to health," an unparalleled advertising expenditure for the toxic products of the cigarette industry is tolerated in clear contravention of the constitutional stipulation that harm to the German people is to be avoided. In 1982, a depressing balance was drawn up at Germany's second government-sponsored cancer conference: although smoking is the most important single cause of cancer, and our health ministry has declared 40% of all new cancers in men as avoidable by not smoking, the topic of smoking was not once placed on the agenda at the numerous sessions in the context of the overall program of cancer control of the federal government. In the 46-page intermediate report from 1979 to 1982, the term "smoking" is completely absent. Of the 44 points of the resolution of the second great cancer conference, not a single point was devoted to smoking! In the meantime, a "working group on smoking" has been formed, which includes several lobbyists of the cigarette industry.

Thus, we have a similar situation in Germany to that in the United States. Just as President Carter dismissed HEW

(continued on following page)

The four German cigarette advertisements for HB, Kim, Camel, and Peter Stuyvesant promise vigor, excitement, fashion, and pleasure. The three German counter-advertisements tell a different story, alluding to stillborn and premature infants of mothers who smoke and the 10,000 limbs amputated in Germany every year due to smoking-related vascular disease. Above: "I'd walk a mile . . . with a smoker's foot?"

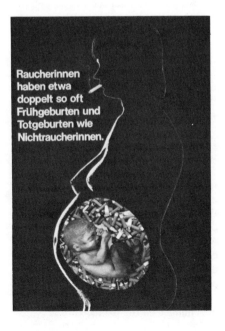

100

Secretary Califano in order to secure the votes of the tobacco farmers, our Federal Labor Ministry, under the pressure of the tobacco industry, withdrew the draft of a new industrial safety law, containing far-reaching protection of nonsmokers at the workplace. Unfortunately, the horizons of our politicians only extend as far as the next election. Advances in the sector of nonsmoker protection in Germany have not been achieved by measures, but rather by legal proceedings. Although the toleration of public advertising for the toxic products of the tobacco industry is not compatible with the oaths of office of our politicians to serve the wellbeing of the people, the advertising expenditure in Germany, as in the United States, reached a new record in 1982. For advocates of consumer protection, there is a worthwhile field of activity ahead in the sector of smoking.

Twenty years after the US Surgeon General's report, the problem of smoking is still unsolved, although it has been known for a long time what should be done, and although the Scandinavian countries have set a good example. Thus, it is by no means an exaggeration to speak of a bankruptcy declaration of Germany's health policy in the sector of smoking. Since the concern for public health is obviously thought less important than are special interest considerations, it is, in my opinion, high time that our politicians are reminded of their official obligations—by legal proceedings, if necessary.

PROF. FERDINAND SCHMIDT, MD
Forschurgsstelle Fur Preventive Onkologie
Klinische Fakultat Mannheim
Universitat Heidelberg
66 Mannheim 1, Maybachsh 14–15
West Germany

Prof. Schmidt is chairman of the Arztlicher Arbeitskreis Rauchen und Gesundheit and a member of the Advisory Panel on Smoking and Health of the World Health Organization.

Norway: a pioneer effort to curb smoking

In 1967, a Norwegian Committee appointed to study smoking habits in Norway (population 4.1 million) concluded that the following practical measures should be implemented or developed in the work to combat the harmful effects of tobacco:

Educational measures. An educational program for school children and young people, physicians and other health personnel, teachers, youth leaders, and parents of children of compulsory school age.

Restrictive measures. Restrictions on advertising; labeling of cigarette packages; changes in taxation on tobacco; restrictions against smoking in public transport.

Therapeutic measures. The expansion of tobacco-weaning clinics and courses.

In 1971 the government appointed a multi-discipline council—the National Council on Smoking and Health—and made it responsible for activities directed against tobacco smoking. The Council was also given the status of an advisory body to the Ministry of Health and Social Affairs in all matters relating to smoking and health, and antismoking activities. Since 1974, the Council has had its own budget and secretariat (in 1982, US $286,000 and five permanent positions).

The three-stage strategy mentioned here has been the basis for the Council in its work against smoking. It has prepared and published general teaching material containing information about the health hazards of smoking, and special material adapted to central target groups (physicians and other health personnel, teachers, women, children). The Council has arranged for and evaluated campaigns in the mass media, as well as in schools, etc.

Each year since 1973 the Council has carried out surveys on smoking to follow trends in smoking habits in the Norwegian population, as well as several surveys among professional groups concerned with health education.

In 1973 the Storting (the Norwegian Parliament) passed an Act banning all kinds of advertising and promotion of tobacco products. The regulations issued in accordance with the Act require cigarette and tobacco packets to be marked with health hazard warnings (also, from 1984, declarations of the content of nicotine, tar, and carbon monoxide). The Act, which has on the whole been accepted by the industry, shopkeepers, and the public has been an instrument working along with the other measures included in the program. (In 1981, the Norwegian Medical Association urged the Norwegian Government to work for a tobacco-free society by the year 2000.)

In 1973, 51% of men in the 16- to 74-year age group smoked daily; in 1982 only 40%. The corresponding figures for women were 32% and 34%. Women's smoking habits have changed very little over these 10 years, with 30% as the minimum and 34% as the maximum figure.

The per capita consumption of cigarettes (manufactured and hand rolled) increased up to 1969-1970. From 1970 onward, there has been a new trend, with only a very small change in annual sales. The leveling out occurred simultaneously with the start of the government's measures against smoking. Since 1981 there have been significant reductions in cigarette sales.

If the increase in the sales figures during the 1950s and 1960s had continued up to today, this would have led to a total tobacco consumption approximately 23% higher than the present level. Among men there is no significant trend toward increased daily consumption. Women's consumption has increased from about 10 cigarettes a day in 1973 to about 11 in 1982.

In the period 1975 to 1982 the Council has carried out several studies on smoking habits among children and adolescents. The percentage of daily smokers has for both boys and girls 13 to 15 years decreased in the period 1975 to 1982, especially among girls. Surveys among persons aged 16 to 20 years show that the reduction continues.

The positive figures for the changes in smoking habits among 2,100 pupils in the 9th grade (15 years old) in 30 schools, which can be followed through surveys in 1975, 1980, and 1982, are:

Subjects	1975	1980	1982
Boys	21.8	18.3	16.5
Girls	28.3	23.5	22.5

Teaching material and school programs on smoking and health have been developed and evaluated. Today extensive material of this kind is distributed to schools with pupils aged 12 to 16 years.

The greatest challenge for future activities will be to strengthen the positive development achieved so far. If the present trend of reduction in smoking among young people continues, it will gradually have a powerful impact on the smoking habits and the total tobacco consumption in the entire population. Yet in spite of the many positive signals from the various surveys, we cannot expect that smoking will be reduced with-

out continued and improved information
activities.

ARNE HAUKNES
KJELL BJARTVEIT, MD
Norwegian National Council
on Smoking and Health
PO Box 8025 Dep., Oslo 1, Norway

Belgium fights tobacco

In Belgium, the smoking population
has declined in the past few years, but
the number of young people who smoke
remains very high (43% from ages 14 to
15, 62% from ages 16 to 18). The number of women and girls who smoke is
actually increasing.

Belgium came late into the struggle
against tobacco and still lags behind
most other European countries. In 1971,
a Royal Decree prohibited the addition
to tobacco of substances able to increase
its toxicity. A mild warning, "Cigarettes
can be detrimental to your health," first
appeared on cigarette packets in 1975. In
1977, the Ministry of Health launched
a campaign against smoking, and a law
concerning the protection and health of
consumers forbade the use of tobacco in
hospitals, some working places (such as
those handling food stuffs or inflamma-
ble products), and most public venues.
On April 25, 1979, there was a National
Day Without Tobacco. Also in 1979, by
Royal Decree the warning was

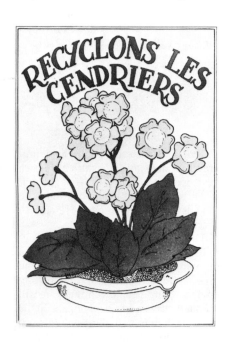

strengthened to, "Tobacco is detrimental
to your health," and limitations were

placed on cigarette advertising.

Besides these official measures, various groups have been involved in efforts
to curtail smoking, including the Antitobacco Association, the Belgian Red
Cross, the Belgian Organization Against
Cancer, and Belgian Heart League.

In 1983, the government initiated a
three-year campaign aimed at 11 to 15
year olds, to be followed by another
campaign for 15 to 24 year olds. The
theme is "the picture of a nonsmoking
star" and will involve stars of cinema and
sports.

THÉRÈSE MANDERLIER, MD
for the Fédération Belge des Chambres
Syndicales de Médecins
Rue du Chateau, 15
1420 Braine l'Allend, Belgium

South Africa: A stepped-up commitment

It is estimated that the economic consequences of smoking in South Africa account for one milliard rand per year (US
$1 billion) and that more than 3,000
people die yearly as a result of illnesses
incurred by smoking. In 1981 the Medical Association of South Africa
(MASA) issued a statement on smoking
on which all its subsequent actions and
strategies have been based. "The MASA
believes that the time has come when
there can no longer be any equivocation
about the ill effects—medical and social—resulting from smoking," the
statement read. "In taking the standpoint the MASA is aware that it is in-

cumbent upon it, as the representative
body of the medical profession in South
Africa, to offer guidance on this important question."

The MASA believes that the weight
of scientific evidence linking cigarette
smoking to the excessively high incidence
of any serious diseases is beyond question. And the MASA believes that it
should be made clear that attempts to
dilute the scientific evidence by various
groups verge on the immoral.

Only a concerted and wholehearted
effort will break the hold that cigarette
smoking has on South Africa's population as a whole. Such steps are vital if we
are to prevent future generations from
suffering a similar fate.

The MASA does not hesitate in calling for the following legislative action:

1. A total ban on all tobacco advertising in all media.

2. All purchases should bear a clear
health warning insuring that the public
is told that tobacco smoking is damaging
to health.

3. A ban on all cigarette vending machines.

4. The removal of tobacco products
from open display shelves in super markets.

5. The discontinuance of allowing tax
relief on any form of tobacco promotion.

6. A ban on sales of cigarettes to minors, to be strictly enforced.

7. The maximum permitted nicotine
and tar yield should be established by
law and enforced.

Additionally, the MASA seeks the
support of important influence groups:

*Doctors and other health profession-
als* to assist and encourage education
campaigns promoted by various organizations including the Department of
Health, Welfare, and Pension; to actively discourage patients from smoking;
and to give up smoking themselves
where they have not done so.

Department of Health and Welfare to
set a target for reducing tobacco consumption by at least 3% per annum; to
begin a major and continuous health education campaign against smoking
among school children with the active
participation of the teaching profession.

Sportsmen and entertainers to avoid
being directly or indirectly involved in
promoting smoking and never to be seen
smoking in public.

Insurance companies to continue the
trend toward offering reduced payments
for those who do not smoke on life insurance policies, and to advertise this fact.

Industry and commerce to encourage nonsmoking in the workplace.

In 1982 the MASA worked in close cooperation with the Council on Smoking and Health to promote a National Smokeless Day. In 1983, a Smokeless Week was held in November, and an increased involvement with youth was one of the main objectives. A regional branch of the MASA initiated a project, "Smokers Anonymous," among school children. The MASA's publications, the weekly *South African Medical Journal* and the quarterly *South African Medical News* (aimed at the public) have actively participated in the campaigns. Also in 1983 the MASA and the Council on Smoking had an interview with the Minister of Health and Welfare to discuss various strategies and to request active cooperation and financial support from the government and the private sector in the campaign against smoking. The Council on Smoking has also requested the Minister to include the word "nicotine" in the act on the abuse of dependence-producing substances.

C. E. M. VILJOEN, MB CHB
Secretary General
Medical Association of South Africa
PO Box 20272
Alkantrant Pretoria 0005

Cigarette smoking in New Zealand: a zealous effort

Prevention has been the major aim of campaigns to counter smoking in New Zealand. There has been an emphasis on programs in the schools and media to educate the young to the disadvantages and dangers of smoking, and to alter the image of smoking from "mature" and "sophisticated" to offensive and self-destructive. A media campaign has recently been initiated, directed specifically at young women. In New Zealand (population: 3.2 million), one in three persons smokes, and between the ages of 15 and 24 more New Zealand women than men now smoke. Public attention has been drawn to the disproportionate number of Maori and Pacific Islanders who smoke. Other programs have focused on the cessation of smoking during pregnancy and discouraging smoking in public places.

As a national organization representing 82% of the medical profession in New Zealand and as the only organization recognized by the Government to represent the profession as a whole, the New Zealand Medical Association (NZMA) has been directly involved in several aspects of the fight against smoking. The major groups conducting campaigns against smoking in New Zealand are the Cancer Society of New Zealand, the National Heart Foundation, and the Department of Health. The NZMA has given strong support to these bodies.

Since the early 1960s, the NZMA has called for a ban on all cigarette and tobacco advertising. In 1973 an informal agreement was reached between the government and the cigarette manufacturers prohibiting cigarette advertising on radio, television, and billboards and in cinemas. The NZMA has continued its demand for a complete ban on all cigarette and tobacco advertising, with particular concern at cigarette company sponsorship of sporting and cultural events.

The Association was involved in the

Cigarette-company-controlled sports in New Zealand. Can the Marlboro Super Bowl and Benson & Hedges 100s World Series be far behind?

establishment of the requirement that all cigarettes manufactured in New Zealand should bear a government health warning on the packet, stating that smoking may endanger your health. This measure was introduced in New Zealand in 1973.

The most recent proposal put forward by the NZMA is a request to government that taxes on cigarettes and alcohol be raised significantly, to act as some form of deterrent. The taxation raised would be targeted toward the government health budget to offset to some degree the massive costs to society resulting from illness caused by tobacco and alcohol consumption.

In recognition of the influential position of medical practitioners in the community as health care educators having immediate and day-to-day contact with members of the public, the NZMA has promoted the concept of the profession leading by example. The Association has urged all physicians not to smoke in their professional rooms and in hospitals. The NZMA has also recommended that the government request that smoking should be banned in all enclosed places.

KAREN MORRIS, BA Hons
Committee Secretary
General Practitioner Services
New Zealand Medical Association
PO Box 156, Wellington, New Zealand

A dilemma for the Philippines

Tobacco is one of the major agricultural products of the Philippines, and a significant portion of the population depends on this industry for its livelihood. This may account for the absence of a strong effort to curtail smoking. This is not to suggest that an awareness of the ill-effects of smoking is nonexistent, but the measures taken are far short of those in many other countries.

For over a decade, there have been prohibitions against smoking in theaters and other public halls, and for a shorter period of time against smoking in public vehicles: these prohibitions are rigidly observed. Increasingly, there are offices, both private and public, in which smoking is prohibited. However, there are no restrictions against cigarette advertisements in any of the media, and advertising in newspapers and magazines as well as on television is heavy for some brands of cigarettes. There are radio spots against cigarette smoking aired as a public service, but no similar ads in the print media or on television.

Except for the Philippine Cancer Society and the Philippine Heart Association, the medical societies have been relatively silent regarding the issue. Inspired by the letter from the Editor of the *New York State Journal of Medicine*, the Philippine Medical Association Executive Council issued a public statement regarding cigarette smoking, and this has been given considerable publicity. It is hoped it will be possible to continue this effort in the coming months.

The statement recognizes the importance of the tobacco industry in this country, and suggests that government should initiate the efforts to encourage farmers to shift to other crops. However, this must be a governmental effort, even if pressure from interested groups may help in getting the government to act. This would not be viewed as a significant priority here today under the present economic and political circumstances, but continued efforts to bring the hazards of smoking to the public's attention may eventually produce results.

V. J. ROSALES, MD
President
Philippine Medical Association
P.O. Box 4039
Manila
The Philippines

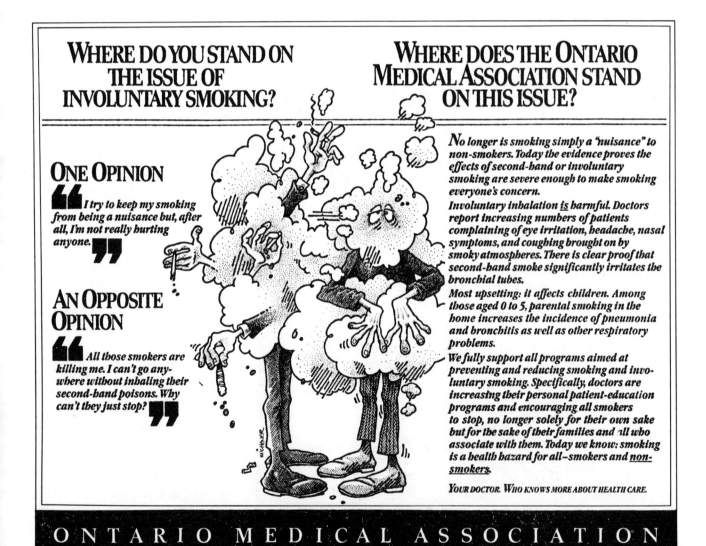

The Ontario Medical Association may be the first medical society to have purchased advertising space in behalf of nonsmokers' rights. This half-page advertisement appeared in *The Globe and Mail* (Toronto) on April 4, 1983. The Association, through its committee on public health, is working with the Non-Smokers Rights Association and other groups to seek a ban on smoking in all Ontario hospitals. The *Canadian Medical Association Journal* and the *Canadian Family Physician* have published several cover stories in recent years on the importance of a nonsmoking environment in health care settings.

The spirit of Chadwick

LAWRENCE D. BUDNICK, MD

In 1982, *The Lancet* decried the pressure from the tobacco companies and their representatives in Parliament on successive governments and called for "a Chadwick . . . to bring home to the Government the results of its pusillanimous agreements with the tobacco companies."[1] Just as "a Chadwick" is needed in the United Kingdom, his inspiration is needed again in the United States to overcome the political interference with the government's disease prevention and health promotion activities.

Edwin Chadwick, born in 1800, initially was a student of law, but later studied under Jeremy Bentham and became a leading proponent of Philosophic Radicalism, or utilitarianism. His first paper, in 1828, described how the life span of the middle class had lengthened with their better surroundings. In 1832, he took his first government assignment, as an assistant on the Poor Law Commission, and, within six years, became secretary of the Commission. In 1842, the Commission issued its three-volume report to Parliament, but the summary volume, *Report on the Sanitary Condition of the Labouring Population of Great Britain*, was written solely by Chadwick.[2] It was the clearest description and analysis, and the most forceful presentation made to date of the insanitary conditions prevalent in England, of the sickness and poverty resulting from these conditions, and of the need for government-sponsored sanitary improvements.[3] As a result of this work, in 1843, a special Royal Commission on the Health of Towns was appointed; it included Chadwick and initiated projects for clean water supply and sanitary sewage disposal. In 1848, the Public Health Act was passed; this was the first time the government accepted some responsibility for the people's health, and, in 1849, a General Board of Health was appointed, with Chadwick as its chief executive officer.[2] After five years, the Board's legislative authority expired and was not renewed. Chadwick, although retired from government service, was still active in public health, and promoted what became the Sanitary Act of 1866. In addition, during all this time, he served as a model for public health reformers in the United States.[3-5]

Many authors attribute Parliament's refusal to reauthorize the General Board of Health in large part to difficulties with Chadwick.[3,6-8] Chadwick, however, thought the problem was more systemic; he discussed the demise of the Board in an address in 1878 to the Fifth International Congress of Hygiene of Paris,[9] and his comments reflect on some of the difficulties faced today by those interested in improving public health.

Although the Board took extraordinary sanitary measures during epidemics, such as ordering people to leave their houses and live in tents, Chadwick believed there was a "general popular acquiescence" because of "the pains taken to show that what [the Board was] doing was the best that could be done in their interest."[9]

The Board was not popular, "however, in the House of Commons, where there were strong manifestations of displeasure, expressed in terms of repugnance to encroachments on popular principles of 'local self-government'." He said, in addition, that many members of Parliament (MPs) placed self-interest above the needs of the people.

Two of the opponents in Parliament were interested in a plan for an outlay of £40,000, which we had condemned. Other opponents were engineers, whose works and profits we had reduced considerably. One member, who owned a great manufactory of soap, from whence noxious smells were diffused amongst the population, told me distinctly, that if there was any interference with that manufacture, it would be the worse for me. But, the most powerful opponents were the directors and shareholders of the trading companies supplying gas and water to the metropolis, whose works we had examined, and proposed to supersede, and whose establishments we proposed to consolidate . . . . With the directors and shareholders of the water companies were allied the directors and shareholders of other companies, the wealthy engineers, interested in large works of the character interfered with, who raised a subscription, with which the Press was largely subsidised, to get up an agitation against the General Board. None of the moving sinister interests appeared on the surface, nothing but a patriotic concern for the large, general political interests of the community, which pretended concern or interest there was no one else there to challenge, but which the community did not support with petitions.[9]

In addition, other government officials who fought against the Board included the solicitor of the Treasury, who served as a water company director, and the Secretary of War and a number of MPs, who reportedly owned shares in the water companies.[1,10]

Chadwick concluded, "Altogether, a formidable phalanx was constituted, and by these opponents at a morning sitting, they effected a surprise, and by a vote which Lord Palmerston declared to be the 'foulest vote' which he had ever known in all his Parliamentary experience, they succeeded in putting the Government in a minority, on the

From the Department of Preventive Medicine and Community Health, State University of New York Downstate Medical Center, Brooklyn, NY.

Address correspondence to Dr Budnick, Injury Control Officer, Center for Environmental Health, Centers for Disease Control, Atlanta, GA 30333.

question of the continuance of the Board of Health in that form." The Board was weakened for, among other changes, the Opposition substituted "for the permanent board of specialists, a board of changing political chiefs, of no special aptitudes." In fact, he stated that the Board had become "a great sham," and had "thrown back the progress of sanitation in England by a quarter of a century."[9]

Chadwick was a tireless and remarkable public health reformer. As *The Times* of London wrote in 1854:

> Future historians who want to know what a Commission, a Board whether working or Parliamentary, a Report, a Secretary of State or almost any other member of our system was in the nineteenth century, will find the name of Chadwick inextricably mixed up with his inquiries. Should he want to know what a job was in those days he will find a clue to his research in this ubiquitous name ... Ask—Who did this? Who wrote that? Who made this index or that dietary? Who managed that appointment, or ordered that sewer, and the answer is the same—Mr. Edwin Chadwick."[11]

For over a century, he has been admired for his work, and for many years he has been considered one of the "fathers of modern public health."[3,4,6,11] Even his modern critics acknowledge that his efforts for the Public Health Act of 1848 and subsequent service with the first General Board of Health were laudatory.[8,10]

Chadwick was no more successful initially against the opponents of the first Board of Health than are modern public health workers against those who protect tobacco and alcohol companies, environmental polluters, and nuclear weapons producers today. Short-sighted and selfish industrialists and politicians interfered with the government's disease prevention and health promotion activities in Chadwick's time, just as they do now. The lesson we can learn from Chadwick, however, is that by persevering, public health workers can secure permanent public health reforms and improvements.

REFERENCES

1. Anon: Voluntary agreements do not stop epidemics. *Lancet* 1982; ii:855.
2. Chadwick E: *Report on the Sanitary Condition of the Labouring Population of Great Britain*, 1842, Poor Law Commission, edited with introduction by Flinn MW, Edinburgh, Edinburgh University Press, 1965.
3. Winslow CEA: Sanitary awakening, in: *The Evolution and Significance of the Modern Public Health Campaign*. New Haven, Yale University Press, 1923.
4. Emerson H: Public health diagnosis. *J Prevent Med* 1927; 1:410-427.
5. Duffy J: *A History of Public Health in New York City 1625-1866*. New York, Russell Sage Foundation, 1968.
6. Meneces ANT: *Sir Edwin Chadwick, Public Health Pioneer*. London, Chadwick Trust, 1972.
7. Hodgkinson R: *Public Health in the Victorian Age*. vol 1. Farnborough Hants, Gregg International Publishers, 1973, vol 1.
8. Ringen K: Edwin Chadwick, the market ideology, and sanitary reform: on the nature of the 19th-century public health movement. *Int J Health Serv* 1979; 9:107-120.
9. Chadwick E: *On the Requisite Attributions of a Minister of Health; and on the Principles of Central and Local Administrative Organisation and Action According to British Experiences*. London, Dr Johnson Press, 1878.
10. Ridgeway J: Chadwick's inquiry, in: *The Politics of Ecology*. New York, Dutton, 1970.
11. Rosen G: *A History of Public Health*. New York, MD Publications, 1958.

PHLOGISTON THEORY REVISITED (1957)

On the floor of the Senate, Senator Maurine Neuberger, citing industry efforts to curb antismoking campaigns in the schools, said there was one theme that runs through all cigarette advertising: "Today's adolescents are tomorrow's addicts." Yet, she added, despite its "cynical manipulation of symbols in an effort to boost sales figures, some tobacco interests have the temerity to criticize efforts to present another view of cigarette smoking. One can almost picture the counterpart of these tobacco spokesmen at the time of Pasteur's discovery of the relationship between fermentation in liquids and the growth of bacteria, a discovery which resulted in the development of pasteurization of milk and is today regarded as a giant forward step in the battle to protect human health."

—SUSAN WAGNER
Cigarette Country-Tobacco in American History and Politics,
New York, Praeger, 1971, p 88.

When "More doctors smoked Camels": Cigarette advertising in the *Journal*

Even well into the twentieth century, cigarette smoking hadn't caught on among most men—and definitely not among women. But through mass media advertising and overseas tobacco funds for the boys at war, cigarettes became firmly entrenched by the 1920s. The tobacco companies were the first to offer women equal rights, of a sort, with slogans such as "I'm a Lucky girl," "Blow some my way," and "Do you inhale? Everybody's doing it!" Readers of the Sunday funnies were told by ballplayers like Lou Gherig and Joe DiMaggio, "They don't get your wind . . . So mild, athletes smoke as many as they please!" To respond to those nagging, fuddy-duddy health doubters, various salutary claims and endorsements by doctors of certain brands began to appear. By the 1930s cigarette advertisements had made their way into medical journals, including the New York State Journal of Medicine. *The following article was written by Alan Blum, MD, Editor, with extensive research assistance by Jessica Rosenberg, a medical student at New York University.*

In 1927 the American Tobacco Company began a new advertising campaign for the nation's leading cigarette brand, Lucky Strike, by claiming that 11,105 physicians endorsed Luckies as "less irritating to sensitive or tender throats than any other cigarettes." The reaction in the *New York State Journal of Medicine* was a swift denunciation from both a moral and a scientific standpoint by the Society's legal counsel, Lloyd Paul Stryker:

> In this present era of advertising and publicity . . . we are accustomed to see portrayals of dramatic critics, actors, and others smoking some particular brand of cigarette and certifying that there is nothing like it. The endorsers, we understand, are not infrequently remunerated.
>
> The propriety of this course on the part of those who furnish their endorsements, where such endorsers are members of the laity, is a matter falling within their liberty of choice, and is properly governed by their own sense of fitness of things. When, however, non-therapeutic agents such as cigarettes are advertised as having the recommendation of the medical profession, the public is thereby led to believe that some real scientific inquiry has been instituted, and that the endorsement is the result of painstaking and accurate inquiry as to the merits of the product.
>
> Despite the frequent attacks upon the medical profession, we believe that the people of this country, take them as a whole, have a regard and wholesome faith in their physicians. All that tends to the building up and strengthening of this faith redounds to the benefit of the medical profession and of its individual members, and that which in any wise tends to shake this faith and confidence works a detriment not only to the profession as a whole but to each individual practitioner. All that tends to strengthen the faith of the people in the belief that medical opinions are founded upon a sound scientific basis, should be fostered by the profession.[1]

Although Stryker could find no canon of the principles of professional conduct of MSSNY that such endorsements definitely violated, he questioned whether or not such involvement by physicians, albeit in this instance most likely unintentional, tends "to advance the science and honor of medicine and to guard and uphold its high standard of honor."

A few months later the *Journal* noted the praise by *California and Western Medicine* (among other journals) for Stryker's commentary:

> It is regrettable that any physicians should have thoughtlessly lent their support to this advertising scheme. The profession that has studiously worked to protect the people from fraudulent claims of drug advertisers should be more alert and discerning.[2]

In the same issue, the *Journal* published new Advertising Standards that declared, "The *Journal* will continue to select, to require proof, to reflect. And its advertising columns will prove increasingly valuable to the readers as a guide to reliability of firm and product." A subsequent editorial announced that advertisements would be edited as if they were scientific articles or news items, to "guard against extravagant statements."[3]

In spite of these assurances, and in the absence of an announcement of a modification of these standards, the *Journal* published its first cigarette advertisement in 1933. For more than 20 years it was to accept more than 600 pages of cigarette advertisements from the six major tobacco companies. Although it is difficult to understand how the *Journal* permitted cigarette advertising, there is no mystery whatsoever as to why tobacco companies sought out medical journals: in the words of an Irish proverb, "Truth may be good, but juxtaposition is better." The tobacco companies were buying complacency.

FULL-BODIED

The first tobacco company to purchase advertising space in the *Journal* was Liggett & Myers. From October 1, 1933, to July 1, 1938, an advertisement for Chesterfield cigarettes appeared in alternating issues, usually on the premium-space back cover. Although some advertisements suggested Chesterfields were healthful ("Just as pure as the water you drink . . . and practically untouched by human hands"—Dec 1, 1933), most were composed of a romantic young couple, a double-entendre catchphrase ("They satisfy!"), and the distinctive Chesterfield logo. The following dialogue was printed below a scene of two lovers snuggled in a one-horse sleigh (Aug 1, 1934):

> Woman: "I thank you—I thank you ever so much—but I couldn't even think about smoking a cigarette."
> Man: "Well, I understand, but they are so mild and taste so good that I thought you might not mind trying one while we are riding along out there."

Perhaps because Lucky Strikes were America's top-selling and most widely advertised brand by the 1930s, the American Tobacco Company may not have wanted to court additional undue medical skepticism concerning its various health-oriented slogans, including, "No throat irritation. No cough." Only one advertisement for Lucky Strike appears to have been published in the *Journal*. Headlined, "A Quarter Century of Research Relating to a Light Smoke," the advertisement discussed American's long-standing ef-

Address correspondence to Dr. Blum, Editor, *New York State Journal of Medicine*, 420 Lakeville Road, Lake Success, NY 11042.

fort to solve "an extraordinarily complex problem":

The objective may be stated as: *the perfection of a cigarette with a minimum of respiratory and systemic irritants, and with a fully preserved character, i.e., a perfected acid-alkaline balance—a cigarette in which rich, full-bodied tobaccos have been successfully utilized to produce "A Light Smoke."*

By means of a graph purportedly illustrating the ratio of total volatile acids to total volatile bases, the company claimed that, unlike Brands B, C, and D, Lucky Strike had struck the proper balance between "acidity and basicity." Why the advertising for this brand was discontinued is unclear, for there is no published correspondence or editorial content discussing the advertisement.

CLINICAL PROOF

Philip Morris English Blend cigarettes made their *Journal* debut in 1935, in single-column advertisements drawn to resemble a cigarette. Citing studies published in medical journals, these advertisements were the first to aim squarely at physicians. The basic claim was that Philip Morris, made with the hygroscopic (moistening) agent diethylene glycol, were less irritating than cigarettes made with glycerine or with no such chemical additive. The Philip Morris claim was largely based on an article published in the *New York State Journal of Medicine*.[4]

In the advertisements, reprints of this study and others in *The Laryngoscope* were offered, along with two free packs of Philip Morris. The study reported a variation of an objective technique for the measurement of irritation—the production of edema in the conjunctival sac of rabbits' eyes. In the authors' experiment, edema produced by the instillation of a smoke solution from Philip Morris cigarettes lasted an average of 8 minutes, while the smoke solution from "cigarettes made by the Ordinary Method" caused edema for an average duration of 45 minutes. The advertisements would note that an article in *Laryngoscope* (1935; XLV, No. 2, 149–154) reported "clinical confirmation. When *smokers* changed to Philip Morris, every case of irritation of the nose and throat due to smoking cleared completely or definitely improved" (eg, Dec 1, 1940).

For 15 years, Philip Morris continued to cite such "proof" for the health benefits of these cigarettes, notwithstanding the fact that the authors of the paper in the *Journal* had concluded that cigarette smoking, regardless of the brand, was the cause of irritation to begin with:

For any one patient we may assume that cigarette smoke may play some part in the pathology of the throat condition for which he has consulted his physician.

In addition, in a subsequent article in the *Journal* criticizing the rabbit eye test as a means of evaluating irritation, Sharlit[5] had written

... the olfactory nerve ends in the mucous membrane of the

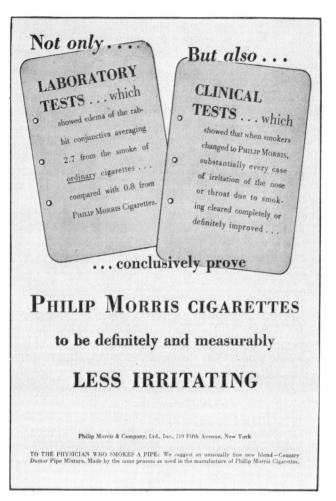

1945

1952

nose are far more efficient than the eye for detecting irritating smoke. Indeed, that is precisely part of the job of these nerve ends. When cigarettes made with diethylene glycol (ie, Philip Morris) were so tested by the writer and several others (smoke quickly drawn up through the nose), they were found, unfortunately, to be quite as irritating as other cigarettes.

Doubtless as the result of this article, Philip Morris issued a retraction of sorts which was published in the issue of Jan 15, 1943:

A DISCLAIMER:
Philip Morris & Company do not claim that Philip Morris cigarettes cure irritation. But they do say that an ingredient—glycerine—a source of irritation in other cigarettes, is not used in the manufacture of Philip Morris.

This did not stop Philip Morris from developing advertising themes throughout the 1940s such as "Why many leading nose and throat specialists suggest . . . change to Philip Morris" (1948–1949) or from boasting about the integrity of its advertising:

INTERESTED IN CIGARETTE ADVERTISING?
Claims, words, clever advertising slogans do sell plenty of products. But obviously they do not change the product itself. That Philip Morris are less irritating to the nose and throat is not merely a claim. It is the result of a manufacturing difference *proved* advantageous over and over again (Nov 1, 1945).

Although little Johnny the bellhop appeared each evening on such popular radio programs as "The Edgar Bergen and Charlie McCarthy Show," his smiling face never appeared in the *Journal*. Nonetheless, Johnny was enlisted in printed advertisements in the mass media to promote the theme of Philip Morris' "definitely less irritating" properties. Among the slogans he was shown calling out were, "Don't let inhaling worry you (if you switch to Philip Morris)!" and "An ounce of prevention is worth a pound of cure." Philip Morris never explained why Johnny's growth was stunted.

SLOW BURN
R.J. Reynolds first advertised in the *Journal* in 1941. Advertisements for Camels appeared in every issue for the rest of the decade, and in every other issue from 1950 to 1953. The early advertisements claimed that Camels, "the slower burning cigarette," produced less nicotine in the smoke. Photographs of men in white laboratory coats peering into test tubes lent a scientific touch. Like Philip Morris, R.J. Reynolds suggested switching brands as the alternative to quitting smoking. Rather than emphasize the irritation issue, R.J. Reynolds chose to play on the use of cigarettes to relieve "the strain of current life," as illustrated in this advertisement from Nov 1, 1942:

In these unsettled times, individuals may tend to display baffling, sub-clinical symptoms. The relationship of these symptoms to smoking and nicotine absorption can be an interesting subject for exploration.

However, the success of the physician's program is dependent upon the patient's full cooperation.

Your recommendation of Camel cigarettes can be an aid in this direction. . . .

Given adequate support by patients, the physician may find case histories more reliable. In addition, the segregation of such data may facilitate valuable group analyses.

Although American Tobacco was first to exploit a patriotic wartime theme ("Lucky Strike Green has gone to war"), R.J. Reynolds quickly followed suit by portraying Camels "as the favorite of the armed forces" (Feb 1, 1943) and appealing to physicians to send a carton to their "friends with the fighting forces." Military physicians became "heroes in white" (Mar 1, 1945), whose only rare comfort was a trusty Camel.

Following a series of postwar advertisements praising America's fighting, smoking physicians, R.J. Reynolds introduced a campaign, based on a survey of 113,597 physicians, that claimed, "More Doctors smoke Camels than any other cigarette." The first advertisement in the series (Jan 1, 1946) included a reprint of a "Dear Doctor" letter from the Camel Medical Relations Division, One Pershing Square, New York, NY, which praised its own survey. The "More Doctors smoke Camels" theme could be heard on most prime-time radio programs, including such children's favorites as "Abbott and Costello." Advertisements nearly identical to those that appeared in medical journals also ran each week in the three most popular magazines of the era, *LIFE*, *TIME*, and *The Saturday Evening Post*, thus as-

suring maximum media saturation.

But R.J. Reynolds managed to top this effort in its direct-to-physician advertising with a campaign for Camels cigarettes that posthumously honored great medical discoverers: Thomas Addison, John William Ballantyne, Sir Charles Bell, John Hughes Bennett, Claude Bernard, Richard Bright, Charles Edoard Brown-Séquard, Paul Ehrlich, Carlos Finlay, Camillo Golgi, William Whithey Gull, Marshall Hall, Herman von Helmholtz, F.G. Jacob Henle, Robert Koch, Joseph Lister, Theobold Smith, William Stokes, Rudolph Virchow, and William Henry Welch. Advertisements in nearly every issue of the *Journal* in 1947 and 1948 praised the perseverence of these men, beneath the headlined slogan, "Experience is the Best Teacher." The advertisments concluded with the line, "Experience is the best teacher in cigarettes too!" and cited statistical proof that Camels were the "choice of experience."

HOUSECALLS

Another way tobacco companies played up to physicians was to provide them with free cartons of cigarettes. This was done either by mail (as part of market research surveys) or by an attractive "detail woman" (who would see to it that a plentiful supply of cigarettes was available in the patients' waiting area) or by exhibits at medical meetings. In 1940 Philip Morris took out space in the *Journal* for an "invitation" to physicians to drop by the cigarette company's booth at the annual convention of the Medical Society of the State of New York. Beginning in 1942, R.J. Reynolds invited physicians to visit the Camel cigarette exhibit at the convention of the American Medical Association (AMA). This

1946

1947

advertisement was not unlike a circus poster:

> See for the first time the dramatic visualization of nicotine absorption from cigarette smoke in the human respiratory tract.
>
> See the giant photo-murals of Camel laboratory research experiments . . . .

In 1949 Reynolds concocted the "30-day test," whereby unnamed but "noted throat specialists" were used to back up the claim, "Not one case of throat irritation due to smoking Camels!" Philip Morris countered with the "nose test," which it urged physicians to try (Mar 1, 1950). In before-and-after pictures, a young woman was shown exhaling smoke through her nostrils—smiling in the photograph labeled "Philip Morris" and grimacing with her "present brand." The advertisement claimed the doctor-smoker would also "see at once Philip Morris are less irritating."

By 1950, Philip Morris had found a new lure: "Make our doctors' lounge your club," invited one advertisement (June 1, 1950). Brown & Williamson Tobacco Company, trying to attract frightened consumers to filter cigarettes, also worked the medical market. One of its advertisements thanked "the 64,985 doctors who visited Viceroy exhibits at medical conventions" (June 1, 1954).

OUT WITH THE BAD AIR . . .

Even though the cigarette companies have never publicly acknowledged any lasting harm attributed to their product, they have always attempted to portray various brands as safer and healthier than others. No aspect is more central to the hoax of safer smoking than is the filter. The first advertisement carried by the *Journal* for a filter cigarette

was for Viceroy (July 15, 1939): "AT LAST . . . a cigarette that filters each puff clean!" ("No more tobacco in mouth or teeth . . . A note on your office stationery will bring two packages with our compliments.")

By 1953, following publication of several major studies that left little doubt about cigarette smoking's role as the primary factor in the growing epidemic of lung cancer among men, nearly all the remaining cigarette advertisements in the *Journal* and other medical publications were for filter cigarettes. The drop-off in cigarette advertising in the *Journal* did not merely come about because the companies' ability to deceive or confuse physicians had run its course. Rather, television had become the predominant medium, and the bulk of advertising budgets was shifted into the sponsorship of the most popular programs.

Philip Morris ran its last advertisement in the *Journal* on August 1, 1953; Reynolds exited at the end of 1953, but not before touting a new slogan, "Progress through research." Meanwhile, Lorillard had launched nationally televised "scientific" demonstrations to show the efficacy and implicit medical benefits of its Micronite filter. This campaign was backed up by a heavy dose of advertising in medical publications.

Although the advertisements never disclosed the composition of "Micronite," there is evidence that the material that Lorillard touted as "so safe, so effective it has been selected to help filter the air in hospital operating rooms" (May 15, 1954) and "to purify the air in atomic energy plants of microscopic impurities" (Feb 15, 1954) was asbestos. A case report from the Thoracic Services of Boston University Medical School, "Asbestos following brief exposure in cigarette filter manufacture," described a 47-year old man who had been exposed to asbestos dust for a period

Helping patients withdraw from smoking

GERALD P. MURPHY, MD, DSC, RUSSEL SCIANDRA, MA

Although all physicians agree that the elimination of cigarette smoking is an essential part of health promotion, most underestimate their ability to succeed in helping an individual patient to give up smoking. Wechsler et al[1] in a survey of 433 primary care physicians in Massachusetts, found that 90% routinely asked patients about smoking and that 58% were prepared to counsel patients about smoking. Only 3% expressed confidence that they were "very successful" with such counseling efforts.

But it appears that even brief but considered advice by the physician has been shown to have a significant success.[2] Indeed, Russell et al[3] point out that if all general practitioners in Great Britain were simply to remember to advise all patients not to smoke, more than half a million individuals a year would stop smoking.

Thus, the physician's pessimism about helping individual patients to give up smoking may be a case of viewing the glass as part empty rather than part full. While an individual physician may at first succeed with only a minority of patients, the number of those who still smoke is so large and the societal problems so great that even a small increase in the cessation rate can have an impact on public health.

While every patient who smokes should be viewed as a candidate for cessation, some patients are more resistant than others. An essential—indeed, mandatory—situation for a full-fledged effort to eliminate smoking is the pregnant woman seeking prenatal care. This includes a visit by a pregnant woman to an emergency room or other kinds of episodic care. Another situation in which a patient is more receptive to counseling is, regrettably, at the time of a severe illness. Pederson[2] has found that patients who have suffered a myocardial infarction are especially amenable to giving up cigarettes. Caution should be exercised in attempting to counsel patients who have severe depression or frank mental illness, but it is inappropriate to accept at face value "stress" as a reason for smoking or to avoid imparting advice because the patient is "too anxious." This can be misinterpreted by the patient as an endorsement of smoking as a means of therapy.

People who smoke are more mindful of the adverse health consequences when they visit a physician's office or other health care setting. Therefore, even the most routine consultation provides an opportunity for the physician to give advice on cessation. Because smoking hampers the man-

---

From the Roswell Park Memorial Institute, New York State Department of Health, Buffalo.

Dr Murphy is President, American Cancer Society.

Address correspondence to Dr Murphy, Director, Roswell Park Memorial Institute, 666 Elm Street, Buffalo, NY 14263.

Smoking Withdrawal Assistance

1. Helping Smokers Quit Kit

    A complete packet of materials designed specifically for physicians to assist their smoking patients to quit. Each kit contains enough materials for 50 patients. Write: Office of Cancer Communications, Box NY, National Cancer Institute, Bldg. 31, Room 10A18, Bethesda, MD 20205

2. Fresh Start

    Fresh Start is a four-session group clinic designed to help participants stop smoking by providing them with all the essential information and strategies needed to direct their own efforts at stopping. The program focuses on an active, pragmatic approach to quitting. Participants are encouraged to apply what they learn in Fresh Start to other aspects of their lives. *For a clinic schedule contact your local American Cancer Society Office.* The address of your local office may be obtained from the head office, The American Cancer Society, 777 Third Avenue, New York, NY 10017

3. Freedom From Smoking Kit

    Packed into two manuals, Freedom From Smoking is a potent self-help program that represents the culmination of four years of research, development, and evaluation. The first manual, Freedom From Smoking in 20 Days, provides a nuts-and-bolts, day-by-day approach to quitting. The second, A Lifetime of Freedom From Smoking, helps smokers reinforce and maintain their new non-smoking lifestyle. Tensions and events that cause backsliding are anticipated; counter-strategies for coping without cigarettes are spelled out. Saying "no" to cigarettes requires practice. These kits are obtained from The American Lung Association, 8 Mountainview Avenue, Albany, NY 12205.

---

agement of some diseases it does not directly cause (eg, diabetes mellitus), the physician should not regard any patient who continues to smoke as "compliant," however well the patient adheres to other recommendations.

What is the best way to counsel patients? Although there are several factors in counseling which are constant in all patients, there is no single best way. The physician must clearly make known his strong feelings against smoking. Smoking should not be permitted by patients or staff in the office setting. Good health posters can reinforce this commitment.

The patient's expectation of success is the best predictor

of nine months in 1953 while working in a factory that manufactured filters containing asbestos.[6] The patient made cigarette filters that consisted of a mixture of Cape Blue asbestos and acetate. According to the second author and a second source,[7] the filters were made for Lorillard, although it is possible that these particular filters were in some way different from the Kent Micronite filters.

Brown & Williamson again drew *Journal* readers' attention to the alleged lower tar and nicotine content of Viceroy, "as proved by testing methods acceptable to the United States Government." (Nov 15, 1953). The last cigarette advertisement appeared in the *New York State Journal of Medicine* on January 15, 1955, paid for by Lorillard to proclaim, "Old Gold—the first famous name brand to give you a filter." This from a company that had advertised Old Gold with the slogan "not a cough in a carload" in the 1930s and 1940s and had ridiculed the early medical reports pointing to the lethal side-effects of smoking with the slogan (also appearing in medical journals), "For a treat instead of a treatment."

Little if any criticism of the policy of accepting cigarette advert... to have been published in the *Journal* d... these advertisements ran. The same is tr... h published cigarette advertising be- tw... . But in 1954 a campaign for Kent, wh... rsement by the medical profession (me... anufacturer had also taken out ad- vert... journals), incurred the wrath of an edito... o denounced the advertising as "an outra... commercial exploitation of the Amer... ion and a reprehensible instance of huc... sequent letter to *JAMA* Irving S. Wri... t not only were the Kent adver- tisemen... implied Kents were the choice for pers... ease) but also especially dan- gerous. V... atient with quiescent throm- boangiitis... red a recurrence after having read a K... that led him to resume smoking.

Thirty ye... dvertisements disappeared from peer-re... als, it seems inconceivable that they eve... ccepted in the first place. Yet many of t... cal magazines continued to accept ciga... oughout the 1960s and 1970s. At leas... azine, *Physician East*, which lists six p... thead and is published in Boston, has ...ued to run cigarette advertising. Others, including *JAMA*, carry advertising for CNA Insurance Company, a division of Loews.

ERRATUM Pages 112 and 113 have been transposed. The article beginning on page 112 ends on page 112 previous article ends on page 113. the article on page 114, and the

COMMENT

Many goods and services offered in the *Journal* in the past half-century have stood the test of time, but a policy of accepting advertisements for cigarettes is a sad saga for this and all other medical publications that have carried them—and for the entire advertising and publishing fields. It may be too late to publish corrective advertising for promotions that ceased 30 years ago, but even in retrospect the credibility of the publication is harmed. The knowledge and common sense about cigarette smoking *were* there— but so were the mass media to undermine knowledge and cultivate mass denial. One clear lesson is that physicians are not immune to propaganda. But the point of this article (and this entire issue) is that the situation in regard to the promotion of smoking is even more pernicious today. The old advertisements in the *Journal* may seem ridiculous in their images and claims, and we can rationalize that we no longer acquiesce in the sale of cigarettes in a medical context. But do we? Whenever we flip past the cigarette ad on the sports page of *The Times* or ignore the one on the billboard downtown or on the bus, subway, or taxi that drops the patient off at our offices, we as leaders in society are doing precisely what the cigarette advertisers want us to do: *not* become angry, but rather to become resigned or complacent. Advertising for a product is not solely designed to sell to potential or current users, but also to assure the complacency or tolerance of non-users.

A common attitude among physicians today is that smoking will gradually die out in the next few years and that the cigarette companies will leave cigarettes to diversify into other kinds of businesses. Unfortunately, this is not on the agenda for a single cigarette company, least of all those which are aiming at developing nations.

It is too simple—and naive—a matter to call for a total ban on cigarette advertising, as so many other medical editorialists have done. Even granting an unforeseen awakening by Congress and local governments to the need for such an action, to judge from the events in countries where there have been such prohibitions, the tobacco industry is adept at incorporating its brand names, images, and packaging colors into other media. At LaGuardia and Kennedy international airports, for instance, the red rectangular symbol with the white triangular cut into it does not require a printed message for it to be instantaneously recognized that Marlboro cigarettes are being advertised. The clear solution is to remove all economic incentives for the cigarette companies and their subsidiaries, and the first step may well be a physician-led selective economic boycott. At the rate these conglomerates are growing, if the medical profession misses out on this opportunity, it may one day find itself working for health maintenance organizations operated by Loews, hospitals run by Philip Morris, trauma centers controlled by R.J. Reynolds, outpatient clinics established by Brown & Williamson, professional provider organizations set up by American Brands, and pharmaceutical manufacturers owned by Liggett. To judge from the increasing number of medical research councils, institutes, and science symposia underwritten by tobacco companies, and the medical schools and business schools accepting endowment money from them, this possibility may not be that far-fetched.

Update: In 1984, GrandMet USA, parent company of Liggett, acquired Quality Care, Inc., a home health care concern, for $125 million.

REFERENCES

1. Stryker LP: The endorsement of commercial products by physicians. *NY State J Med.* 1927; 27:1264 1265.
2. Editorial: Cigarette testimonials. *NY State J Med.* 1928; 28:355 356.
3. Advertising standards. *NY State J Med.* 1928; 28:361.
4. Mulinos MG, Osbourne RL: Irritating properties of cigarette smoke as influenced by hygroscopic agents. *NY State J Med* 1935; 35:590 592.
5. Sharlit H: Cigarette smoke as a health hazard. *NY State J Med* 1935; 35:1159 1161.
6. Goff AM, Gaensler EA: Asbestos following brief exposure in cigarette filter manufacture. *Respiration* 1972; 29:83 93.
7. Personal communication, EA Gaensler, CB Carrington.
8. Anon: Cigarette hucksterism and the AMA. *JAMA* 1954; 154:1180.
9. Wright IS: Cigarettes. *JAMA* 1954; 155:666.

of smoking cessation.[4,5] The physician should encourage the patient to believe he can get along quite well without cigarettes and should assure him of the physician's own confidence in the patient's ability to stop. Counseling which relies too heavily on fear or guilt may cause the patient to "dig in" even further and increase smoking.

It is helpful to seek a commitment from the patient to agree upon a target date for ending all smoking. The date should be put in writing on the patient's chart. The physician must offer continuing encouragement and advice in all subsequent visits, even after the patient has stopped smoking.

It is essential to prepare the patient for possible side effects such as headache, smoking withdrawal, irritability, drowsiness, and insomnia. As with all good history-taking, the physician should also aid the patient in identifying situational cues to smoke. Alternate activities to substitute for smoking should be discussed.

The physician should become acquainted with materials available from the American Cancer Society, the American Lung Association, and the National Cancer Institute (Table). These materials should be scrutinized with the aim of developing improvements in individual approaches to the problem.

Smoking is a multifaceted problem that can be successfully solved through the commitment of the medical profession. An investment of time and interest by the physician during routine contacts with patients can go a long way toward ending the smoking pandemic.

REFERENCES

1. Wechsler H, Levine S, Idelson RK, Rohman M, Taylor JO: The physician's role in health promotion—a survey of primary care practitioners. *N Engl J Med* 1983; 308:97-100.
2. Pederson LL: Compliance with physician advice to quit smoking: A review of the literature. *Prev Med* 1982; 11:71-84.
3. Russell MAH, Wilson C, Taylor C, et al: Effects of general practitioners' advice against smoking. *Brit Med J* 1979; 2:231-235.
4. Ockene JK, Benfari RC, Nuttall RL, Hurwitz, I, Ockene, IS: Relationship of psychosocial factors to smoking behavior change in an intervention program. *Prev Med* 1982; 11:13-28.
5. Pederson LL, Baskerville JC, Wanklin JM: Multivariate statistical models for predicting change in smoking behavior following physician advice to quit smoking. *Prev Med* 1982; 11:536-549.

CIGARETTES AND DEATH CERTIFICATES
(*from the* Florida Medical Association Journal, *1973; 60:92*)

All of us are well aware of the role cigarette smoking plays in the causation of pulmonary emphysema and squamous cell carcinoma of the lungs. Most of us also realize the aggravating effects of cigarette smoking on coronary ischemic heart disease. For years we have neglected to mention tobacco on certificates of death except under the most unusual of circumstances.

Physicians are expected to render a clinical judgment as to the causative factors of death when a certificate is completed. There is no reason why we should continue to omit the most significant causative factor in the production of pulmonary emphysema and squamous cell carcinoma of the lungs when we certify. Certainly the use of tobacco is the major underlying causative factor in these two diseases.

The collection of accurate final statistics has always been a function of the State's Division of Health. It would be of great service if every physician in the State of Florida were to receive a directive from the Division of Health with a request that cigarette smoking or tobacco use be specifically mentioned on the death certificate when, in the clinical judgment of the certifier, this was a factor when death was caused by either pulmonary emphysema or squamous cell carcinoma of the lung or any other smoking-related diseases. An alternative would be a box to be checked off on the certificate which would designate whether or not the patient had been a heavy user of cigarettes. This would be simpler for the physician since it would require no additional judgment decision on his part in regard to the relationship of the death and cigarettes. Statistical analysis of the data so collected would, in the long run, accomplish the same desired purpose.

In the meantime, there is no reason why we physicians, on our own, could not begin to certify as has our colleague, Charles F. Tate, MD.

—JOSEPH H. DAVIS, MD
Medical Examiner, Dade County
1050 NW 19th Street
Miami, FL 33136

(*Editor's note: Dr. Davis prepared the comment below at the request of the* New York State Journal of Medicine.)

Ten years later, the death certificate in Florida is being emended to include a box not for indicating cigarette smoking but for recording the presence or absence of pregnancy. This is in spite of the fact that the catchment system of maternal mortality committees already assures a high level of success in documenting pregnancy-related deaths.

From a priority standpoint, what is needed is a box pertaining to cigarette smoking. Because the vast number of cigarette-related deaths is not being documented, the enormity of the problem remains largely unaddressed by government.

Changing death certificates to improve the reporting of maternal mortality while continuing to avoid the opportunity to document the two leading causes of death—tobacco and alcohol—is akin to studying a speck in the eye of a gnat while bearing down on us is a thundering herd of elephants.

—Joseph H. Davis, MD

Myths and realities of smoking cessation

JEROME L. SCHWARTZ, DRPH

Every physician can play a leading role in helping patients to give up smoking. However, misconceptions abound in regard to the process of ending dependence on cigarettes and thus have hindered clinical and political involvement of physicians in attacking the cigarette pandemic. Physicians overestimate their patients' awareness of the hazards of smoking and underestimate their own ability to get patients off cigarettes. This article will examine some of the myths and realities of smoking cessation which are raised time and again in the course of discussions with health professionals, individuals who no longer smoke, and persons who have continued to smoke.

MYTHS

"It takes too long to counsel patients." Although primary care physicians are busy people, and many claim they just do not have the time to go into detail with patients about smoking, it takes very little time for a physician to offer advice on how to stop smoking.[1] Most physicians ask each patient about smoking habits, and many do point out the evidence of smoking's harmful effects on the respiratory and cardiovascular systems. But many others—ironically often out of fear of offending or appearing to make a moral judgment—fail to present a strong statement about the importance and joy of not smoking.[2]

Blum[3] points out that the approach to each patient should be personalized, taking into account social, cultural, ethnic, and occupational factors, as well as the brand of cigarettes smoked (to get a better idea of the image the smoker may have of himself or herself). He suggests that the best approach to advising a construction worker on smoking might be to talk about the chances of increased fitness and enhanced sexual performance. On the other hand, an executive is more likely to take to heart an explanation of relative risk factors, while a teenager will be more concerned about self-image, and thus more susceptible to statements concerning the physical unattractiveness of yellow teeth and "zoo breath"—not to mention money down the drain that could be spent (or saved) for more pleasant activities.

"The general public is aware of the hazards of smoking." A report to the Federal Trade Commission has pointed out that the general public has *not* "heard it all before."[4] Approximately one fourth of the total population and about one half of all those currently smoking have still not accepted the proposition that "cigarette smoking is dangerous to your health" and can cause lung cancer. The report states that there is even less general acceptance of propositions linking smoking to specific health consequences such as heart disease, emphysema, chronic bronchitis, and lowered birth weight.

"People continue to smoke because they want to." Many people continue to smoke, not because they want to, but because they cannot easily stop. Smoking is a potent form of drug dependence, and a cigarette is a highly efficient device for administering nicotine,[5] as well as sugar and other flavoring agents for which the body has acquired a taste.

"Switching to low-nicotine cigarettes reduces risk." Those who switch to low-nicotine cigarettes compensate by smoking more, taking larger or more frequent puffs, and by inhaling more deeply.[6] Although use of low-tar cigarettes may result in lower mortality rates for lung cancer, this does not mean that rates for coronary heart disease or emphysema are reduced.

"95 percent of persons who stop smoking do so on their own." Although it is true that most people stop smoking without going through an organized method, many people act on the advice or warning of their physician.[7] The patient has to understand his dependence and be aware that stopping requires effort. Cessation may be easy for some, but it is difficult for most. A serious discussion would inform the patient that smoking cessation may be difficult but that it is necessary.

"Tranquilizers help people quit." The results for stopping smoking by using tranquilizers are very poor; prescriptions for tranquilizers for patients who suffer from acute anxiety when trying to stop smoking are contraindicated.[8] Instead the patient needs moral support to see him through the anxious period. Support, once the patient has stopped smoking, can include telephone conversations, reminders through the mail, face-to-face meetings, or devising a "buddy system" in which two or more patients keep in touch and support each other's efforts. Patients might even be advised to call the office (a sort of "smoking hotline") at the first urge to smoke. Even the suggestion that they have a place to phone is a powerful help. Office personnel can offer encouragement for continued abstinence and make suggestions regarding exercise, relaxation, or deep breathing. Those persons having a tough time can be put through for a brief conversation and morale boost with the physician; patients greatly appreciate this caring attitude on the part of the physician.

"Certain methods are just right for certain people." There is no particular method that is just right for a given individual. Sometimes it takes several practice tries before an individual can stop for good. It is often not the method but the point at which a person attempts to stop smoking. Like falling in love, timing is important.

Although it is claimed that good results have been achieved with hypnosis and acupuncture, evaluations are

Dr Schwartz has evaluated smoking cessation programs for the Centers for Disease Control, Public Health Service.

Address correspondence to Dr Schwartz, 746 Hawthorn Lane, Davis, CA 95616.

often faulty. A review of 17 studies of hypnosis revealed that after six months, abstinence ranged from 40% to 88%.[9] Better results were achieved with several hours of treatment and intense personal interaction. Investigators who used acupuncture with 405 subjects reported that it helped only between 5% and 15% to stop smoking for six months.[10] It was concluded that the effectiveness of acupuncture in smoking cessation is the result of a large psychologic component. From the results of several European studies of well-motivated individuals, it appears that nicotine-based chewing gum is a promising method, but the results of the studies vary greatly.

REALITIES

"About 4,000 known compounds are generated by burning cigarettes." The burning tip of a cigarette reaches 1900° F; by the time smoke reaches the inhaling tip, the temperature falls to about 100° F. Although carbon monoxide, nicotine, and tar are the main culprits in damaging health, there are many other noxious compounds, such as nitrogen oxides, nitrosamines, hydrogen cyanide, sulphur compounds, aldehydes and ketones, aromatic amines, alkanes and alkenes, carboxylic acids, arsenic, and various insecticide residues. Some of these compounds are poisons, and others are carcinogens and mutagens.

"Cigarette smoking is the most important preventable environmental factor contributing to illness, disability, and death in the United States." This has been the conclusion of successive surgeons general. In 1979 it was reported that the health damage resulting from cigarette smoking costs this nation an estimated 325,000 premature deaths each year, and $27 billion in medical care, absenteeism, decreased work productivity, and accidents.[11]

"Specific step-by-step instructions on how to stop smoking is the method preferred by patients." The Smoking Control Research Project conducted a survey of the willingness of individuals to accept 10 smoking withdrawal methods.[12] Instructions received the highest positive response of any of the methods, public health clinics the lowest positive response. Instructions received a 69% favorable response; medication, 66%; television programs, 64%; and books, 53%. This compares with 36% to 42% for individual counseling, hypnosis, lectures, tranquilizers, group discussion, and clinics. This means that individuals prefer to quit on their own, utilizing instructions, books, and television programs.

The physician can help the patient decide whether to quit cold turkey or to taper off. Environment must be considered, since it is difficult to stop when one is surrounded by others who smoke. Contrary to popular belief, persons strongly dependent on cigarettes can be advised to quit cold turkey; of course, they will suffer withdrawal symptoms but these must be faced.

"Health is the major reason for stopping." Most of those who stop smoking have become convinced that smoking is bad for their health. Some stop for other reasons: they no longer enjoy cigarettes, they begrudge the expense, others want them to stop, or they wish to serve in an exemplary role.[13] Some people stop once they decide that cigarettes are harming their health, particularly following diagnosis of a chronic disease condition or after a reduction in smoking because of an upper respiratory tract infection.

Visits for coughs and colds are perfect opportunities for physicians to point out the folly of continuing to smoke and the waste of money on medications and doctor bills.

"Most methods achieve about the same results." Although a few methods have been reported to produce better results (perhaps the counselors were more experienced or because follow-up support was more effective), most methods achieve approximately the same success rate after one year. This implies that the committed physician may do wonders. Of great importance is an atmosphere within the office that emphasizes good health. The staff should not smoke; there should be no ash trays; nonthreatening, no-smoking signs or posters should be prominently displayed; and literature about stopping smoking should be available.

"Evaluation of smoking cessation programs lacks proper design." By and large, evaluations of smoking methods do lack proper design.[14] Many investigators conduct limited follow-ups, base their results on those who reply, and measure success inadequately—based on reduction in smoking rather than on total abstinence. Although reduction in smoking lowers risk, it is difficult to interpret results and compare programs unless "percent who quit" is used to measure the results. The rule should be a one-year follow-up, and success should be defined as one who has refrained from smoking for one year. One noticeable improvement is the number of investigators who choose to validate smoking behavior through blood or urine tests or measurement of expired air carbon monoxide. All programs should consider some form of validation, particularly methods linked to medical offices.

"Filters advertised as aids to break the cigarette habit don't work." Two studies of Teledyne Water Pik's "One Step at a Time" showed that the filter system for stopping smoking is not effective. In one study not one single person quit smoking at the end of the eight weeks when they were supposed to quit.[15] Follow-ups revealed that 10% stopped smoking, but they did it cold turkey after disposing of their filtration devices. In the second study, "One Step at a Time" was compared with "quitting on your own."[16] At the end of one year, "quitting on your own" recorded 33% abstinence, while the group on the filters achieved 22%. The investigators concluded that the data fail to document the utility of the filter system for stopping smoking.

"Follow-up support is necessary to maintain the quitting effort." Most persons need reassurance once they have broken the smoking habit. Physicians need to become aware of the importance of spending time supporting efforts of their patients to achieve good health habits.

"Success in breaking the habit depends on both the participant and the method." Persons who smoke must be committed to stopping; this commitment is stronger with people who believe that dangers of smoking are personally relevant, and in those who have a compelling reason to stop. This is why the role of the health practitioner is so important in helping patients to stop smoking.

CONCLUSION

Because of the overwhelming evidence implicating smoking as a major health hazard, all patients who smoke should be urged to stop. Unfortunately, many cigarette-related diseases are diagnosed too late to be reversed by cessation. There is evidence, however, indicating improvement in most conditions when the patient does stop smoking. Physicians can be successful in their efforts to control premature disease among their patients through a strategy focusing on health promotion: helping patients to stop smoking; and counseling all teenager patients not to start, so they will not have to go through the frustrations and discomforts of stopping once they realize, years later, that smoking really is harmful to their health.

REFERENCES

1. Frederickson DT: How to help your patients stop smoking. *J Med Assoc Georgia* 1969; 58:421–425.
2. Peabody HD: A practical approach to office management of cessation of cigarette smoking, in Richardson RE (ed): *Proceedings of the Second World Conference on Smoking and Health*, London, Pitman Medical, 1972, pp 185–189.
3. Blum A: Butting in where it counts. *Hosp Phys* 1980; 16(4):22–35.
4. Fishbein M: Consumer beliefs and behavior with respect to cigarette smoking: A critical analyses of the public literature, in *Federal Trade Commission, Report to Congress: Pursuant to the Public Health Cigarette Smoking Act, for the year 1976*, Washington, May 1977, 113 pp.
5. Russell MAH: Smoking addiction: Some implications for cessation, in Schwartz JL (ed): *Progress in Smoking Cessation*, New York, American Cancer Society, 1978, p 207.
6. US Department of Health and Human Services: *The Health Consequences of Smoking: Cancer—A Report of the Surgeon General.* DHHS Publication No. (PHS) 82-50179, 1982, p 9.
7. Russell MAH, Wilson C, Taylor C, Baker CD: Effect of general practitioners' advice against smoking. *Br Med J* 1979; 2(6184):231–235.
8. Schwartz JL, Dubitzky M: *Psycho-Social Factors Involved in Cigarette Smoking and Cessation.* Berkeley, CA, Institute for Health Research, September 1968; 628 pp.
9. Holroyd J: Hypnosis treatment for smoking: An evaluative review. *Int J Clin Exp Hyp* 1980; 28:341–357.
10. Martin GP, Waite PME: The efficacy of acupuncture as an aid to stopping smoking. *NZ Med J* 1981; 93:421–423.
11. US Department of Health, Education, and Welfare: *Smoking and Health—A Report of the Surgeon General.* DHEW Publication No. (PHS) 79-50066, 1979.
12. Schwartz JL, Dubitzky M: Expressed willingness of smokers to try 10 smoking withdrawal methods. *Public Health Rep* 1967; 82:855–861.
13. Green DE: Psychological factors in smoking, in Jarvik ME, et al (eds): *Research on Smoking Behavior*, Washington, National Institute on Drug Abuse Research Monograph 17, December 1977, pp 149–150.
14. Schwartz JL, Rider G: *Review and Evaluation of Smoking Control Methods: The United States and Canada, 1969–1977.* National Clearinghouse for Smoking and Health, Center for Disease Control. HEW Publication No. (CDC) 79-8369, 1978.
15. Miller GH: Devices to help smokers stop don't. *Am Pharm* 1980; NS 20: 53–54.
16. Hymowitz N, Lasser NL, Safirstein BH: Effects of graduated external filters on smoking cessation. *Prev Med* 1982; 11:85–95.

EMPHYSEMA BLUES

when you get down   and your lungs don't sound so good
you're coughin' up stuff   it's gettin' rough
to breathe the way you should

just give us a call   it won't take long at all
we'll clear up your chest   give you all the best
therapy in the store

we'll give you routine treatments   q.i.d.
volume ventilators are such a breeze
postural drainage   helps clear your lungs
i know you're gonna love it   it's so much fun

cardio-pulmonary   resuscitation
cheynne-stokes   respiration
acidotic alkalotic   laminar flow
gas, humidity and aerosol

got the coughin' wheezin' emphysema blues
coughin' wheezin' emphysema blues

nasal basal cannulas
saturate your bronchi
positive pressure helps force that gas
right down to your alveoli

so when you get down   and your lungs don't sound so bright
just give us a call   we'll run down that hall
and light your lucky strike

coughin' wheezin' emphysema blues
hackin' crackin' O_2 lackin' blues
rootin' tootin' gruesome sputum blues
coughin' wheezin' emphysema blues

—lyrics from one of two songs
of a record by Kirk & Blake;
available for $5 (incl postage) from
Kirk Torney Publishing, PO Box 7108,
Berkeley, CA 94707.
© Coventry Publications ASCAP

A positive health strategy for the office waiting room

JOHN W. RICHARDS, JR., MD

In 1979 the American Medical Association (AMA) congratulated a group of magazine publishers for their refusal to accept tobacco-product advertising. The AMA was unstinting in its praise: "In view of the overwhelming evidence against smoking, your policy of refusing to accept tobacco advertising can only be construed as an unselfish act. America's physicians applaud your action."

The following year the Congress of Delegates of the American Academy of Family Physicians (AAFP) approved a resolution to "commend publications which have refused to accept tobacco advertising and to circulate to its members a list of these publications."

These actions came at the request of physicians in the AMA and the AAFP who also belong to DOC (Doctors Ought to Care, c/o Thomas Houston, MD, Floyd Medical Center, 304 Turner-McCall Blvd, Rome GA 30161). DOC had compiled a list of such magazines and had explored attitudes on the part of physicians and publishers on the subject of cigarette advertising in magazines placed in the office waiting room.

In 1979 DOC conducted a mail questionnaire survey of members of the South Carolina Medical Association, to examine their knowledge of smoking-related illness and patient education.

With regard to the various risk factors for premature deaths, most of the 156 respondents were aware that cigarette smoking was responsible for the highest number of premature deaths in the United States. It was also the one factor for which physicians felt the need for more patient education materials.

Although 70% of the respondents felt that the waiting room is a good place to learn about health (and 60% felt that patients thought so, too), 70 of 145 respondents to one question admitted spending nothing on health education materials for the waiting room; only 18 physicians claimed to spend more than $60 a year on such material, preferring to accept free pamphlets from the voluntary health agencies and governments. In contrast, more than half (83) subscribed to six or more commercial magazines for the waiting room, and two thirds of the respondents spent $50 or more each year on such subscriptions. The most frequently subscribed-to magazines were *TIME* (49), *Newsweek* (47), *Sports Illustrated* (33), *Better Homes & Gardens* (32), *People* (28), *US News & World Report* (27), and *Ladies Home Journal* (27). Only three of the top ten magazines subscribed to by physicians for their waiting rooms did not contain cigarette advertising: *National Geographic* (25), *Good Housekeeping* (22), and *Reader's Digest* (21). Intrigued by the DOC survey, one physician reported 390 pages of cigarette advertising in the magazines in his waiting room!

The most advertised product in the magazines most subscribed to by physicians for the patient waiting area is cigarettes. In magazines such as *TIME* and *Newsweek* cigarette advertising comprises between 15% to 80% of total color advertising for a given issue (except for the June 6, 1983 issue of *Newsweek* which contained a story on non-smokers rights; *Newsweek*, not the tobacco companies, pulled the cigarette ads). Although they have published cover stories on AIDS, Legionnaire's disease, Tylenol, and toxic shock syndrome, these magazines have not carried a cover story on smoking since 1970—when the bulk of cigarette advertising switched into the printed media. In 1977, in an article on carcinogens, *Newsweek* listed tobacco as number 8 (arsenic was listed as number 1; the list was in alphabetical order). Each year, *TIME* and *Newsweek* accept in excess of $30 million in cigarette advertising, or approximately 20% of total advertising income. *TIME*, *Newsweek*, *Better Homes & Gardens*, and other magazines buy mailing lists of physicians to offer reduced "professional courtesy" subscription discounts.

When questioned by physician-subscribers about the policy of accepting cigarette advertising, *TIME* has sent form letters which say, "We respect your right to disagree with us." The publisher of *Better Homes & Gardens*, which has made a concerted effort to be portrayed as a health magazine (notwithstanding the 15 to 20 pages of cigarette advertising in each issue), has expressed his hope that "those people who do not smoke will turn past the cigarette ads." *Newsweek* has perhaps the lengthiest stock reply:

> We know that many of our readers object to the publication of cigarette and liquor advertisements. We feel, however, that if we were to accept some ads and reject others, we would be, in effect, endorsing products and making the very kind of editorial statement through our advertising columns that we so scrupulously avoid in our news copy. Therefore, we accept ads from the makers of all legal products, as long as these ads conform to the standards of good taste and ethical practice established by the Better Business Bureau and the Magazine Publishers Association.
>
> We hope you realize, though, that our editorial department is completely independent from our advertising department, and our running ads from tobacco companies and distilleries has never prevented us from conscientiously reporting on the health hazards and social problems related to smoking and drinking. We keep our readers informed about new findings establishing the connection between smoking and, for example, heart disease, ulcers and lung cancer. We examine the abuse of alcohol among teenagers, the dangers of mixing drugs and alcohol, and the link between drinking and birth defects. We think that through these reports we fulfill our responsibilities as an independent news source, whatever the content of the ads that appear in the magazine.

There are a few bright spots, most notably that of *Runner's World*, whose editor and publisher, Bob Anderson, has made a special appeal to physicians:

From the Department of Family Medicine, Medical College of Georgia, Augusta, Georgia.

Address correspondence to Dr Richards, Assistant Professor, Department of Family Medicine, Medical College of Georgia, Augusta, GA 30912.

There's a serious problem sitting in your waiting room.

It's magazines. Magazines filled with full-page advertisements promoting one of the most serious health problems in the world: Cigarettes. Just a glance through any one of hundreds of popular periodicals will indicate that they derive a major portion of their revenues from the thriving tobacco industry. And while your patients are sitting there waiting for you to help them improve their health, these high-powered ads are encouraging them to ruin it. Successfully, too. Because despite all the efforts to dampen America's voracious appetite for tobacco, the deadly weed is doing very well.

We'd like to make a modest suggestion. Subscribe to a publication that refuses to accept cigarette advertising. It's *Runners's World* Magazine. In *Runner's World*, you'll find the same national advertisers found in those other magazines, but you won't find one advertisement promoting poor health. In fact, nearly every advertisement, and absolutely every article, *promotes* good health, exercise and proper diet. There are no advertisements for distilled spirits either . . .

On October 10, 1983, *The Saturday Evening Post* announced that effective with its March 1984 issue, it would no longer accept tobacco advertising. For a publication that had been fighting a tough battle for survival in recent years, the move suggests that publications that cultivate nontobacco advertising revenue no longer "must" accept cigarette ads. The *Post*'s publisher is Cory SerVaas, MD.

Some physicians, such as Hunter Fry of Melbourne, Australia, prefer to call attention to cigarette ads by writing ridiculing slogans on the ads with a felt-tip pen as a means of making patients more aware of how the ads undermine health. Other physicians buy a rubber stamp or stickers that say "This advertisement is a rip-off." Others, such as Stephen Barrett of Allentown, PA, head of the Lehigh Valley Committee Against Health Fraud, fill out the blank subscription forms in the magazines with the statement, "It is immoral to accept cigarette advertising." He has yet to receive a reply.

The physician has a golden opportunity to enhance the healthful environment of the office by scrutinizing magazines for misleading and antihealth advertising. If 400,000 American physicians vowed not to let their office waiting rooms be vehicles for cigarette sales, this would contribute significantly to health promotion. Canceling subscriptions to such publications—informing the publisher for the reason—might set the ball rolling toward changes in publishing policy.

Following is the most recent listing of magazines that do not accept cigarette advertising.

W = weekly; M = monthly; BM = every other month.

GENERAL INTEREST

Consumer Reports   (M—$12)   256 Washington St, Mount Vernon, NY 10550
The Futurist   (BM—$20)   4916 St Elmo St, Bethesda, MD 20814
Good Housekeeping   (M—$12.97)   959 Eighth Ave, New York, NY 10019
Mother Jones   (M—$18)   625 Third St, San Francisco, CA 94107
The New Yorker   (W—$32)   25 West 43rd St, New York, NY 10036
Parents Magazine   (M—$7.95)   685 Third Ave, New York, NY 10017
Reader's Digest   (M—$12.93)   Reader's Digest Rd, Pleasantville, NY 10570

TRAVEL

Adirondack Life   (BM—$10)   420 East Genesee St, Syracuse, NY 13202
Arizona Highways   (M—$15)   2039 West Lewis, Phoenix, AZ 85009
Missouri Life   (M—$15)   1205 University Ave, Columbia, MO 65201
National Geographic   (M—$15)   17th and M Streets, NW, Washington, DC 20036
Nevada Magazine   (BM—$7.95)   101 South Fall St, Carson City, NEV 89410
Travel Holiday   (M—$9)   Travel Bldg, 51 Atlantic Ave, Floral Park, NY 11001
Vermont Life   (Q—$4)   Vermont Development Dept, 61 Elm St, Montpelier, VT 05602
Yankee   (M—$14)   Main St, Dublin, NY 03444

SPORTS

Bicycling   (9/yr—$10)   35 East Minor St, Emmaus, PA 18049
The Runner   (M—$15)   One Park Ave, New York, NY 10016
Runner's World   (M—$14.95)   1400 Stierlin Rd, Mountainview, CA 94043
Sail   (M—$21.75)   PO Box 10219, Des Moines, IA 50380

YOUTH

Boy's Life   (M—$10.80)   1325 Walnut Hill La, Irving, TX 75062
Humpty Dumpty Magazine   (8/yr—$11.95)   1100 Waterway Blvd, Indianapolis, IN 46206
Jack and Jill   (8/yr—$11.95)   1100 Waterway Blvd, Indianapolis, IN 46206
Mad Magazine   (8/yr—$9.75/10 issues)   485 Madison Ave, New York, NY 10022
Ranger Rick's (*nature magazine*)   (M—$9.50)   National Wildlife Federation, 1412 16th St, NW, Washington, DC 20036
Sesame Street   (10/yr—$6.95)   1 Lincoln Plaza, New York, NY 10022
Seventeen   (M—$11.95)   850 Third Ave, New York, NY 10022

(continued on following page)

These four magazines lead in income from cigarette advertising.

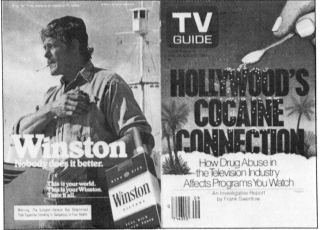

AVOCATIONS

American History Illustrated   (10/yr—$16.95)   Box 822, Harrisburg, PA 17105
British History Illustrated   (BM—$12)   Cameron & Kolker Streets, Harrisburg, PA 17105
Collectibles Illustrated   (BM—$11.50)   Main St, Dublin, NH 03444
Crafts   (M—$15)   PO Box 10103, Des Moines, IA 50347
Dance Magazine   (M—$22)   1180 Avenue of the Americas, New York, NY 10036
Fishing Facts   (M—$17.88)   PO Box 609, Menomonee Falls, WI 53051-9984
Historic Preservation   (BM—$15)   National Trust for Historic Preservation, 1785 Massachusetts Ave,
                Washington, DC 20036
Horticulture   (M—$18)   300 Massachusetts Ave, Boston, MA 02115
Model Railroader   (M—$20)   1027 North Seventh St, Milwaukee, WI 53233
Modern Photography   (M—$7.98)   PO Box 10785, Des Moines, IA 50349
Organic Gardening   (M—$12)   35 East Minor St, Emmaus, PA 18049
Personal Computing   (M—$18)   50 Essex St, Rochelle Park, NJ 07662
Popular Communications (*ham radio*)   (M—$12)   76 North Broadway, Hicksville, NY 11001
Popular Computing   (M—$12.97)   PO Box 307, Martinsville, NJ 08836
Railfan & Railroad   (M—$17)   PO Drawer 700, Newton, NJ 07860
Theatre Crafts   (9/yr—$15.75)   Suite 312, 250 West 57th St, New York, NY 10017
Writer's Digest   (M—$18)   9933 Alliance Rd, Cincinnati, OH 45242

SCIENCE

Animal Kingdom   (BM—$7.95)   185th Street and Southern Blvd, New York, NY 10460
Audubon   (BM—$13)   950 3rd Ave, New York, NY 10022
Natural History   (M—$15)   Central Park West at 79th St, New York, NY 10024
Nutrition Action   (10/yr—$10)   Center for Science in the Public Interest, 1755 S St, NW, Washington, DC 20009
Scientific American   (M—$21)   415 Madison Ave, New York, NY 10017
Smithsonian   (M—$17)   900 Jefferson Dr, Washington, DC 20560
The Sciences   (10/yr—$12.50)   2 East 63rd St, New York, NY 10021
Zoo News   (M—$8)   PO Box 551, San Diego, CA 92112

"Non-smoking, please"
A money-saving proposition

In both the marketplace and the workplace, there is a growing demand for a smoke-free environment. The travel, food, and lodging industries are responding to this demand, and some businesses are providing cleaner indoor air environments for their employees and customers.

For Muse Air, a Dallas-based airline flying mainly between California and Texas, the decision to make no smoking the rule on all of its flights was strictly a matter of economics. Muse saves on maintenance costs, such as by having cleaner air filters, and the policy pleases its passengers. It also pleased the American Association for Respiratory Therapy, which presented Muse Air with the first AART Special Recognition Award at a midair ceremony aboard a flight from Dallas to Houston in 1983.

Chicago's Midway Airlines lent support to the Great American Smokeout in November 1983 by leaving on the "no smoking" signs throughout its flights.

Passengers on touring buses run by Maupintours are also assured of a clean-air environment. The Kansas City-based company prohibits smoking on all of its buses.

Between May and September Cebu Cruises (Room 2, 1017 168th Ave SE, Bellevue, WA 98008) offers 8- or 11-day non-smoking cruises along the Pacific Northwest coast.

La Quinta Motor Inns began offering no-smoking accommodations in 1981, at the suggestion of an allergist in Charleston, SC, who requested smoke-free rooms for his patients coming into the city for treatment. The idea proved so popular that many other inns in the

San Antonio-based chain have added as many as 16 clean-air rooms.

In 1978, Ramada Inns, Phoenix, set aside rooms in all of its motels for people who do not smoke. The rooms have nearly a 100% occupancy rate. The Executel chain, Seattle, and Canada's Four Seasons Hotels, Ltd, are other examples of innkeepers that offer smoke-free rooms.

For another innkeeper, profit is only part of the motive for offering no-smoking accommodations. Lyndon Sanders, SC, the 54-year-old owner of the Non-Smokers Inn, Dallas, believes that the deaths of his father and at least

a dozen close friends were caused by cigarette smoking. A plaque by the flagpole in front of the Inn reads:

When this flag flies at half staff, it does so in memory of over 1,000 Americans who die daily due to the effects of tobacco. And as a challenge to the social acceptance of smoking in public places. Lyndon Sanders, Sr. November 18, 1982.

Sanders requires prospective employees to undergo polygraph tests to prove that they haven't smoked for the past six months. Guests at the Non-Smokers Inn sign an agreement acknowledging that if they smoke in the room, they must pay a $100 fine to cover the cost of cleaning and deodorizing. The 134-room inn began turning a profit six weeks after it opened and is booked solid most nights. There has been no damage from cigarettes placed on furniture or

dropped on carpeting. Sanders says that the lack of cigarette damage enables him to run the Inn at a cost of 30% less than a comparably-sized hotel.

Despite the interest among some hosts to offer no-smoking rooms to their guests, travelers to large cities may still be hard-pressed to find such accommodations. *Journal* telephone inquiries to the reservation desks at six New York City hotels (New York Hilton, New York Sheraton, Sherry Netherland, United Nations Plaza, Helmsley Palace, and the Plaza) found none that set aside rooms for guests who do not smoke.

The business with clean-air environments that are springing up around the country are slowly being tied into an informal network aided by travel agencies. Thrifty-Rent-A-Car and some major hotels in cities served by Muse Air now offer completely smoke-free arrangements that travel agents can book when they make Muse flight reservations.

For example, a person who does not smoke can hop aboard a Muse Air flight from Dallas to Los Angeles, rent a Thrifty-Rent-A-Car on arriving at Los Angeles International, and drive to Sunset Boulevard, to check into one of the no-smoking rooms at the Hyatt Regency.

Also taking advantage of the proliferation of businesses that cater to people who do not smoke is the Nonsmokers' Travel Club (8928 Bradmoor Drive, Bethesda, MD 20817). Founded in 1974, the Nonsmokers' Travel Club now has 1,400 members in the United States and Canada. The club sponsors three domestic and foreign trips a year. Members travel in the no-smoking sections of airplanes and employ nonsmoking drivers and guides on bus tours. As part of each tour, arrangements are made for meals in the nonsmoking sections of restaurants.

A trip to Atlanta, GA, for example,

The above round-up of news of progress on the non-smoking front was compiled by Marc Kusinitz. PhD. a New York-based science writer.

may include a meal at Mary Mac's, one of the city's largest restaurants. Mary Mac's offers "Southern Hospitality, 'DamYankee' Efficiency," and a no-smoking section that includes over half of its 375 seats. There is a demand for even more smoke-free seating.

In New York, the local chapter of Group Against Smoking Pollution (GASP, 7 Maxine Avenue, Plainview, NY 11803) encourages patronage of restaurants that have a no-smoking section or room available at all times. A recent issue of GASP's newsletter commends such restaurants as Baron's III (Veteran's Memorial Highway, Bohemia), Milleridge Inn (Broadway, Jericho), Pumpkin Eater Natural Foods (Broadway at 91st, Manhattan), and The Beanstalk (Sixth Avenue at 48th Street). The Scobie Diner (Northern Boulevard, Little Neck), which attracts patrons from throughout the New York City area, has a spacious nonsmoking area that is filled round-the-clock.

Other service industries have also found that many customers appreciate a smoke-free environment in which to transact their business. The Northport, WI, branch of H & R Block restricted all smoking by its consultants to ventilated restrooms after clients complained about the smoke-filled consultation rooms.

Not only customers, but employees, too, are the beneficiaries of clean air policies. The W W Richardson Insurance Company, Warren, RI puts workers who smoke into rooms separate from those who do not smoke. For the past six years, Radar Electric Inc, Seattle, WA, has had the question, "Do You Smoke?" at the top of its employment application form. The hundreds of prospectives employees who answered "yes" have been turned away. IBM headquarters in Armonk, NY prohibits smoking in common areas such as elevators and photocopying rooms. The company's cafeterias set aside no-smoking sections.

The Wall Street Journal reported in 1982 that managers are increasingly requesting employment agencies to send them people who do not smoke. A Los Angeles employment agency, Bright Futures, receives the most requests for people who do not smoke from accounting, legal, and banking firms. Very few such requests come from health-care institutions.

Businesses that restrict or ban smoking may gain more than the gratitude of their employees. At the Fifth World Conference on Smoking and Health, William L. Weis, Associate Professor of

Business at Seattle University pointed out that, compared to those who do not smoke, the average employee who smokes uses about 50% more sick leave and uses the health care system at least 50% more often. The worker who smokes suffers more than twice the mortality rate of nonsmokers during his working years and wastes an estimated 6% of his working hours in the "ritual" of smoking (handling the cigarette, lighting up, putting out the cigarette). Moreover, cigarette smoke forces industries to spend about six times the capital and operating expenses to maintain adequate air circulation. It also increases maintenance costs for cleaning, repainting, and replacing furniture. The person who smokes also may impose a costly liability on an employer for damages sustained by

co-workers forced to work in a smoky environment, and decreases the morale of those workers because of the irritation and discomfort of working in a smoke-filled environment.

The tobacco industry is aware of the growing concern among workers and consumers of the health threat posed by cigarette smoking. As far back as 1973, the *U.S. Tobacco Journal* reported: "...the most potentially dangerous threat to the future of the tobacco industry is. ..the developing psychological attitude that smoking is somehow socially unacceptable. ...".

How has the cigarette industry responded? Apart from a series of pamphlets and newspaper and magazine advertisements attacking the "anti-smokers" for attempting to undermine personal freedoms, individual companies, especially RJ Reynolds, in its ads for Winston and Vantage, have glorified the hard-driving, smoking worker. But the trend is clearly going against Reynolds, as illustrated by the passage of a stringent clean air ordinance for the workplace by voters in San Francisco.

According to an item in Regina L. Carlson's report, *Smoking or Health in New Jersey*, a 1980 Louis Harris poll found that while 33% of US workers smoke on the job, 51% of co-workers object to smoking on the job. Carlson, the executive director of the New Jersey Group Against Smoking Pollution (GASP), also cited a US government poll that found that 70% of the population, including a majority of those who smoke, agreed that public smoking should be limited.

Carlson's publication, sponsored by the New Jersey State Health Department, contains a review of judicial decisions resulting in compensation to workers exposed to cigarette smoke. In one decision (Fuentes vs the Workers Compensation Appeals Board), the California Supreme Court upheld a $10,000 award to a worker for a lung injury resulting in permanent partial disability, 25% of which was judged to be attributed to cigarette smoking, a third of which occurred on the job.

In addition to healthier workers, a safer working environment, and lower overhead for businesses that restrict smoking, another possible benefit of not smoking can be lower life insurance premiums. In 1984, when the first Surgeon General's report was published, the State Mutual Life Assurance Company was the first insurance company to undertake an exhaustive study of the mortality rate differentials between those who smoke and those who do not. Because people who do not smoke were found to be much better health risks, the company began providing discounts to those people who had not smoked within the past 12 months.

Fifteen years later, State Mutual compared the death rate of policy holders who smoked with those policy holders who did not.

In their report on this study for State Mutual entitled, "Mortality Differences Between Smokers and Non-Smokers," Michael J. Cowell, Vice President and Chief Actuary, and Brian L. Hirst, Associate Actuary for the company, pointed out that State Mutual's intent is not to take a moral position. State Mutual merely acknowledged that people who don't smoke are better insurance risks than those who do smoke:

Against this background, we conclude that non-cigarette smokers could be considered as the population that defines "standard" risks, while smokers could be considered substandard, with the degree of rating increasing with the extent of their smoking habits. Nonsmokers who are better than average in other underwriting considerations (e.g., build or blood pressure) could be considered preferred risks.

Among the many other insurance companies that offer discounts to people who don't smoke are Kentucky Central Life, Home Life Insurance Company, Prudential, and Phoenix Mutual. Phoenix Mutual also offers lower group life insurance rates to small companies that prove that none of their workers smoke. The trend in nonsmokers' discounts is gradually extending to fire, health, and even automobile insurance (since persons who smoke are likely to drink more heavily than those who do not smoke).

For better or worse, then, the movement away from a smoking society may have as much to do with the money saved as with ending the hazard to health or the odor in the air.

The AMA tackles smoking
"A strong stand"

For thirty years, since banning cigarette advertising from JAMA *in 1953, the American Medical Association (AMA) has been in the thick of efforts to curb smoking and its promotion. The following review of AMA actions on smoking, gleaned from* JAMA *and* American Medical News, *was prepared by Jessica Rosenberg, a medical student at New York University, who served as a research assistant at the* Journal *during 1983.*

SUPPORT FOR RESEARCH
In December 1963, following approval by the House of Delegates, the Board of Trustees of the AMA appropriated $500,000 for a long-range program of research on tobacco and health, "to be devoted to the study of human ailments that may be caused or aggravated by smoking, the particular element or elements that may be the causal or aggravating agents, and the mechanisms of their action."[1] The Board's hoped-for outcome was the identification and removal of the harmful components in tobacco as a means of making smoking safe. The program, to be directed by the AMA's Education and Research Foundation (AMA-ERF), was described in *JAMA* as "a vigorous and farsighted response to the smoking problem."[2]

The Surgeon General's *Report on Smoking and Health* was issued two weeks before the first meeting of the five-man AMA-ERF Research Committee on January 31, 1964. The three committee members who had also served on the Surgeon General's Public Health Service Advisory Committee emphasized that the AMA program in no way contradicted the purpose and conclusions of the Surgeon General's report.[3]

The AMA-ERF Committee was authorized to solicit funds for the research, provided that they were "given without restrictions." Within weeks, six tobacco companies* contributed $10 million to the research, to be given over a five-year period. "On that basis, the members of the board of directors of the foundation were pleased to accept the generous offer to these companies," said Raymond M. McKeown, MD, AMA-ERF president.[4]

Three years into the program, Committee chairman Maurice H. Seevers, MD, stated that "certainly there are no scientific data that would contradict the basic tenets of the Surgeon General's report.[5] He added, "while the medical profession and tobacco industry have somewhat divergent reasons for promoting tobacco research, both are committed to basic scientific research as the best means of developing specific answers to the questions raised by our smoking population." In 1968, the six tobacco companies pledged an additional $8 million toward the AMA-ERF research.[6]

In 1978 the Committee published the 365-page report, *Tobacco and Health*, recording and summarizing the results of the research. A major conclusion of the report was "that cigarette smoking plays an important role in the development of chronic obstructive pulmonary diseases and constitutes a grave danger to individuals with preexisting diseases of the coronary arteries."[1] Other findings concerned the "effects on behavior and on biochemical mediators elicited by nicotine," and "mechanisms by which nicotine may influence the production of peptic ulcer." Although the Committee had limited the number of awards for cancer research because this area is otherwise generously financed, potent cocarcinogens were identified in tobacco tar, and the inducibility of aryl-hydrocarbon hydroxylase was identified as a determinant of susceptibility to lung cancer.

The Committee's statement of a decade earlier that "research under the aegis of the project had not altered the conclusions of the 1964 report of the Surgeon General" was reiterated in the forward to the 1978 AMA-ERF

* American Tobacco Company; Brown & Williamson Tobacco Corporation, now a unit of BATUS or British-American Tobacco; Liggett & Myers; Lorillard, now a unit of Loews Corporation; Philip Morris, Inc; and R.J. Reynolds Tobacco Company.

volume.

The report appeared at a time when Health, Education & Welfare Secretary Joseph Califano, Jr., was an outspoken critic of the tobacco industry. The date of release coincided with a visit by President Jimmy Carter to North Carolina. On learning the conclusions of the industry-financed report, Carter publicly repeated an earlier statement that:

> . . .nobody need fear the facts about tobacco use. Certainly, no one need fear the emphasis on research that will make the use of tobacco in the future even more safe than it has been in the past.[7]

In a news release, Horace Kornegay, president of the Tobacco Institute, castigated the AMA, accusing it of contriving the timing of release of the report to coincide with and discredit President Carter's trip to visit tobacco growers in North Carolina. Kornegay also attacked the report as old news and blamed the AMA's subcommittee for "generalizations" that would prejudice future research—"to the public detriment":

> The (tobacco) industry deplores the politics of the release of this document by the AMA. In a spirit of corporate responsibility and a genuine sustained desire to find necessary answers, the tobacco industry will continue to devote funds to scientific research to find a resolution to the smoking and health controversy.[8]

WARNING LABELS

In 1957 the Legal and Monetary Subcommittee of the Government Operations Committee of the United States House of Representatives held hearings on the responsibility of the Federal Trade Commission (FTC) regarding advertising claims for filter cigarettes. The chairman of an AMA cancer research committee testified that a human being would have to smoke 100,000 cigarettes a day to get the equivalent exposure of tar to that which produced skin cancer in mice.[9] Following publication of the Surgeon General's report on smoking, the AMA supported research as the proper way to deal with the cigarette problem. The AMA specifically opposed the addition of warning labels to cigarette packages, and testified as such to the FTC in a letter from AMA Executive vice-president, FJL Blasingame, MD: "The health hazards of excessive smoking have been well publicized for more than ten years and are common knowledge," Blasingame wrote. "Labeling will not alert even the young cigarette smoker to any risks of which he is not already aware.[10]

Although the successful camouflaging of the warning labels by cigarette manufacturers lends ironic credence to Blasingame's viewpoint, the AMA position on labeling led to the charge that the AMA was engaging in political tradeoffs with the tobacco industry. Representative Frank Thompson, Jr., (D, New Jersey) accused the AMA of siding with the tobacco industry as part of a deal to get tobacco state congressmen to vote against proposed Medicare legislation.[11] Blasingame responded by calling Thompson's charge "slanderous," but his description of the AMA position raised questions about the AMA's acceptance of tobacco industry money: "We believe that since people will continue to smoke, the answer lies not in restrictive rules and regulations but in research into the effect of tobacco on smoking, the results of which conceivably could eliminate the hazards of smoking. The AMA has embarked on such a research program, with the assistance of a $10-million grant from the six major tobacco companies," Blasingame replied.[11,12] Warning labels were mandated by Congress in 1965, and the AMA later reversed itself on the labeling issue. The 1980 Report of the Council on Scientific Affairs of the AMA, *Smoking and Health*, recommended that health warnings on cigarette packages be made even more explicit, and that they be displayed on all cigarette advertising as well as on the packages.[13]

RECOMMENDATIONS

The House of Delegates at the AMA Annual Convention in 1964 adopted a statement that recognized "a significant relationship between cigarette smoking and the incidence of lung cancer and certain other diseases, and that cigarette smoking is a serious health hazard."[14] The House further recommended that health education programs on the hazards of smoking be developed by the AMA for members of all age groups, and be made available through various media.

At the AMA Annual Convention in 1969, the House of Delegates passed a resolution that dealt with several aspects of the smoking problem. The AMA resolved to "again urge its members to play a major role against cigarette smoking by personal example and by advice regarding the health hazards of smok-

ing."[15] It also criticized the "incongruity" of government spending of tax dollars to promote the production and sale of tobacco while also spending more tax dollars to discourage smoking as a health danger. Finally, as part of a resolution "to discourage smoking by means of public pronouncements and education programs," two anticigarette posters were developed, designed to provoke an emotional response against smoking.

At the 1970 Convention, the House of Delegates resolved to urge the Federal Aviation Administration to require separate nonsmoking sections on all public air transportation, when the size of the aircraft permitted. A resolution that the AMA urge Congress to enact legislation to end tobacco subsidies was referred back to the Board, since it was considered that they, through the AMA President, were already taking appropriate action.[15]

The House of Delegates took personal action against smoking at the 1972 Annual Convention, adopting a resolution discouraging (but not banning) smoking during sessions of the House.[17]

In the last decade, several physicians within organized medicine, including an editor of *JAMA*[18] have called for greater involvement in the smoking problem by the AMA.[19-22] In an editorial in *JAMA*, Sheldon B. Cohen, MD, questioned the AMA's failure to take strong action to prevent and eliminate smoking, while spending $200,000 to eliminate television violence, "an area where the data are much less firm and that is much less directly connected with the everyday practice of medicine."[23]

In 1978, the Resident Physicians Section (RPS) adopted a resolution 121(I-78) that called for the development and funding of a multimedia antismoking and "positive health" campaign. The RPS further called for the AMA to commend publications that refuse to accept cigarette advertising, and for physicians to communicate the hazards of cigarettes and the necessity of not smoking to their patients.

At the 1979 Annual Convention, the Board rejected a resolution for a "positive health" program on the grounds that its intent was already being implemented and that the expenditure was not warranted. The AMA did support the resolution by the RPS calling for the AMA to publicly commend publications that refuse to accept cigarette ads, and to provide the list of publications to AMA members. It also supported a resolution directing the AMA to request television networks to halt the use of athletes to endorse tobacco products. Finally, in adopting the report of Council on Scientific Affairs, *Smoking and Health*, the AMA allocated $45,000 to an anti-smoking campaign that emphasized smoking cessation and research.

In 1980, the AMA Board rejected resolutions that the AMA support efforts to pass legislation banning cigarette advertising and restricting smoking in public places, on the grounds that the Council Report adequately dealt with those issues. The Board further rejected a resolution to support "The Cigarette Safety Act" requiring that cigarettes be self-extinguishing, arguing that the bill was not specific on how the self-extinguishing cigarettes were to be made, and that further research was needed. However, in 1982 the House of Delegates endorsed the Cigarette Safety Act.

Until September 1981, the AMA Members Retirement Plan held approximately $1.4 million in stock in Philip Morris and R.J. Reynolds. In June the House of Delegates had rejected an RPS resolution to divest the stock, but responding to adverse publicity and pressure from some of its members, including the RPS and medical student sections, the AMA Plan divested itself of all tobacco stocks. (None of the newspaper editorialists who chastised the AMA over this matter chose to examine their own publishers' unquestioned acceptance of cigarette advertising money or to praise the AMA for voting to urge an end to tobacco subsidies.)

At its Interim Meeting in December 1982 the House of Delegates took action to disapprove and discourage the promotional distribution of free cigarettes, and to develop model local and state legislation to prohibit the practice on public policy. The issue had been introduced by the AMA's Medical Student Section, which expressed concern that samples are often illegally handed out to minors.

The AMA's Reference Guide to Policy & Official Statements[24] leaves no doubt about the increasing commitment of the AMA to a reduction in smoking:

The American Medical Association urges its members to play a major role against cigarette smoking by personal example and by advice regarding the health hazards of smoking.

The AMA discourages smoking by means of public pronouncements and educational programs, and takes a strong stand against smoking by every means at its command.

REFERENCES

1. *Tobacco and Health.* Compiled by AMA-ERF Committee for Research on Tobacco and Health. Chicago, American Medical Association Education and Research Foundation, 1978.
2. AMA's response to the smoking problem. *JAMA* 1964; 187(6): 27.
3. Committee for research on tobacco and health holds first meeting. *JAMA* 1964; 187(6): 26.
4. Tobacco firms contribute to AMA-ERF smoking study. *JAMA* 1964; 187(7): 27.
5. AMAgrams. *JAMA* 1967; 202(6): 9–10.
6. AMAgrams. *JAMA* 1968; 205(4): 9.
7. Anti-smoking campaign. *Weekly Compilation of Presidential Documents.* Administration of Jimmy Carter. Washington, 1978; 14(12): 536–7.
8. AMA denies tobacco book release was an attempt to embarrass Carter. *Am Med News*, August 18, 1978, p 8.
9. Wagner S: *Cigarette Country: Tobacco in American History and Politics*, New York, Praeger, 1971, p 86.
10. AMA stand on cigarette labeling. *JAMA* 1964; 187(11): 16–17.
11. Controversy over cigarette labeling. *JAMA* 1964; 188(1): 15–16.
12. AMA presents cigarette labeling views to FTC. *JAMA* 1964; 188(1): 29–31.
13. Council on Scientific Affairs: *Smoking and Health. JAMA* 1980; 243: 779–781.
14. Cigarette smoking called hazardous to health. *JAMA* 1964; 189(1): 26.
15. AMAgrams. *JAMA* 1969; 209(12):1799.
16. AMAgrams. *JAMA* 1970; 213(9): 1402.
17. AMAgrams. *JAMA* 1972; 221(7): 639.
18. Moser RH: The new seduction. *JAMA* 230: 1564.
19. Walker WJ: Government-subsidized death and disability. *JAMA* 230: 1529–1530.
20. Miami physicians take lead in drive to curb cigarette smoking. *Am Med News*, February 13, 1978, p 3.
21. Greene GE: Nonsmokers' rights: a public health issue. *JAMA* 1978; 239:2125–2127.
22. Segregate smokers in public places, MD-crusader urges. *Am Med News*, June 15, 1979, p 11.
23. Cohen SB: Should medical associations discourage smoking? *JAMA* 1978; 239: 158.
24. *Reference Guide to Policy & Official Statements*, American Medical Association, Chicago, 1980.

Using athletes to push tobacco to children
Snuff-dippin' cancer-lipped man

In 1985 nearly 4,000 cigarettes are expected to be sold for every adult in the United States; in 1880, the per capita consumption was 25. The astronomic increase in cigarette smoking during the past 100 years has corresponded to the decline of all other forms of tobacco (cigar, pipe, plug, snuff), not to mention the disappearance of the spittoon.

Ironically, the popularity of cigarettes began in large part as the result of concerns about health. The spread of tuberculosis in the latter half of the 19th century led to an increase in antispitting laws and a resultant shift by tobacco companies into the promotion of cigarettes—mass produced on newly invented machines.

Until the 1960s consumption of smokeless tobacco products steadily declined. With the publication in 1964 of the Surgeon General's *Report on Smoking and Health*, sales of smokeless tobacco began to rise. Although subsequent reports of the Surgeon General have discussed the carcinogenic properties of all forms of tobacco, between 1960 and 1970 sales of snuff and chewing tobacco rose 25%, and between 1970 and 1980 sales doubled again (*Adweek*, July 13, 1981).

Until recent years snuff dipping was a practice confined largely to black women in the rural Southeast, in whom the chance of contracting oral cancer has been found to be 50 times that of nonusers of snuff.[1] Similarly, tobacco chewing was a custom of rural southern men. In 1980 Christen, McDaniel, and Doran[2] called attention to widespread snuff-dipping and tobacco chewing among baseball and football players in college, high school, and elementary schools in Texas. These practices have been described as "the latest crazes" among teenage boys in the suburbs in the

How to enjoy tobacco without lighting up.

I've learned a lot since coming to Chicago — and not just about baseball. I've learned how to get full tobacco enjoyment without lighting up. I use smokeless tobacco. And you guys that are just starting out...well, you should try mild Happy Days mint. It's the perfect smokeless to begin with because it's got a taste that's mild and easy to enjoy. And just a pinch between your cheek and gum is all it takes. It's just right whether you're cutting the lawn or cutting down a baserunner.

If you're interested in trying a few pinches, write: Smokeless Tobacco, U.S. Tobacco Company, Dept. ST-078, Greenwich, Conn. 06830.

Smokeless tobacco. A pinch is all it takes.

Northeast and in Washington, DC (*Washington Post*, November 12, 1980). One in 10 Colorado high school students surveyed by Greer uses smokeless tobacco; the age of the average user is 15.

There is no mystery to this phenomenon. Unlike cigarette advertising, commercials for these carcinogenic products

have not yet been withdrawn from television, and manufacturers have taken advantage of the situation. The heroic imagery evoked in expensive promotional campaigns for snuff and chewing tobacco is—in a word—matchless. The array of celebrities employed to cultivate the puberty rite of tobacco use includes baseball players George Brett, Carlton Fisk, Catfish Hunter, Sparky Lyle, and Bobby Murcer, and football players Terry Bradshaw, Nick Buoniconti (now a tobacco and candy distributor), Earl Campbell, Joe Klecko, and Laurence Taylor (*Advertising Age*, June 23, 1980; *U.S. Tobacco Journal*, March 8, 1982). Singer Charlie Daniels appears on a collection of high-priced paraphernalia for a brand of snuff, Skoal, a product of

Official Sponsor

the United States Tobacco Company, Greenwich, CT. A race car driver, Harry Gant, drives a car painted with "Skoal Bandit"; his entourage includes a group of cheerleaders called the Skoal Bandettes. In 1983, a commercial record, "Skoal Dippin' Bandit," sung by New York Yankee Bobby Murcer, was frequently played on teenage-oriented radio stations. "The people at the stock car races walk around in their Skoal T shirts and Skoal caps and they greet one another as people who belong to something special," said Per Erik Lindqvist, vice-president of marketing at United States Tobacco (*U.S. Tobacco Journal*, March 8, 1982).

Responding to a question from the *U.S. Tobacco Journal* about why so many young males are buying smokeless tobacco, United States Tobacco Company chairman and president Louis

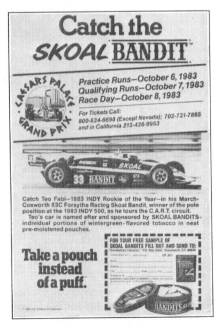

Bantle said, "I think there are a lot of reasons, with one of them being that it is very 'macho'."

Bantle estimated that 80% to 85% of his company's customers are new users and not just those who switch from cigarettes out of concern for health. He also reported that United States Tobacco is intensely aiming at a budding international market.

A public relations operation, the Smokeless Tobacco Institute, in Peekskill, New York, issues press releases to let the public know about the shortcomings of medical research reports implicating snuff as a cause of oral cancer (*Advertising Age*, April 13, 1981).

With the recent 16¢ rise in the federal excise tax on a pack of cigarettes, United States Tobacco has begun a national $2 million advertising campaign for Skoal Bandits—little pouches of snuff, like teabags. The campaign was launched in July in New York City on radio and TV and in newspaper sports sections, including *The New York Times* and *Newsday*. The television advertisements on such programs as ABC TV's Wide World of Sports and NBC TV's Football Game of the Week teach the potential young "Bandit" the technique for using snuff. (*Advertising Age*, June 27, 1983)

During the 1980 Olympic Games, the United States Tobacco Company, an official sponsor, spent $2,500,000 promoting snuff. For 1984, it has created a United States Tobacco Sports Medicine Program. Various sports writers, TV editorialists, athletic commissioners, team owners, players, and nontobacco sponsors of professional sports have vied for media attention in 1983 to condemn drug abuse among athletes and teenagers. Yet none has publicly challenged the campaign of the United States Tobacco Company.

It could be argued that the morbidity and mortality attributable to smokeless tobacco is so much less serious than that of cigarette smoking as to be an acceptable lesser of two evils. But the more likely hypothesis, in light of the cigarette companies' not having objected to the exclusion of smokeless tobacco from the ban on television advertising, is that the Skoal ads serve as an initiator to a milder form of tobacco use and may start even younger children on the road to cancer.

Can there be a more cynical attempt to capture the youth market than that by the makers of cigarettes, snuff, and chewing tobacco? Apparently so. A child walking through almost any candy store, supermarket, pharmacy, airport souvenir stand, or variety store cannot fail to come across a prominent display for candy cigarettes (with brand names identical

to the real ones), cigars, pipes, and pouches of Big League Chew, a shredded bubble gum that produces "man-size wads" and that in the words of its inventor, former baseball player Jim Bouton, is "designed to look like chewing

tobacco used by baseball players "(*Advertising Age*, June 23, 1980). Then there is Chaw, powdered bubble gum in a round little box resembling a tin of snuff. A display for Chaw features a cowboy with a bulging cheek and the slogan, "Best chew this side of the Pecos."

What next can we expect from the candy companies—bubble gum cocaine?

ALAN BLUM, MD
Editor

REFERENCES

1. Winn DM, Blot WJ, Shy CM, Pickle LW, Toledo A, Fraumeni JF: Snuff dipping and oral cancer among women in the Southern United States. *N Engl J Med* 1981; 304:745-749.
2. Christen AG, McDaniel RK, Doran JE: Snuff dipping and tobacco chewing in a group of Texas college athletes. *Texas Dental Journal* 1979; 97:6-10.

GOVERNMENT INVOLVEMENT IN SMOKING AND HEALTH

The Office on Smoking and Health is the focal point for all smoke-related activities of the Department of Health and Human Services.

The Office prepares and disseminates the annual Surgeon General's reports on smoking, the last five of which have honed in on specific aspects of the problem: *The Health Consequences of Smoking, The Behavioral Aspects of Smoking, Education, and Prevention* (1979); *The Health Consequences of Smoking for Women* (1980); *The Changing Cigarette* (1981); *Cancer* (1982); and *Cardiovascular Disease* (1983).

Using computer and microfilm, the Office's Technical Information Center serves researchers by providing literature searches, references, abstracts, and copies of articles. Last year, approximately 4,500 inquiries were received.

In addition, the Center, publishes the periodic *Smoking and Health Bulletin*, an annual cumulation of abstracts of research papers (*Bibliography on Smoking and Health*), the biennial *Directory of Ongoing Research in Smoking and Health*, and an annual summary of legislative actions (*State Legislation on Smoking and Health*).

The Office is responsible for analyzing scientific information for the purpose of maintaining Federal smoking policies. It is one of four centers serving the bibliographic needs of the World Health Organization on smoking and health.

The Office develops educational programs and public service announcements targeted to women, ethnic minorities, teens, and children, and disseminates model programs both for preventing teenage smoking and for encouraging smoking cessation.

To be placed on the Office mailing list or to receive further information about its services, write to:

Department of Health and Human Services   5600 Fishers Lane
Office on Smoking Health   Park Bldg., Rm. 1–10   Telephone: (301) 443-1690
Technical Information Center   Rockville, MD 20857

LETTER TO THE EDITOR

19th April 1984

TO THE EDITOR: I have recently had the privilege of reading the December 1983 issue of the *New York State Journal of Medicine* devoted to "The World Cigarette Pandemic." May I take this opportunity of congratulating you and your contributors on a remarkable achievement which will be of lasting importance far beyond the State of New York? As you point out in your outstanding editorial, in most medical journals, "smoking is considered only piecemeal, if at all . . ."; indeed, only *The Medical Journal of Australia,* under your editorship, has thus far preceded the *New Yorks State Journal of Medicine* by devoting an entire issue to the topic of smoking.

And yet, smoking remains far the largest avoidable cause of death and disease in the world today. In the recently published WHO Expert Committee Report on Smoking Control Strategies in Developing Countries, it was noted that, ". . . in the world as a whole, cigarette smoking is now responsible for more than 1 million premature deaths each year." This itself is without doubt a considerable underestimate, and regrettably the decline in cigarette smoking noted in some industrial countries is being more than counterbalanced by an increase in cigarette sales in developing countries.

For more than thirty years tobacco manufacturers have known about the uniquely dangerous nature of their product. At any time since then (for example, after the first reports of the Royal College of Physicians of 1962 or the Surgeon General in 1964) they could have chosen to recognize the dangers of smoking, to cease all advertising and promotion of tobacco products, and to ensure that future generations would not be subjected to the smoking holocaust. Such a course of action would of course have required courage, honesty, and some concern for public welfare; it would also have entailed the recognition that no amount of profit can justify the premature deaths of more than 300,000 Americans each year, let alone the many, many more deaths outside the US for which major international American tobacco companies are responsible. Some tobacco companies have indeed diversified, but along with this diversification they have for more than three decades attempted to deny the overwhelming evidence on the dangers of smoking, to advertise their products as extensively as possible, to ensure the highest possible levels of sales, and to encourage new smokers (particularly children) to start smoking. Additionally, tobacco companies both individually and collectively have sought to minimize and counter the impact of health education: the recent outrageous advertising and publicity campaign by the R.J. Reynolds company (claiming it does not advertise to children) is only the latest example.

If cigarette manufacturers had acted responsibly, there would be no need for a forceful anti-smoking campaign. As it is, the companies have acted so irresponsibly that future generations will find it hard to understand why governments did not take firmer action, as recommended by report after report after report from the most eminent medical bodies. They will be forced to conclude with entirely jusifiable cynicism that the reason for inadequate governmental action was simply the ruthlessly applied political and economic power of the tobacco interests. But future generations will also ask why doctors, who make such efforts to care for the health of individuals, did so little to counter an epidemic of such magnitude. They will note that with a few honorable exceptions, the medical profession did no more than pay lip-service to the problem —and hoped that someone else would deal with it. Even worse, an organization such as the American Medical Association seemed so concerned, for so long, at the power of the tobacco lobby that it apparently sought to play down the importance of smoking. Medical historians of the future may well, indeed, ask whether in its distressingly inadequate and sometimes counter-productive response to the smoking problem the AMA itself was not guilty of malpractice?

It is to be hoped that doctors concerned for the public health will have been stirred by this volume into taking action both individually and through their organizations to counter the smoking problem. They can be greatly encouraged at evidence from around the world indicating that a comprehensive governmental program consisting of measures such as a ban on tobacco advertising and promotion, strong health warnings, regular tax increases, and worthwhile funding for health education (none of which infringe the freedom of the individual, as opposed to that of the manufacturer of a known carcinogen) can indeed be effective in reducing cigarette smoking in both adults and young people. And having taken heart, they should treat the smoking problem as they would other major political issues, by writing to politicians and otherwise lobbying them, by publicizing their views, and by ensuring that representative organizations such as the AMA become part of the anti-smoking campaign.

It is politicians who will ultimately settle the smoking problem, and thus decide whether or not more than a million premature deaths from smoking worldwide will continue to occur each year. But at present politicians can be forgiven for believing that the medical profession does not see smoking as a major problem: all the pressure is coming from the other side. The important initiative taken by the *New York State Journal of Medicine* in devoting an entire issue to the smoking problem can be a milestone in moving doctors towards a type of action that can and must be taken—but its ultimate success will depend on the willingness of its readers to ensure that politicians are made aware of its implications.

MIKE DAUBE
Department of Community Medicine
University of Edinburgh

Mike Daube is director of health promotion for the government of Western Australia, which is perhaps the most committed anti-smoking government in the world.